Portable Australian Authors

THE JINDYWOROBAKS

PORTABLE AUSTRALIAN AUTHORS

This series provides carefully selected volumes introducing major Australian writers and movements. The format is designed for compactness and for pleasurable reading. Each volume is intended to meet a need not hitherto met by any single book. Each is edited by an authority distinguished in his field, who adds an introductory essay and other helpful material.

General Editor: L.T. Hergenhan

Also in this series:
Henry Lawson edited by Brian Kiernan
Marcus Clarke edited by Michael Wilding
Five Australian Plays edited by Alrene Sykes
The 1890s edited by Leon Cantrell
Rolf Boldrewood edited by Alan Brissenden

In preparation:
Hal Porter edited by Mary Lord
Joseph Furphy edited by John Barnes

*Portable
Australian Authors*

The Jindyworobaks

*Selected and edited with an
Introduction and Bibliography by*

Brian Elliott

University of Queensland Press

Published by University of Queensland Press,
St Lucia, Queensland, 1979
Introduction © Brian Elliott, 1979
This compilation © University of Queensland Press, 1979

This book is copyright. Apart from any fair dealing for the
purposes of private study, research, criticism, or review, as
permitted under the Copyright Act, no part may be reproduced
by any process without written permission. Enquiries should be
made to the publishers.

Typeset by Academy Press Pty Ltd, Brisbane
Printed and bound by Silex Enterprise & Printing Co., Hong Kong

Distributed in the United Kingdom, Europe, the Middle East,
Africa, and the Caribbean by Prentice-Hall International,
International Book Distributors Ltd, 66 Wood Lane End, Hemel
Hempstead, Herts., England

Published with the assistance of the Literature Board of the
Australia Council

National Library of Australia
Cataloguing-in-Publication data

The Jindyworobaks.

(Portable Australian authors)
Bibliography
ISBN 0 7022 1296 2
ISBN 0 7022 1297 0 Paperback

1. Australian poetry—History and criticism.
I. Elliott, Brian Robinson, ed. (Series)

A821'.009

Contents

xv Acknowledgments
xvii Introduction

PART 1 MAJOR JINDYWOROBAK POETS

Rex Ingamells

3 Editor's Note
4 Luis de Torres
4 Boomerang
4 The Afghans
5 Forlorn Beauty
5 Evening in the MacDonnells
6 The Bullocky
7 Excited Crows
7 Garchooka, the Cockatoo
7 Garrakeen
8 Rivers and Mountains
10 Black Children
10 Long Ago
11 Moorawathimeering
11 Forgotten People
14 Sun-Freedom
15 Shifting Camp
15 Outback
15 Earth-Colours
16 Ngathungi
16 Boolee
17 Black Mary
17 Memory of Hills

18	From a Dying People
19	Black Boulder
19	Desert Dawn
19	Dark Cry
20	The Swagman
20	*From* The Gangrened People
21	Billai
21	Yaraandoo
21	*From* Unknown Land
22	Australia
25	To Mirrabooka
26	Martin's Pub
27	Macquarie Harbour
27	Captain William Bligh
28	The Tourist Dump
28	Slight Autobiography
29	*From* **The Great South Land**
	Columbus and Balboa
	The *Tryal*
31	The Pensioner
33	*Extracts from* Uluru, An Apostrophe to Ayers Rock

W. Flexmore Hudson

37	Editor's Note
38	Song
38	The Poet and the World Today
38	Sonnet, 1935
39	The Farmer
39	To a Boy on His Eleventh Birthday
41	Mallee Farm at Dusk
42	Drought
43	As the Fugitive Grass
43	Mallee Scene
43	Mallee Courage
44	Mail Night; Mallee Store
44	Andrew
45	Prayer
45	Song of an Australian
46	Gum Tree
47	To Myrle: And Then You Sang
47	Magpies
47	Black Cockatoos
48	Sundown
48	To Edgar H. Mercer, *from* Sonnets on the War
48	Galahs

49	War
49	*Conclusion from* As Seeds Through Years of Drought
51	*Extracts from* **Indelible Voices**
55	Hare in Summer
55	Words
56	Kirsova
56	Giovanni Rinaldo, P.O.W.
57	Nostalgia
58	The Kiss
59	Bashō
59	Mallee in October
60	A Hymn for the Dark Age
62	Coach in Training Camp

Ian Mudie

64	Editor's Note
65	As Are the Gums
65	This Land
66	Street Vision
66	Corroboree to the Sun
67	Earth
68	Underground
68	Morialta Memory
69	Galah
69	Have Anger
70	Belong
71	This Is Australia
73	I Would Not Go
73	The Young Warriors
74	Glory of the Sun
75	If This Be Treason
76	*From* **The Australian Dream**, Part 2, Pioneers
80	New Guinea Campaign
80	Unabated Spring
81	No Phoenix Australis
81	They'll Tell You About Me
83	The O.T.
84	The Wreck of the *Ethel*, Low Tide
85	One Day, Perhaps in Spring
86	The Blue Crane
87	Sitting-Room, Strzelecki Homestead
88	Bushfire
89	I Wouldn't Be Lord Mayor
90	In Neon Pastures
90	To Me the Poem

Contents

90	River Port
91	The Crab or the Tree
92	The Day the Rain Came
95	Intruder

William Hart-Smith

96	Editor's Note
97	Avenger
98	La Perouse
99	Summer Day
99	The Fishing Lubra
100	We Are the Elders
100	April 28th, 1770
101	Moondeen
102	Black Cockatoos
103	Prologue to Christopher Columbus
104	Space
104	The Pear-Shaped Earth
105	Water-Lily
105	Immarna
106	Candle on a Stump
107	Flame the Cat
108	Post Mortem
109	Baiamai's Never-Failing Stream
109	Because the Caterpillar
109	The Surplus
110	Eaglehawk
111	Open Air Pictures
111	Mary
112	Nullarbor
115	Picture in Bright Colours
115	Willie Wagtail
116	The Life of Rocks
117	Death of an Ant
117	Legend
118	Sparrows
118	Smoke on the Plains
119	In Sydney
119	Number

Roland Robinson

121	Editor's Note
122	The Creek
122	I Made My Verses

122	And the Blacks Are Gone
123	Flowering Tea-Tree
123	The Invocation
123	Coming with Darkness
124	Climbing the Gully
124	Communion
124	Morning
125	Departure
125	Call on the Sea to Be Still
125	The Drovers
126	Black Cockatoos
126	Would I Might Find My Country
127	Deep Well
127	Casuarina
128	I Had No Human Speech
129	Rock-lily
129	Emu
129	The Desert
129	The Blanket
130	The Brolgas
130	The Dancers
131	The Pæan
132	The Rabbit
132	The Wanderer
133	The Ibis
133	For Rex Ingamells
134	Thrush
134	Passage of the Swans
135	Sundowner
135	The Pioneers
136	One Eyed Nalul Speaks
136	The Child Who Had No Father
138	Jarrangulli
139	Mapooram
140	Captain Cook
141	Kimberley Drovers

PART 2 THE JINDYWOROBAK ANTHOLOGIES 1938–1953

145	Editor's Note

1938

147	Wolfe Fairbridge: The Banksia
147	Paul L. Grano: Out Samford Way

148	Victor Kennedy: Queer Little Almond Eyes
149	Geoffrey Reading: Silas
149	Ian Tilbrook: Gums
150	Russel Ward: The Kangaroo
151	Brian Elliott: Blackboy

1939

152	Wolfe Fairbridge: Written After Flying Perth-Adelaide
153	John Opie: Tallabilla
154	P. Pfeiffer: At the Window

1940

155	Nancy Cato: River Scene
156	James McAuley: Envoi for a Book of Poems

1941

157	C.B. Christesen: Dawn at Flying-Fish Point
158	Max Harris: Harris the Hobo
158	Paul L. Grano: Prime Minister to Go Home
159	The Austral-Anglo
159	James Devaney: Bamba
160	"Rickety Kate": Waratah
161	Garry Lyle: Rainmaker's Stone

1942

162	"E": Return
162	F.T. Macartney: Didjeridoo
163	Leonard Mann: To Young Soldiers
164	Brian Vrepont: The Fishers
165	John Ingamells: Protest
166	Dorothy Hewett: Flame Woman
166	John Shaw Neilson: The Sundowner

1943

168	Kenneth H. Gifford: Galah Song
168	James McAuley: Terra Australis

1944

170	Gina Ballantyne: Nostalgic

170	Olive Pell: Reaction
171	F.B. O'Connell: Rain at Caloundra
172	R.G. Howarth: Love is Cruel to the Lover
172	Brian Elliott: The Golden Eagle

1945

175	Peter Middleton: Cane Saga

1946

177	Ken Barratt: Burke and Wills
179	John W. Eyles: Desert Crossing
179	George Farwell: Mallee Song
180	Harley Matthews: The Vineyard

1947

183	Edna Tredinnick: Arunta
184	Llewellyn Rhys: Aroultja
184	E.M. England: Corroboree for a Dead Warrior
185	John T. Kirtley: Written for Ian Mudie

1948

186	Colin Thiele: Swagman Day
187	Arthur Murphy: Swagmen

1949

188	Mary Gilmore: The Word
189	Lilith Norman: The Colour of Sorrow
190	Alexander Craig: Elegy
191	Geoffrey Dutton: Wool-Shed Dance

1950

192	Judith Wright: Wonga Vine
193	Ernest G. Moll: Farm Day
193	K.E. Murray: *From* Nullarbor
194	Ray Mathew: Whose Country?
195	Kevin E. Collopy: Children of the Desert
195	Nancy Cato: Mallee Farmer
196	Rosemary Dobson: Child with a Cockatoo
197	R.A. Swan: Epitaph to the Vanished Tribes
197	David Rowbotham: Roofs
198	Irene Gough: Narrinyerri

1951

- 199 Douglas Stewart: The Aboriginal Axe
- 200 David Campbell: The Waterhole
- 200 Francis Webb: Henry Lawson

1952

- 202 Peter Hopegood: Sons of the Surreal Refabricate the Dragon

1953

- 203 Margaret Irvin: Paddy Melon Country

PART 3 JINDYWOROBAK PROSE

Fiction

- 207 James Devaney, Two Extracts from "Sanctuary", *The Vanished Tribes*
- 211 Rex Ingamells, Two Extracts from *Aranda Boy*
- 217 Roland Robinson, Two Narratives from *Aboriginal Myths and Legends*

Origins and Theory

- 219 James Devaney, Extracts from *The Vanished Tribes*
- 221 Rex Ingamells, Extract from a Letter to Miles Franklin, 16 March 1948
- 223 P.R. Stephensen, Two Extracts from *The Foundations of Culture in Australia*
- 227 Rex Ingamells, Three Extracts from *Conditional Culture*
- 227   Gum Trees in Italy
- 229   Environmental Values
- 231   The Word "Jindyworobak"
- 232 Victor Kennedy, Extract from *Flaunted Banners*
- 235 Rex Ingamells, Extract from a Letter to W.F. Hudson, 27 June 1941
- 236 Rex Ingamells, Statement in *Jindyworobak Anthology*, 1945

Criticism

- 239 Jindyworobak and *The Bulletin*

239	Revival in Poetry? [1941]
241	Notes on a Banner Bearer [1941]
243	Rex Ingamells, Something More Than an Editor's Note [1941]
248	Jindyworobak and *Southerly*
248	A.D. Hope, Culture Corroboree [1941]
252	Editorial [1941]
254	Extract from Editorial [1942]
256	R.H. Morrison, The Verse Anthologies: For and Against [1948]
259	Max Harris, Dance Little Wombat [1943]
264	Critical Extracts from *Jindyworobak Review 1938–1948*
264	James Devaney (Foreword), Rex Ingamells (Introduction), E. Morris Miller, Mary Gilmore, Gina Ballantyne, Ian Mudie, Nettie Palmer, Judith Wright, Max Harris, Brian Elliott, W. Flexmore Hudson, R.G. Howarth, Alec King
273	F.J. Letters, The Jindyworobak Theory, *In a Shaft of Sunlight*, 1948
278	Judith Wright, Extract from *Because I Was Invited*, 1975

PART 4 JINDYWOROBAK AFFINITIES

283	Editor's Note

Fiction

289	D.H. Lawrence, Two Extracts from *Kangaroo*
292	Xavier Herbert, Extract from *Capricornia*
293	Xavier Herbert, Extract from *Poor Fellow My Country*

Verse

Kath Walker
296	The Teachers
296	We Are Going
297	The Bunyip
298	Ballad of the Totems
300	*Extracts from* The Wonguri-Mandjikai Song Cycle of the Moon-Bone

Les Murray
304	*From* The Bulahdelah-Taree Holiday Song Cycle

308	The Flying Fox Dreaming
309	The Euchre Game
310	Visiting Anzac
312	Laconics: The Forty Acres

Peter Porter
| 314 | On First Looking into Chapman's Hesiod |

Richard Tipping
| 316 | Personal object |

317	Glossary
319	Textual Sources
329	Select Bibliography

Acknowledgments

For permission to reproduce material in this volume, acknowledgment is made to the following.

Part 1:

Mrs E.E. Ingamells (for the work of Rex Ingamells); Mr Flexmore Hudson; Thomas Nelson (Australia) Limited and Renee Mudie (for the work of Ian Mudie); Angus & Robertson Publishers and William Hart-Smith (for the work of William Hart-Smith); The Macmillan Company of Australia Pty Ltd, A.H. and A.W. Reed, Edwards and Shaw Pty Ltd, Angus & Robertson Publishers and Roland Robinson (for the work of Roland Robinson).

Part 2:

David Campbell and Curtis Brown (Aust.) Pty Ltd (for the work of David Campbell); Nancy Cato; C.B. Christesen; Alexander Craig; Freda Francis (for the work of James Devaney); Rosemary Dobson; Geoffrey Dutton; Edith M. Anders (as E.M. England); Dorothy Holledge (for the work of Wolfe Fairbridge); Noni Farwell (for the work of George Farwell); Kenneth H. Gifford; Public Trustee of New South Wales (for the work of Mary Gilmore); Irene Hall (as Irene Gough); Max Harris; Dorothy Hewett; Mrs M.P. Hopegood (for the work of Peter Hopegood); Mrs L. Howarth (for the work of R.G. Howarth); John R. Ingamells; Margaret Irvin; Lenore Filson (for the work of "Rickety Kate"); Dorothy Kennedy (for the work of Victor Kennedy); Angus & Robertson Publishers (for the work of James McAuley); Frederick T. Macartney; Leonard Mann; Mrs A.J. Davis (for the work of Harley Matthews); Ernest G. Moll; Angus & Robertson Publishers (for the work of John Shaw Neilson); Lilith Norman; David

Rowbotham; Angus & Robertson Publishers (for the work of Douglas Stewart); R.A. Swan; Colin Thiele; Edna Tredinnick; Russel Ward; Angus & Robertson Publishers (for the work of Francis Webb); Judith Wright McKinney.

Part 3:

The *Bulletin* Newspaper; Freda Francis (for the work of James Devaney); Public Trustee of New South Wales (for the work of Mary Gilmore); Max Harris; Angus & Robertson Publishers (for the work of A.D. Hope); Mrs E.E. Ingamells (for the work of Rex Ingamells); Dorothy Kennedy (for the work of Victor Kennedy); Catherine King (for the work of Alec King); Kathleen Letters (for the work of F.J. Letters); Ailsa Morris Young (for the work of E. Morris Miller); R.H. Morrison; The Macmillan Company of Australia Pty Ltd (for the work of Roland Robinson); John W. Lockyer (for the work of P.R. Stephensen); Oxford University Press (for the work of Judith Wright).

Part 4:

Ronald M. Berndt; William Collins Publishers and Angus & Robertson Publishers (for the work of Xavier Herbert); Laurence Pollinger Ltd and the Estate of the Late Mrs Frieda Lawrence (for the work of D.H. Lawrence); Les Murray and Angus & Robertson Publishers (for the work of Les Murray); Oxford University Press (for the work of Peter Porter); Richard Tipping; Jacaranda Wiley Ltd (for the work of Kath Walker).

Details of textual sources for each section are given at the back of the book.

Introduction

JINDYWOROBAK

In the beginning was the word: Jindyworobak. It *was* Rex Ingamells and it was *with* him. Until he uttered it darkness covered the face of the waterless land. The word was light and it dawned. Australia was re-created.

We enter a mythological world, but it is our own. We take possession of the magic that is our own. We are initiated men.

This was the Jindyworobak creed. I present it at the outset in noble proportions. I think we should not forget its noble hopes. It began in a spirit of memorable bravery. We should remember that too. We should remember the odds that were against it. But these in themselves are noble resolutions and our strength, or our charity, may not always be equal to keeping them.

The truth is, the Jindyworobak movement was a generation of Australian poets at school. The nation in the decade 1930–1940, which saw their rise to articulation, was still emotionally and intellectually a colony in adolescence, awaiting cultural maturity. It must come. But when? The need of change was the more urgent because the times were gloomy and a great cloud of ugliness and terror was descending upon the older European vision. Spain, Italy, Germany, Russia smouldering: and then upon all these, industrial depression relieved only by a feverish anxiety to build up weapons of destruction. The older world suffered from disastrous forms of heart disease. The young Australians wished, if they could, to assert their youth and difference, to relish the natural freedom of the human spirit, and they wished to look for it, since other resources had clearly failed, only in their own country. There was a sense that poetry—the loftiest, if not the only focus of spiritual values—in particular had failed, and it had failed because it no longer represented fundamental experiences of living. It had become a decorative frill. The impulse of the young Australians was to say, We must find it again; and we must find it here.

So they set themselves to learn how. First to find out, and then to teach others.

They were inexperienced and earnest; in a word, novices. They may be thought of as the class of '38, because it was in that year they graduated—matriculated, rather—and produced their first magazine and manifesto, the 1938 *Jindyworobak Anthology*; also Ingamells's declaration of war against the provincial philistines, the pamphlet *Conditional Culture*. It is of course true that spade-work had been done long before then, but this was the definitive move. The *Anthologies* were produced annually from 1938 to 1953. By then the class was ready to disperse, but it had done its work.

Reginald Charles, known as Rex Ingamells, was clearly the founding father of Jindyworobakism. He attacked the idea with a fiery devotion and a fanatical enthusiasm, which were catching and attracted in time a number of followers and disciples. The first of his active supporters, however, Wilfred Flexmore Hudson, who was at one with him for poetry as the national desideratum, was never a thorough-going convert to the Jindyworobak theory of it. Nevertheless his reservations did not prevent him from contributing all he could. After him came Ian Mayelston Mudie, who brought energy to the movement, some of it at times a little strident. These three, with the backing of a large number of loyal lesser voices, made up the first phase. All three were Australian born; in point of fact, all South Australians and natives of the same city, Adelaide. Though a state capital it was still then a provincial city, but perhaps for that very reason closer than the larger, more sophisticated Melbourne or Sydney to the mood of the hinterland. At any rate, between them these three produced a wild, bright, fresh music.

The two principal figures of the phase which followed, William Hart-Smith and Roland Edward Robinson, were both born abroad. Hart-Smith was English, Robinson Irish. It may be a question whether being Australian only by adoption, even when quite young, may have an important bearing upon a nascent Jindyworobak. Be that as it may, Jindyworobaks they became; Hart-Smith for a season though not for ever, and Robinson with final commitment. But the main difference between the phases was that the second was for art and poetry mainly and for Jindyworobak theory only as the way to reach them; for the first three, the theory itself was primary and obsessive.

It is not yet possible to claim that any one of the five principal Jindyworobaks stands out in isolated distinction. Time may modify this view; for the present at least, they cohere as a group. It will in the end be necessary to judge Hart-Smith and Robinson by tougher, more traditional standards than the others; they will have to stand by their achievements alone, whereas for the first three, idealism and good intentions will also enter into consideration. It is they more particularly who seem the novices; it is they who appear more eagerly full of novelty and promise. They occupy the desks at the front, with a lively *esprit-de-corps* coming up from behind. But on the whole their sanguine hopes outshone their achievements. The poets might have done better to apply their minds with greater concentration; the results have inclined somewhat towards distraction and slipshod conclusions. A misguided idealism has led too often to impractical solutions. At the very worst, ignorant and obstinate. But by and large a good group, working well together, and genuinely concerned for the spiritual welfare of the nation.

The first section of this introduction is a very general account of the origin and early development of the Jindyworobak movement, centred inevitably upon Ingamells. Then follow brief introductory comments on the five major poets separately, and a section on the *Jindyworobak Anthologies*. The book begins with the verse selections, followed by a quantity of critical and controversial material (mostly early), much of which will need to be looked on with a historical eye. At the end there is a short list of bibliographical references. If this list seems meagre, it is partly because the Jindyworobaks have never, either as individuals or as a group, attracted a really active body of critical commentary. It is also partly because, as much as I could in the limited space, I have tried to embrace the controversial part of that criticism within the covers of this volume, and hence render it reasonably self-contained in the critical way. This was possible because most of the controversy was in any case contemporary or near-contemporary. There is at present a discernible rise of interest in the Jindyworobak movement, which may mean that the time is ripe for serious reappraisals; but this interest replaces an attitude which for a number of years has been one of something like contempt.

There were always two more or less clearly defined streams of poetical development in Australia; probably in all colonial poetry. The settlers in America set the pattern. They had two aims: first to re-enter the lost paradise (which the discovery of new worlds out of Europe seemed to promise), and second, to exploit it. In the early years of Australia practical hardships (coupled with the awareness that the place was a convict settlement anyway) tended to stress material progress, though never to the utter exclusion of hopes and visions. Among writers many were motivated strongly by the settlers' struggles for mastery over farm and station land, but for others landscape and vista were what mattered. By 1900 there was a conventional dichotomy which divided "Sydney" from "the bush"; this could signify the division between sophisticated and natural art; or, more narrowly, between cabinet or drawing-room literary conventionalism, album lyricism and the like, and the vigorous outdoor traditionalism of the bush yarn and the balladry of action and heroism. Victor Daley, Sydney Jephcott, James Hebblethwaite with innumerable others, including a host of literary ladies, represented the one; writers like Lawson, Paterson, Ogilvie, Brady and the balladists generally the other. All found a home in the *Bulletin*, which, for all its active (and successful) campaigning for a national literature in line with its motto, "Australia for the Australians", saw no inhibiting incompatibility between the genres. A result was that even in that enterprising paper (which one of its detractors once disparaged as the *Bul-let-in*) a high degree of favour was bestowed upon the best of both kinds. The "action" strain led to poems about horses and heroism; the "cabinet" persuasion developed into paeans to "Beauty". By the time the first Jindyworobak had managed to mature a year or two beyond callow puberty he was ready to rebel against the complacent colonial acceptance of both. He found it all weary, stale, flat and unprofitable; and worse, boringly *unrelated* to the experiences of wonder that were daily before his eyes: the sights and sounds of the landscape he knew, the response of his own blood and muscle to the physical environment about him. Above all, there was no spirituality, nothing of a true bond between the man and his natural world, in what the poets appeared to feel. He was conscious, as were his friends and contemporaries, of something not yet adequately expressed yet very real in what his generation more than earlier ones sensed of that vital bond. Not that it had never been noticed before; emphasis had been placed upon the *strangeness* of Australian nature and the *uniqueness* of the sensations which it induced. A poem like Charles Harpur's "Midsummer Noon in the Australian Forest" is not hard to interpret as a child's—a young boy's—recollection of delicious moments of communion with the natural bush environment as direct, unliterary emotion:

a fully and articulately *related* experience. This appeared to him genuine; of the "opal-hearted country, a wilful, lavish land" about which Dorothea Mackellar had rhapsodized, he was not so sure. But there really was a dreamland of Australia into which the young could enter; they were all aware of it, now more than ever before. As the vision of the old world lost its appeal (who could long for Europe now?), the vision of the new one, the immediate experience, grew more compelling. How to grasp it was the problem; convention did not yet sanction these values. But the time was ripe for change, and a key was provided. The old dream*land* became the new Dream*time*. This shift enabled Ingamells and the others to put a name to the quality of Australian uniqueness they had so piquantly experienced but not been able to express. It was *Aboriginal*.

It was this new fact they went to school to learn; it was this they became missionaries to teach. It cannot be stated too early, or asserted too positively, that the Aboriginal element in the Jindyworobak programme, whatever may be the common impression, was not part of any impulse to write Aboriginal history or to propound Aboriginal law or morality, or even to describe Aboriginal culture. They were not archaeologists and anthropologists, and if they were missionaries—as I have unhesitatingly called them—their mission was directed not to the blacks, but to the whites, to the civilization which now exists and is in control. They cannot be faulted by pointing out that their ethnological information was often faulty; they were never scientists, and their use of the material was always directed to literary ends. They were poets—for the most part lyrical poets. Even that makes them un-Aboriginal, as will appear.

But the Aboriginal linkage calls for explanation. The Jindyworobaks were not even the first to posit it; they had predecessors whom it is proper to place in the picture. When, earlier, I specified which were the two prevailing poetical *genres* of turn-of-the-century Australian writing, I might well also have listed a third, almost as prevalent: the didactic. There was enough of the preaching strain in Australian verse already for the Jindyworobaks themselves to inherit a rather uncomfortable infusion of it. I would rather not think of this preaching as characteristic of them—though, unfortunately, it too often was. The style was already present in Adam Lindsay Gordon but its high priest was Bernard O'Dowd, who learnt his art from listening to Moody and Sankey hymns and to Salvation Army preachers on street corners. But he was earnest and sincere, not less so than the Jindyworobaks when they carried on in the same strain; and it was Bernard O'Dowd who first rationalized the Dreamtime for white Australian consumption.

O'Dowd's imagination (if that was what it really was) ranged over political-philosophical and ideal themes, and expressed itself with all the glamour of a university extension lecture on some industriously knowledgeable topic; but he had read a notable book and referred to it. This was Spencer and Gillen, *The Native Tribes of Central Australia*, 1899. Significant allusions to it occur in his long and not always wholly unattractive poem, *The Bush* 1912. Spencer's was not the first study of the native culture to be published, but it was by far the most systematic yet to appear, and it was followed by others; not only that, but scholars abroad took notice of it. Among Australian poets, however, O'Dowd was the only one of distinction to refer to it, and no doubt his interest in it was at the time attributed to the same kind of overworked eccentricity which applied to his other obscurities. The public as a whole was not yet ready to pay attention to the Aborigines; interest so far had not advanced beyond mere curiosity. Nor was the reference to Spencer the only aspect of *The Bush* which might be expected to capture the attention of an Ingamells. O'Dowd's national-political idealism was harmonious with Ingamells's, and so was his disposition to see the real Australia in terms of physical experiences. I think particularly of the lines,

> When, now, they say "The Bush!", I see the top
>   Delicate amber leaflings of the gum
> Flutter, or flocks of screaming green leeks drop
>   Silent . . .

He was aware of O'Dowd's theme of destiny and waiting:

> For Great Australia is not yet: She waits
>   (Where o'er the Bush prophetic auras play) . . .

Never mind what she waits for; for Ingamells it was not the same. O'Dowd also saw the Australian *mystery* and declared

> She is the scroll on which we are to write
>   Mythologies our own . . .

He insists constantly on the indwelling *spirits* of the bush, though in a way perhaps to have more meaning for Irish Robinson than for Ingamells of Orroroo: "And you have Children of the Dreaming Star . . ." Above all this, the poem has two references to Alcheringa: in one O'Dowd says he has

"In Alcheringa found the Golden Age" (which is not ridiculous, allowing for a measure of poetic licence), and the other is a direct tribute to Spencer:

> And Spencer sails from Alcheringa bringing
> Intaglios, totems and Books of the Dead.

More poetic licence; these 'intaglios", and possibly the "Books of the Dead", otherwise meaningless, may be tjurungas (churingas) . . . but what does it matter? The book had been read.

Though this precedent might be relevant, one cannot see Ingamells or any other Jindyworobak simply following it. *The Bush* is a poem still too much encrusted with fustian and old-fashioned poeticisms of the Victorian-romantic kind (what O'Dowd himself referred to as "the cheap parterres of Europe" —another idea Ingamells would have accepted, though not its wording) to be of any value as a model. But it exhibits the Aboriginal vision, at least in the form of a faint glimmer, and the next example provides more. If few Australians had read *The Native Tribes of Central Australia*, readers elsewhere valued it and a new edition of the same work was called for and brought out under the title *The Arunta* in 1927. By then the public was more ready to receive it and this was the edition which the young Jindyworobaks read. Ingamells was only fourteen in 1927 but it cannot have been long before he discovered it. It was also read by Mary Gilmore, and prompted her to produce two volumes of poetry near to the Jindyworobak kind, and which could have influenced Ingamells had he been aware of them. I shall come to them presently. Mary Gilmore too was something of a didactic poet, though less pontifical than O'Dowd, and more feminine in her way of going about it. Clearly there was nothing shocking to the Jindyworobak imagination about using poetry for a missionary purpose. But what was so attractive about Spencer's Alcheringa to allure the poets at all? The answer, so far as it touches Ingamells, may appear in the circumstances of his early life.

Rex Ingamells (1913–1955) was born at Orroroo in South Australia, a location of some symbolic importance since it was a town on the edge of the salt-bush plain, on the railway line to Broken Hill: a last-outpost meeting-place of the civilized and the savage. This meant actually that he was born at one of the far limits of the Arunta[1] tribe, the Central Australian people of whom Spencer wrote. This fact does not imply close proximity, especially in 1913, but occasionally, on journeys, he may as a child have seen a little of some Aboriginal encampments. It was experience of which, likely enough, the detail could be forgotten but the effect carried long in his memory. He left Orroroo at a young age to go to school in Adelaide, afterwards to the university where he studied history. He was in fact to become for a time a teacher, but abandoned that eventually to be a publisher's agent. His historical reading did not, as far as I am aware, concern itself intimately with Australian documentation but it was no doubt at the university that it led him to his discovery of *The Arunta*.

Neither of us read the book with scholarly attention; we read it impatiently. The work is large and detailed; I am sure Ingamells read it more carefully, and more often, than I did. It crystallized for him a number of ideas and attitudes. Above all it presented him with the concept of the Dreamtime. "Dreamtime", however, is only an anglicization (and an often abused and sentimentalized one) of the Arunta terms used by Spencer. Properly the word should be Alchera in Arunta; the form Alcheringa is an adjective formed from it (but the distinction is pedantic). It should be added that the same mythical concept (or one very like it) is common to all Australian Aboriginal tribes, though different languages have different words for it.

This is no place to attempt a scientific explanation of the Alchera; nor is it necessary to an understanding of the Jindyworobak use of it. One does not need an anthropological explanation of Hades to understand *Orpheus in the Underworld*, or of the *Nibelungenlied* to follow *Das Rheingold*. The Jindyworobaks used the Alchera symbolism with as much or as little detail as they required; and it was not usually complicated. In effect it is a myth of a time outside the limits of history in which whatever exists has the reality of myth, not of fact; it exists in eternal terms as "then" or "now" or "in the future" or "always"; it is the time to which all other time goes back, in which the first things were done, the first creatures came to life, the creation-time. The first men and the first animals and plants came together then and were, not physically but totemistically, identified and (as the legends relate) interchangeable. It is a vision of the world which is so like a dream that it is also called the "Dreaming" (a more accurate expression than "Dreamtime"). All men of today belong to their proper totems and are reincarnations of the creatures (animals, human heroes, spirits, wanderers) of the original creation-time. Taken in conjunction with aspects of Aboriginal ritual and law, social structure and moral and religious institutions, it is easy to see how O'Dowd could find the "Golden Age" in Alcheringa. We do not, however, need to see the phenomena in terms of such ideal perfectionism to realize that their "dreaming" aspect, which means one thing to an Aboriginal and another to a youthful white poet, has a sufficiently elastic validity to work on a number of levels and with satisfaction to the user on many of them.

An important question is whether such an image can be as useful to a reader as it obviously has been to a group of writers. For Aboriginal minds it is not merely a plausible image, the philosophical–intellectual–religious–ethical medium in which all their myths, legends, ceremonies, institutions and even their very thoughts cohere, it is the very basis of their faith; it is at the root of their concept of reality. It is of no use to pretend that white Australians, even Jindyworobak poets, can give that kind of sacred belief to it. So for them it is a figurative image, a symbol, a large metaphor. And as such it either does or does not work. Flexmore Hudson, as we are aware, found it hard to swallow. Ian Mudie could take it or leave it; for him it was an instrument, to be used or left alone. Hart-Smith accepted it as a device of the mind: he tended to stand off and use it imaginatively, but always preserving his own perspective. Robinson let it work like a yeast in his mind, an intoxicant, much as the poets of Ireland used the Red Branch. Only for Ingamells, really, was it in any closely resembling sense an article of faith; and it was a white Dreamtime, really, that sustained his faith most of the time. The Aboriginal Dreamtime excited him. But it was the Australian one—the Great Australian Uniqueness—that he most deeply believed in.

If the edges of this explanation seem fuzzy, they must be left so; I think no permanent good can come of an attempt to reduce the concept of the Australian Dreamtime to precise definition. Some of it must certainly be left to be taken on trust. Yet the curious thing—for really it is an astonishing concept, quite a wild kind of fantasy and not one it might have seemed likely a nation as pragmatic as the Australian would easily accept—is that it has, upon the whole, been favourably taken. Among the poets, the Jindyworobaks themselves apart, few have been ready to accept it unqualified; but it has gone somehow into the background of their thinking. Some even who have been openly critical, even derisive, towards the Jindyworobaks, have been influenced by it, sometimes to an extent they hardly realize. What one can say, is that a myth may exist and be recognized even if nobody accepts it at face value; the Jindyworobaks' Dreamtime is such a myth and can well function in that way. Even for Ingamells it was a part of literature and not, like the Arunta Alchera, part of life as a whole. That is where, for us now, its real value lies and must lie. It is not the Real Presence; it is a tjurunga (churinga), a totemic symbol, a stone elaborately carved or painted with a sacred design, the serious representation of its contained truth, not the fact itself.

Put to the political application that O'Dowd made, the Golden Age of the Alchera was a pastoral simplification not equalled by the prettiest fancies of a Theocritus or a Virgil: for both those poets knew well enough that a farmer is at bottom a farmer. It is true, though, that, seen wholly under a colour of idealism, the tribal life of the Aborigines, politically ordered by a rule of democratic custom and mutual consent, and spiritually controlled by the mythological authority of the Alchera, seemed to constitute the kind of perfect human community which nothing in the inherited white civilization could equal. This thought, however unreal (and I imagine nobody was actually deceived) had a genuinely imaginative appeal for a group of young poets who, in the bad times of the 1930s, all felt trapped within a national and political "environment" which appeared hopelessly and inescapably evil, and threatened to close in on them and destroy them and Australia utterly.

Ingamells was already writing short poems and lyrics with a Jindyworobak drift in 1930. Two modest volumes appeared, in both cases with the friendly encouragement of Edgar Preece, an Adelaide bookseller who published *Gumtops* in 1935 and *Forgotten People* in 1936. There were some amiable verses here, but from the Jindyworobak point of view they were still tentative. In 1936, however, there was also a tentative use of the magic word: "Jindyworobak". It appeared in *Chapbook*, the second (and final) issue of a small magazine, also issued by Preece, along with some other experimental writings which included the poem "Moorawathimeering" to be discussed presently. Ingamells brooded over these innovations for two years, preparing for the Jindyworobak *annus mirabilis*, 1938. In that year three significant works appeared—slender pamphlets, but with a strong impact. These were his third volume of poems, *Sun-Freedom*; the prose manifesto, *Conditional Culture*, and an even more vital challenge, the first *Jindyworobak Anthology*.

In *Conditional Culture* he wrote:

"Jindyworobak" is an aboriginal word meaning "to annex, to join", and I propose to coin it for a particular use. The Jindyworobaks, I say, are those individuals who are endeavouring to free Australian art from whatever alien influences trammel it, that is, bring it into proper contact with its material. They are the few who seriously realize that an Australian culture depends on the fulfilment and sublimation of certain definite conditions, namely:
1. A clear recognition of environmental values.
2. The debunking of much nonsense.
3. An understanding of Australia's history and traditions, primaeval, colonial and modern.

As he saw it, the need was to "annex" or "join" the white to the black, or the black to the white—it is not clear how, except that the process would involve some "debunking", and require some revaluation of "Australia's history and traditions". As a manifesto it might have been more precise and lucid, but that does not mean nothing can be made of it. In the light of what followed it can be interpreted. "Environmental values" means what it says: the relationship, subjective or objective, between a man and the world about him. In poetry this mostly comes to mean the relationship between personal or individual sensibility and the physical or social landscape. With the Jindyworobaks it often comes to a way of looking at the "primaeval" landscape, whether that implies the Aboriginal, mythical and original Australia or something rather closer to mere geology. It is epitomized in a man-landscape equation. As for the second "condition", it is obvious enough what Ingamells had in mind; it mainly refers to proprieties of local diction, and was a complaint with more urgency to it when he wrote than it has now. Especially in the poetry of Kendall, but also in the drawing-room lyrics and album and magazine verse of the half-century which followed, there was an excessive abundance of what Ingamells regarded as inappropriate "English" poeticisms—mostly mere words, but also conventional concepts and allusions—O'Dowd's "cheap parterres":

> I know she is fair as the angels are fair,
> For have I not caught a faint glimpse of her there,
> A glimpse of her face and her glittering hair,
> And a hand with the Harp of Australia?
>
> Kendall, "The Muse of Australia"

Ian Mudie considered that this Jindyworobak objection was justified well enough, and effectively made;[2] but it is odd that Ingamells should choose to use an American colloquialism ("debunking") to make the point. Others, of course, felt similarly and the Jindyworobaks may not claim the whole credit for reforming the "parterres", but their vehemence was a natural ingredient in the programme. The third "condition", especially as it includes the term "primaeval", is more important and original. "Primaeval" implies more than merely "old" and its powerful message had not been heard in Australia alone —at least there may be a tone here that echoes Longfellow's American "forest primeval". Whether or not, it is the Aboriginal association that Ingamells had most specifically in mind, and this implied the other terms. "Australia's history" did not begin in 1788; it began thousands of years before that (the archaeologists now say something like fifty thousand, but in 1938 the figures advanced were less). Ingamells's point is to promote a recognition of *total* Australian identity; a range of history in which the Aborigines have much the largest part, but which requires to be seen in the three aspects mentioned, Aboriginal, colonial-pioneering and modern-contemporary. *All three* are component parts of Ingamells's "Dreamtime". "Alchera" or "Alcheringa" is the specifically Aboriginal Dreamtime, but the Jindyworobak Dreamtime is "Australia's history" as a whole, or whatever part of it he chooses to emphasize. That is, it is the national identity viewed *sub specie aeternitatis*.

It should be clear enough from these principles that (although they were accused of it) the Jindyworobaks never set out to write Aboriginal poetry in English words. Their desire to "annex and join" was not a desire to invade and conquer. Nor did they design to be conquered: they always retained their white character, shown in the most unmistakable way in their continuation in the European tradition of lyrical styles. Possibly there is an assertion concealed here which calls for amplification. If we go to what seem to be the purest, the least contaminated and therefore the most fundamental conceptions of Aboriginal poetry accessible to us, the Arunta or Aranda epics which are the subject of T.G.H. Strehlow's elaborate study, *The Songs of Central Australia*,[3] it is plain that the earliest and most primitive kind of poetry—and poetry it certainly is, in spite of certain dissimilarities to what we are accustomed to—is impersonal and cannot be lyrical. The Aranda *Songs* are ceremonial and ritual epics, sacred texts, never ascribed even inferentially to any single personal author, and handed down through the generations without (conscious) modification. The conventions of language and diction, which are complex, but need not concern us, are in themselves preservative even though the literature is, historically, entirely an oral tradition. As the Jindyworobaks paid no visible attention to the actual "literature" of the songs there is little point in attempting to examine technicalities. Even though Ingamells was acquainted with Strehlow and discussed his ideas and received some encouragement from him, I doubt very much that his acquaintance with the songs was extensive; in any case, most of Strehlow's published studies came later. (He published "Ankotarinja, an Aranda Myth" in *Oceania* IV, 1933, but I have seen no evidence that Ingamells used it.) It is, in fact, an unprofitable exercise to try to establish any connection between Aboriginal and Jindyworobak poetry, and even the striking forms and designs of Aboriginal visual art seem to have made only a picturesque impact. Most people, including the poets, who were acquainted with Aboriginal artifacts in the 1930s regarded them as quaint, decorative, but impenetrably symbolic and made no attempt to understand them more than very superficially. The white writers could not write with anything resembling the commanding impersonality of the Aboriginal epics, whether or not they knew them.

That impersonality is a mark of the extremely early primitive state of Aranda poetry. It is difficult to be positive, but as far as I am able to tell from a comparison with the northern (Arnhem Land) poetry of which careful and admirable translations are available by Ronald Berndt (see bibliography), it remains my impression that the completer isolation of the Central Australians has preserved more closely intact the primitive function of poetry with them than was the case elsewhere. In the north some degree of contact with visitors from beyond the sea (or some other cause) had introduced at least a minor degree of quasi-literary sophistication into their styles. According to the impression conveyed by Strehlow, at least, there appear to be few Central Australian verses which do not derive from the epics, even those that serve as charms and incantations; and above all, nothing that could be called lyrical in a European sense.[4] It is impossible for an inherited, ritualistic poetical system whose origins are lost in the remote past (are, in fact, accepted as being part of the creation itself, the heroes who are the subject of the poetry being themselves regarded as the creators of the verses) to retain personal accents, and therefore to function, even when fragmented, as European lyrics do. The essence of European lyric is that it expresses a personal emotion; the *passion* in the verse is an outflow of the poet's own heart ("the spontaneous overflow of powerful feelings", said Wordsworth). There are passages, certainly, in the epics which arouse strong, even excited emotion (and this comes through impressively in translation, though we may not understand them exactly as a primitive Aborigine would). But the Jindyworobaks never aimed at poetry of that tribal and ritual kind; they were lyrical poets, lyrists in the classical, European and even (deny it as they might) the English tradition; and they were never anything else. They were romantics still, whether they liked to think so or not; and their romanticism persisted even when they stood ranting and preaching on the hustings, uttering what was perhaps barely even poetry at all.

What one will claim for the Jindyworobaks, especially for the first three and Ingamells above all, is that they had *some* of this impersonal detachment. They caught it in the first place from their own prophetic seriousness: teachers and propagandists, it was not for them to dwell, or to dwell exclusively, on emotions they did not share freely with others. Second, it appears to be something absorbed from the landscape, the "environment" or "spirit of the place", and in this respect a response of their own to something which had great importance in the Aboriginal mind. It must be interpreted for the Jindyworobaks, principally as a broad, pervading influence, an atmosphere; but as the Aborigines understood it, it came down to specific detail. Every location, every feature of the visible landscape was inhabited with mystical, mythical and totemistic presences—places where mythical events had occurred, where the wandering ancestors had rested, and (of vivid importance to individuals) spots where the quickening had occurred which first identified them as the living unborn and assigned them to their totems. Naturally in these circumstances there was a profound suggestiveness in all places, ritually important to the natives, imaginatively so (in a more or less Wordsworthian sense) to the poets; a mystical experience, in fact, which may be designated for both the white and the black, though with different implications, as Australian site-magic.

For Ingamells the mystical sensations of site-magic were the key to his imaginative expression. His inspirations, and also his limitations, were for the most part visual; at any rate, sense-impressions. And as they were impressionistic, so were they, for the most part, brief. A single image or image-vista may constitute the whole content, the whole essential content, of his poem. Always he writes best about what he can touch or see: rocks, most often; or effects of light; the open landscape, people who animate it. His "Black Mary" is human but is equally a living sculpture: she "walks wonderfully". He is vividly responsive to moods of dawn or dusk, the splash of light on a cliff face. He also has another and a particular responsiveness, to language—that is, to words heard in a romantic ear. In "Jindyworobak" there is a striking instance; in fact he uses the word out of context and perversely, but it still serves his creative purpose and retains the magic which it had first for him when he discovered it. Undoubtedly the sound of the words Alchera and Alcheringa enchanted him before he had fully digested their meaning. This enchantment found in words is a European characteristic; to the Aborigines, though they might be sacred, those words were not exotic. But it is now convenient to turn to a poem which raises and perhaps may answer a few queries of the kind which has just come into context, touching both language and the vision of Alchera; and at the same time to refute the accusation that Ingamells attempted to compete with Aboriginal poetry by writing lines of his own in imitation of it. It will be apparent at once that this last charge is nonsense.

The poem "Moorawathimeering" will be found on p. 11; the reader may care to turn over the pages and find it. It may be guaranteed to have an instant effect, but whether sympathetic or hostile may be unpredictable. Here at any rate is at first sight an array of impenetrable Aboriginal words: yet a quick glance at the glossary will show that they can all be interpreted painlessly:

> Into moorawathimeering, where atninga dare not tread,
> Leaving wurly for a wilban, tallabilla, you have fled . . .

This was a "debunking" of English artificiality in diction with a vengeance. Was the effect merely an exchange of nonsense for nonsense, or was there new magic in it? Obviously the attempt was experimental, and even if successful in the way of novelty, not likely to be very freely repeatable. But in this one poem, if not so clearly in the others (a few only) which accompanied it, it does seem to me that he captured the magic he sought. It makes little difference to point out that here again there has been some minor verbal confusion. When the poem first appeared (obviously it was one of the very early products of his Jindyworobak awakening) he spelt the word "moonawathimeering", and that was the spelling used in the first reprint in *Sun-Freedom* 1938. But at this stage he must have glanced back at its source in *The Vanished Tribes* and realized he had miscopied it. All later printings (and it remained a favourite poem) replace "moon—" with "moor—". Captivated as he was by native words (which he never troubled to relate with any system to their proper original languages and dialects), he could also be careless with them and in one instance, may I be forgiven for suggesting, amusingly reckless —as when, in another of his early experiments he wrote,

> Flat upon her mooloona
> Innerah eats the kombora ...

Yet against the bathos of this set the line

> fine as late allinga light[5]

These are trifles: "Moorawathimeering" is perhaps rather more.[6] Clearly it has an Aboriginal subject. It is not an Aboriginal poem. It makes vivid use of Aboriginal and Dreamtime ideas; it respects the decorum of site-magic and time-magic equally. But it never loses touch with the European lyrical tradition.

It is time to look at the literary influences which did affect the Jindyworobaks. I place a considerable importance on the nineteenth century theme of "the coming Australia", a cliché of sentimental prophecy which was uttered by, let us say, all and sundry, but with strong confidence and belief, and culminated in Bernard O'Dowd, who accompanied his hopes with an anxiety lest the splendid promise should somehow go awry:

> Are you for Light, and trimmed, with oil in place,
> Or but a Will o' Wisp on marshy quest?
>
> "Australia" (sonnet)

Ingamells and the Jindyworobaks were certainly for Light, but the marsh was all about them in their youth; the Will o' Wisp, however, was not an Australian but the grim, defecting European spook. Light always inspired Ingamells. There was another nineteenth century image on which he built, but again without taking it over unchanged. This was the dawn-image, the symbol of enlightenment on the point of breaking through the colonial dark. For the early poets it was almost wholly a political prophecy. "She is not yet," wrote Brunton Stephens in 1877, but the listener with a fine ear

> Hears in the voiceful tremors of the sky
> Auroral heralds whispering "She is nigh".
>
> "The Dominion of Australia, a Forecast"

For James Lister Cuthbertson it was more literal—

> Give us from dawn to dusk
> Blue of Australian skies . . .
>
> "The Bush"

For George Essex Evans there were spiritual overtones:

> From sunlit plains to mangrove strands
> Not as the songs of other lands
>   Her song shall be.
>
> "An Australian Symphony"

The poem was a protest against another cliché, that of the "weird melancholy" Marcus Clarke found in Gordon. Tired as the poets were of it, however, the "weird melancholy" theme could never quite be persuaded to lie down and die; and it turned up again in Ingamells's day in an unexpectedly vivid version, in D.H. Lawrence's *Kangaroo*.

These were all notions that Ingamells felt called upon to deal with, but without knowing how. He was encouraged as quite a young man to feel that he possessed a poetical destiny. In his introduction to the 1938–1948 *Jindyworobak Review* he tells us, "Between 1933 and 1935 Professor L.F. Giblin, Mr Edward Garnett and Mr John Masefield encouraged me to write Australian nature poems". Giblin's encouragement was important, the others possibly more incidental. But the first really powerful stimulus—a fire to kindle him—came from his discovery in *The Australian Mercury* in 1935 of the first instalment of *The Foundations of Culture in Australia* by P.R. Stephensen (the complete text was published in the following year). Through his friend Edgar Preece he was able to make contact with Stephensen. What Stephensen urged (and urged with some belligerence) was that Australia should discover and stand by her own cultural attitudes and standards. His point of view was largely, but not wholly political; and it might almost have been that he spoke Ingamells's thoughts, but more loudly.

At the same time, Ingamells recalled, "*The Australian Mercury* induced me to turn to *Kangaroo* by D.H. Lawrence, wherefrom I gained a strong sense of the *primaeval* in Australian nature". *Kangaroo* had appeared in 1923 but had passed unnoticed; now it became a challenge. Lawrence, who had no doubt read about the "weird melancholy" formula before arriving in Australia, was stunned by its impact when he walked into the bush; he of course refashioned it to suit himself, but essentially the "strangeness" he ascribed to Australia was derived from that literary precedent. He was also responsive, as Ingamells believed everyone should be, to the

Great Australian Uniqueness which made its impact through the Environment. What he had to say renewed and intensified for many Australians certain impressions which had somewhat faded because they had been repeated so often. Lawrence, once heard, could not fail to be listened to. But Ingamells felt he must stake out his own independent claim as well: "... on the subject of the *primaeval*, I rejected Lawrence's view of strangeness in the Spirit of the Place ..." How could he not? For Lawrence's reaction, vivid as it was, was that of a man who was a stranger himself; and for Ingamells and other Australians, it was only necessary to show that this "strangeness" had been familiar all their lives. The difference was one of terminology, but what Ingamells saw was the mystery that Lawrence gave a name to ... an *Aboriginal* power. So for him it was of the Dreamtime; Lawrence did not think in that precise formula.

Ingamells says of Stephensen's influence that it was greater after 1941; it is not necessary to follow this, which may merely imply a closer personal acquaintance. The main effect was upon his early programme of thought, and that was determined by 1938 if not before. Lawrence's effect on him was wholly literary and imaginative. Quotations have been assembled from both writers to illustrate their influence and will be found in Parts 3 and 4.

Of influences purely literary, two more must be mentioned, though of one I remain dubious. They are James Devaney, especially for his *The Vanished Tribes* (1929), and Mary Gilmore, who has been mentioned before. Of the actual relevance of her two volumes *The Wild Swan* (1930) and *Under the Wilgas* (1932) I am far from certain; and yet they cannot be passed over. Ingamells was acquainted with Mary Gilmore later and she contributed both to the Jindyworobak *Anthologies* and (very briefly) to the 1938–1948 *Review*. But he does not anywhere mention the two volumes named as formative, and I do not see that he could have failed to do so had he known them while they were fresh.

Nevertheless it would appear that Mary Gilmore and Ingamells in this instance shared two models in common. *The Vanished Tribes* was one of them, apparent to every eye in certain themes and occasional phrases and expressions. The other, even more indispensable, was *The Arunta*. Mary Gilmore had not hitherto written much about Aborigines (she had been writing verse since 1910), and did not write much outside these two volumes. But whether or not he read them at the time, Ingamells must have recognized something of himself in such lines as these:

Fallen the flame and the spear, and fallen the hunter;
The child's bones lie in the grass, by the weed o'ergrown;
The gunyah once home is fallen like fallen Arunta,
Only a womerah left, and a mouldered bone.

The hunted of the dogs; whom no man has righted;
Their blood is black on our hands that nothing can purge.

And the refrain:

O the lost tribes! . . .
He came a ghost
Where once there walked a host.
O the lost tribes! . . .

"The Aboriginals", from *The Wild Swan*

In fact this is not Jindyworobak writing, but its compassion for the Aborigines marks strong affinities in it, and these come out even more in certain other pieces, notably "Land of Mirrabooka", "Wariapendi: a Dirge" and "The Children of Mirrabooka" in *Under the Wilgas*. A significant difference is that Mary Gilmore has a perspective of age and experience which the young Jindyworobaks lack; and the key to her thought is pity. The Jindyworobaks are not without it but it is by no means their linchpin. Mary Gilmore on the other hand is without their lust for hard, bright visuals, an especially marked disposition in Ingamells.

Since I cannot properly place Mary Gilmore prominently among the Jindyworobak selections in this volume, yet do not think it right to omit her, I must contrive an opportunity to quote at least one entire poem; and it may well fit in here. Here is the lyric "Australia". It falls into two seemingly discontinuous parts, which however do cohere in the final perspective. It is a perspective of time—not, however, Jindyworobak time. This is not Alchera poetry; the calendar is Classical, not Aboriginal.

I

There was great beauty in the names her people called her,
Shaping to patterns of sound the form of their words;
They wove to measure of speech the cry of the bird,
And the voices that rose from the reeds of the cowal.[7]

There, where the trumpeting frog boomed forth in the night,
Gobbagumbalin! he said, Gobbagumbalin!

And even as Aristophanes heard, in the far-off deeps
Of his Grecian marshes, the frogs, so we in that word,
Gobbagumbalin! . . . Gobbagumbalin! . . .
Harken, and measure the sound!

II

Mark where, fallen, the tribes move in the shadow;
Dark are the silent places where Arunta walks—
Dark as the dim valleys of Hades where stalk,
Grey-shaped, the Gods and Heroes of the Greeks.
These were the young; for even then Arunta was old.
Very old was Arunta when Alexander wept;
Old, old was Arunta when over Bethlehem
Was seen the star that told the birth of Christ;
Old, old was Arunta when upward from the deep
Was swung the hammer-symbol of Poseidon.
They rose and fell, but Arunta lived on.
Then was Arunta put out in a night.

The Jindyworobaks did not turn to Greece for comparisons. It is a sobering thought, nevertheless, that the Aborigines, with a history extending back infinitely further than Alexander, or for that matter the heroes of Troy, could be destroyed with such grim and dramatic suddenness as followed in Australia upon the entry of the alien white invader.

When projecting the 1938–1948 *Review* Ingamells wrote to Mary Gilmore. She replied, "About Jindyworobak . . . I am an Alice-sit-by-the-fire in relation to it". But her note was sympathetic. (*Review*, p. 35)

The case of James Devaney is different. "In 1936," Ingamells wrote (*Review*, p. 11), "I discovered a copy of *The Vanished Tribes* . . . and I have seldom felt more excitement than upon my first reading of these beautifully told stories." He continues: "From the glossary I took the name 'Jindyworobak' because of its Aboriginality, its meaning, and its outlandishness to fashionable literary taste." It is true that in the glossary at the end of *The Vanished Tribes* "Jindyworobak" is given as meaning "to annex, to join"; but at this stage he had evidently not read the story in which the word is used, where it carries no such signification. What matter? It was the magic word for which he had been waiting and he "adopted" it at once. It is fair, though, to add that it was only one element of the large debt he owed to Devaney. *The Vanished Tribes* (and I think also, but to a lesser extent, an earlier novel, *The Currency Lass*, 1927) remained always at the back of his mind, occupying a place and preserving an authority comparable with that of *The Arunta*. He drew upon it for both thematic material, descriptive or narrative, and Aboriginal words. Friendship followed his discovery of the stories and in 1948 Devaney was invited to contribute a foreword to the *Review*. "I am not a Jindyworobak," he began, claiming neither authority nor responsibility. But added sympathetically, "except perhaps by adoption". He never accepted assimilation into the movement, but that was partly a difference between generations. In 1948 Mary Gilmore was eighty-three, James Devaney two years short of sixty.

Not long before Devaney's death I visited him in Queensland and asked him about his association with the Jindyworobaks and especially about the sources of *The Vanished Tribes*, which I too had come to regard as a remarkable book. He was vague about both and I believe had forgotten much of the detail; but he spoke with a strong respect for Ingamells's literary enterprise. He could name no documentary sources for the stories and perhaps had none. As a young man he had gone among the northern blacks as a teacher, and had sat with the elders and learned from them. It would appear that most of the material in his book was drawn from tribal talk. He had been sensitively but not scientifically interested. He gathered no particularly sacred narrative, and had no anthropological pretensions, but cared a great deal for the stories as stories; and this may perhaps be why his book reads more naturally than most. There is more of the Dreamtime in them than may at once be apparent. The incidents could belong to present or past or mythical time and distinctions are not insisted upon. Their substance is Aboriginal. But the perspective is never far removed from western realism. For this reason they struck Ingamells forcefully. Certainly the Jindyworobak movement could not have developed as it did had its founder never discovered them.

THE POETS

REX INGAMELLS

Ingamells has already figured largely in this introduction, so what follows relates more pointedly to the anthologized material. The more I reflect about the Jindyworobak achievement, the more I am inclined to believe that the vigour was his and that he at his best epitomized it—but when I say so, it is the occasional brilliant, light-flooded image that comes to my mind, not his reasoning about the experience. He was the first, the most passionate and perhaps in the high moments of his success the most effective of the Jindyworobak "joiners": but I will not assert that he always knew with complete precision what were the elements he was joining. It is important to see him feeling his way: often enough in the dark.

There is a love of light and warmth, but not much that is specifically Jindyworobak, in his early experimental pieces. One of the earliest to survive (dated 1930; but as we have it, a later revision) is his fragmentary "Luis de Torres", in which there is a plentiful romanticism but nothing Aboriginal. Ingamells did not, at any rate consciously, begin with an Aboriginalized vision. It was only that the Dreamtime, when it came, captured for him with astonishing vividness the sense of Australia's magical uniqueness which was his first conscious poetical preoccupation. It was something imbibed in childhood and "Luis de Torres" symbolized it: the mythical experience of history, the glamour of the "Great South Land". All Australian school children were told about that at the age of perhaps nine or ten. We were the heirs of that marvellous late discovery, the last and best to be made in an expanding world of golden, mysterious wonder. The heritage was not for him only: we all shared it. Especially it was the sea-voyagers who captivated us: theirs was the irresistible appeal. If I remember rightly a second wonder hung about the stories we were told in junior classes about the enviable lives of Little Aborigines, who lived in wurlies, on lizards and snakes and kangaroos, and ran free and naked in a world of sunshine and kindness.

It is possible to be ironical about this childish mythology but for many it was a formative force; it was for Ingamells. I do not think it too extravagant to suggest that when he formulated his Jindyworobak theories, these myths were a potent ingredient. Ultimately they entered into the Jindyworobak impulse; what was to be joined and mutually annexed was surely not two histories but two mythologies.

When he was first aware of poetical sensibility he produced verse like "By the Fire", which is characterless:

> I am sitting by the fire,
> Watching the warm raying of its light,
> And treasuring remembered conversations . . .
>
> (1931)

But in "The Old Telegraph Station, Strangways" (also 1931) he has already caught a little of the passionate, though as yet unformulated, Jindy colour:

> It is the most unhappy place these eyes
> Have seen: forlorn old ruins . . .

From here we go to "heartless cries of crows", a plangent Jindy emblem. If the way to Alcheringa lay first through the evocation of old and nostalgic times (and it almost certainly did)—with "drear floods" and "affrays with blacks" in lonely country, "small campfires in dark wastes", this was well on the track. We come closer still with "The Afghans", which I reprint; but the first convincing Aboriginal landmark is "Boomerang" (1932). Ingamells never considered it good enough to reprint. Perhaps the best of this early trial-and-error poetry was "The Bullocky", which has perception, feeling and some poetical substance. The bullocky comes at noon in a cloud of dust and pauses outside a bush school to hear the children singing:

> the smoke
> From his old black pipe curled up;
> Then, when the singing ceased, he called
> To his blowing team—"Gerrup!"
>
> (1932)

"Forlorn Beauty" (1933) shows some regression: half the poetical energies of the late colonial lyrical impulse exhausted themselves in singing the praises of Beauty (more often than not capitalized and personified). And yet in this (on the whole jejune) poem occurs one of Ingamells's most splendid Jindyworobak images . . . glimpses, rather:

> O I have seen one flaming peak at dawn
> Across a sea of sand . . .

The true Jindyworobak fusion is attained with a group of short bird-pieces in 1935: "Garchooka the Cockatoo", "Garrakeen" (the parakeet), and one or two other associated fragments. "Garchooka" in seven lines is his first unimpeachable lyric in the Jindyworobak mode. A flight of cockatoos passes, screeching, along a reach of some river—I fancy the Murray is meant—and the noise of the birds, the flash of their colour, the mood of evening, the gold light and the rippled water, all cohere in a brilliantly native Aboriginal impressionism. Its Dreamtime significations could easily escape notice, so may be pointed out. For Ingamells there is, to begin with, the magic of the bird's name, a response which never failed in him; but it is reinforced with tribal echoes, since it is natural to assume the birds are totemic tribal spirits as well as physical creatures. Of course this requires a contribution from the informed imagination, but it is not at all difficult to supply.

Perhaps these bird poems were lucky successes: he was by no means so happy with frogs.

> I hear, ere sleep, the medleyed notes
> Escape the wet, moon-gleaming throats.
>
> There's one old bull-frog's bass . . .
>
> . . . giant reed-growths in a marsh
> Where starlight streamed insipid on
> The slime of Labyrinthodon.
>   (1935)

Imageless and banal; nothing of Alchera here. Nor is there anything of Mary Gilmore's grotesque magic in the Aristophanic frog-poem quoted earlier. This piece, which is three years later than hers, is full of faults which break the poet's own canons: weakly artificial diction, lumbering rhyme. The "one old bullfrog" has a personality—but as a rule Ingamells is happier with light than with sound. These fragments come near to his true landscape:

> Look at the rocky range . . .
> The black crows are calling, forlornly crying out . . .
>   "Evening in the MacDonnells" 1933
>
> There are rock-rooted ranges . . .
> There are crows settling on the boundary gate
> or poised in the sky . . .
>   "Memory of Hills" 1939
>
> Black boulder,
> gust-chilled,
> dew-filmed for starlight . . .
> I know you are
> a raging-red coal of the sun
> earth-flung
> to set this mountain on fire . . .
>   "Black Boulder" 1940

Sound may support vision, but vision is first. If he wholly forsakes the visual his talent may fall limp:

> How can a stranger hope to understand?

(Dorothea Mackellar said that: "All you who have not loved her, You will not understand".)—But if that individual line was abysmal, its companion was not:

> Dark ghosts go with me all about the land.
>   "Forgotten People" 1936

In "The Gangrened People" 1941, where he preaches grossly, there are not even dark ghosts to save him:

> We, the Gangrened People,
> swollen up with fabricated virtue,
> virus of hypocrisy,
> call ourselves the champions of Justice
> and Liberty and O Democracy . . .

Jindyworobak indignation of this quasi-political kind was pious and well-intentioned but in effect nothing to the poetical point. The Jindyworobak imagination could never (even in Ian Mudie, a somewhat more robust political personality) be made with any grace to work like a horse on the hustings. Yet they were both tempted to mount the noble hobby. Ingamells in particular was an ineffective satirist—in the romantic, rhapsodical, lyrical and visionary vein he could be memorable, but as a Jindyworobak Jeremiah, performing concertos for the political didgeridoo, he is almost always flat and tedious. The truth is, he lives by his insights and they tend to be of a brief, almost flashing duration: he does not well sustain a large design. His attempt at a narrative of some length, "The Bloodwood Tree" 1936, meant to be harsh, grim and heroic, is merely gothically uninspired. He did not so much lack imaginative passion as humour; often it was simply this that failed his design. And perhaps if he had possessed a more lively sense of proportion he would never have embarked upon that poetical old-man-of-the-sea, *The Great South Land* (1951). This work, which he boasted ill-advisedly was longer than *Paradise Lost*, has passages of a certain not unadmirable rhetorical eloquence. His earnestness shines right through it. But it never rises above the grandeur of a nobly planned compilation. It is the childhood history lesson conscientiously expanded; it is a young man's homework laboriously performed. All that it contains of the real Jindyworobak spirit returns to those happy nursery days before he had yet heard of Alcheringa. But it celebrates the great Australian uniqueness; the mystery, not the consummation. It would not be just to pass it over without notice but it is not represented at length in the selections here, partly because space was not available to include passages long enough to be typical; partly because it seems to me to depart, even if it does not mean to, from the Jindyworobak vision. The few fragments reprinted will not, I hope, exhibit it in an unattractive light. They are moments of lyricism in a design which I believe is in itself lyrical, but portentously carried out.

There are signs of a restlessness in some few of Rex Ingamells's later lyrics which might lead us to suppose he was moving towards a more balanced and mature complex of poetic values than had carried him forward—joyously and brilliantly at his very best—so far. Unfortunately in December 1955 he was killed in a motor accident. The poem "The Pensioner", reprinted here, is one which could suggest a change in his style and outlook. But it was not to be.

FLEXMORE HUDSON

The earliest of Ingamells's serious supporters was Flexmore Hudson, born also in 1913. There were, however, temperamental differences as well as a strong common interest. Hudson was from the beginning as deeply committed to the intimacy and uniqueness of the Australian "environment" as Ingamells was, but he took less kindly to the imposition of an Aboriginal visionary scheme over the landscape. He chose rather to see with his natural eyes. He took his stand upon sensibility and rejected, or at best accepted only very uneasily, the additional mystification of an arbitrary programme. He was young enough and nationalistic enough at heart to write, in 1938,

> I am proud to be an Australian and I love
> all trees Australian, birds and beasts,
> all ranges and their rivers . . .

In essence this was not very different from Ingamells; but the manner and the approach were unlike. Both poets were young visionaries in their way, equally captivated by the light and outline of the physical world, and equally impressionistic in their sighting of it. Each seems to say "Look!" and the reader's gaze falls upon some vivid, precise detail. Usually in Ingamells's case it is one commanding point of light; in Hudson's something slightly more diffused, rather a vista than a point. Ingamells's images burn, Hudson's gleam. The difference is brought out in a comparison between Ingamells's "Black Boulder" and Hudson's "Mallee Scene": Ingamells strikes like a blacksmith, Hudson exhibits a delicacy like Conder or the early Streeton. He is more accessibly, more gently emotional. Emotion has its dangers and Hudson's style is vulnerable; but especially in his impressions of life in the Mallee country there is a beautiful balance between the physical illumination of what he describes, and the warm human sympathy which goes with it.

In the event Hudson could bring only a part of his mind to the Jindyworobak scheme. The mind, not the spirit jibbed; he could not surrender critical independence. It was for some such reason that he attempted valiantly to keep going a separate poetical magazine of his own—not in rivalry to the

Jindyworobak Anthologies, so much as in order to preserve detachment. This was *Poetry Quarterly*. He financed it virtually alone and published it as near to quarterly as he could, from December 1941–December 1947. A magazine with as broad a basis as its editor could command, it ventured a little into international territories. It was a noble struggle but a financial drain and had to be abandoned; it never attracted as much notoriety as the annual Jindyworobak issues. The two editors worked together—mostly in harmony, occasionally disagreeing, but generally giving each other generous and friendly support.

Hudson had several styles, the best, in my opinion, being his landscape impressions; it was also the style closest to Ingamells. This, which I call his "Look! See!" landscapism, has nothing Aboriginal about it yet is intensely actual and no less strongly imbued with the "Spirit of the Place" (Ingamells's term). I would wish to call it site-magic. However, as that is an Aboriginal phenomenon, the term is not quite suitable. Next in order after this style I would place his poems of love and friendship, of which several are represented in the selections. These are quite personal, not Jindyworobak. They are not wholly satisfying, but some of them, about children, have a delicacy comparable with the landscapes.

There is a third style which I only wish I could declare equally non-Jindyworobak. But, sadly, other Jindyworobaks were all too prone to it, Ingamells among them: that is the political–moral–homiletic strain, previously referred to as the hobby horse. I have no praise for it but recognize it, especially in Hudson's handling, as a well established if rather outmoded genre. I have already referred to Lindsay Gordon (who had the justification that his contemporaries thought well of it) on the moral side and Bernard O'Dowd on the propagandist. The poem which most recalls O'Dowd is *Indelible Voices*, which in the present selection has had to be reduced to a series of skipping fragments. There is enough, I hope, to represent the character of the poem, which is long, not merely moralistic, and bears acutely on the dilemma of youth at the time; which was, in effect, as needs no repetition, the characteristic Jindyworobak dilemma.

Another style of Hudson's which calls for notice, and has an affinity with the Jindyworobak interest but is not identical with it, is the Whitmanesque. Whitman's American nationalism in the first place had fortified the Australian nationalism of O'Dowd; it had a compelling sweep about it which also appealed to Hudson. And by way of standing out against Ingamells's Aboriginal Australianism, he seems to have approved the strain in Whitman which claimed that pride in the merely national ideal, while it might be much . . . "I am proud to be an Australian" . . . was also not enough; it was ultimately important to strive for the brotherhood of all men.

> I am with you, you men, and women of a generation, or of ever so many generations hence;
> I project myself—also I return—I am with you, and know how it is.
>
> Whitman, "Crossing Brooklyn Ferry"

Hence, passionately as he was attached, strongly as he felt the peculiar uniqueness of being Australian, Hudson believed that to be committed too deeply to the Dreamtime was to accept too narrow a philosophy. Sympathetic to Whitman's universalism, he was also attracted to his rhetoric and his prosody, and the result was several attempts of his own in the same manner. I think they are not to be dismissed as imitations; there was no meanly sycophantic motive in them. They are serious attempts to express a corresponding idealism for Australians. I draw attention especially to the 1941–42 poem "With the First Soft Rain" as a perfectly sincere example. If such a poem needs further justification, perhaps it may help to point out that Hudson here returns conspicuously to his Mallee landscape, though in a less lyrical mode. That there was a certain amount of hesitancy in his rejection of Jindyworobak Dreamtime nationalism is shown by what he wrote in the 1938–1948 *Review*.

"Many critics," he conceded, "do not object to the regionalism and localism of Jindyworobak writing: they would approve of an Australian Hardy presenting a particular locality in great detail." I take this to mean he would approve of a high degree of local colour in Australian writing; it is the mysticism he distrusts. The same anonymous critics (Hudson himself is their voice) "detest the idea of strengthening the sense of nationality, because this can so easily degenerate into an intolerant and bragging provincialism". It is better to abandon national sovereignty and preach Whitman's world citizenship. "But that concept, unfortunately, still seems fantastic to most people." (Ah! how young we all were then! Yet three of the Jindyworobaks were 35 in 1948, and two were 37; I was 38.)

"I cannot help suspecting," Hudson said in the same contribution to the 1948 summing-up,

> that Mr Ingamells's stressing of the cultural importance of the Aborigines is sheer primitivism, a sentimental glorification of a far distant stage of human development . . . There are in it, too, hints

> of a windy Platonic doctrine of recollection and of a Spenglerian conviction that modern society has degenerated ... This primitivism has its source in the shock which all sensitive spirits suffer in misery and in the contemplation of misery ... It is for the Jindyworobaks now to show how the Aborigines' way of life offers a solution to our problems or even a balm for our hurts. I cannot see that they have done so yet ... This idealizing of our Aborigines is, to my mind, escapism.

There is an apparent firming here of opinion against Ingamells's experimentalism; not to be accounted hostile by any means, though the judgment has an elegiac fall. Hudson had always thought the doctrine not quite right; by 1948 he seems at last fairly convinced it was quite wrong. And yet a little sadly.

It seems to me that, in spite of Hudson's growing distrust, these two, Ingamells and Hudson, were the real Jindyworobak innovators. Each took the movement seriously, whether to foster or to doubt it; the element of debate between them helped rather than hindered the development of the movement, whose main initiative remained with Ingamells in any case. But in a sense—a paradoxical sense—they were both eclipsed, or at any rate somewhat shaded, by a third recruit who at times appeared more Jindyworobak than the Jindyworobaks themselves; and sometimes denied affiliation. This was Ian Mudie.

IAN MUDIE

If any one single, simple expression of poetic faith which is also national faith could be said to epitomize the Jindyworobak code it might be Ian Mudie's short lyric "Underground" (see p. 68). It would be hard to think the author of that brief but decisive statement was ever really at odds with Jindyworobak theories and principles and I am inclined to discount his protests. When he differed from Ingamells it was usually on a matter of detail or for some temperamental reason. Mudie was a man of robust and energetic personality and very much his own sociable, easy-going man; impatient by disposition and an unhappy conformist to any other man's rules; but a natural enthusiast, eager to proclaim what he believed in. "Underground" speaks out for the younger Jindyworobak movement and possibly he outgrew the more aggressive colours of its sentiment—particularly his anger at "the blindness/ ship-fed seas bring us/ from colder waters". Mudie was in fact the only one of the three early Jindies who had any personal knowledge of life abroad. He had lived in London for a time, several years before the Jindyworobak proposition was invented at home, and enjoyed the experience; after his Jindyworobak fever abated he returned on an extended vacation and died suddenly while he was away. It is hard to know whether this beginning and ending are relevant information or not. During the years we are actually concerned with he was passionately nationalist in political feeling, and if not a constant Jindyworobak in his poetical moods, it would be hard to find any other epithet for them. "Underground", as it happens, exploits not merely the predictable Alcheringa mythology, but also a typical white-settler imagery of water in the dry land, the archetypal symbolism of artesian springs. One can see that the Dreamtime image and the water image both really serve the same end; separately or together they contribute assurance to the Australian imagination, a form of spiritual or even physical and material support, comforting to the poets' sense of identity with the "land". Seen like this, it is not difficult to distinguish the Jindyworobak faith as a mythology created or developed for the movement's own needs; it was not merely an attempt to take over, holus bolus, an Aboriginal ideology which never belonged to the white world and could not be transferred to it. It was because of confusion about this issue that the Jindyworobak adherents were sometimes in rebellion. No one of them seems to have been quite clear in his analysis of the general mythology, though I believe Ingamells understood better than any of the others what was involved; he felt about the differences instinctively, but never actually defined them.

In his contribution to the 1938–1948 *Review* Mudie appears no longer wholly and heartily to identify with the Jindyworobaks—it may be only my fancy, but it seems to me he deliberately avoids using the word there, but still upholds what it stands for. "During the past ten years," he begins, "Australian poetry has orientated itself in its own continent." Landscape poetry has thrown off the "pale echoes" of English poetical models, and poetry in general has rejected the old, unnatural diction of imitation English verse. The need had been for a convincing "background to the environment"—in other words, a frame of native reference. In an unhappily turgid but earnest paragraph he refers to the principal Jindyworobak innovations as "the rich lode of the dream-time and the pay-dirt of aboriginal life". As a result, "Academics can no longer sneer, as they did less than ten years ago, that to use such terms as Alcheringa, coolamon, Byamee, is affectation, or that to use them as symbols . . . spear-sharp . . . is unscientific. Such terms have become part of the tribal background of our poetry . . ." His complaint against formal Jindyworobakism, not precisely defined but implied, is that its tribalism remains too exclusively Aboriginal. "Dream-time," he says, "is always with us; it never ends. The poets—the storytellers, the myth-makers, the corroboree-makers—would be failing in their purpose if they allowed the post-aboriginal national scene to remain unpopulated" . . . in effect, the Aboriginal Dreamtime is over, but the broader Australian Dreamtime must not be supposed destroyed with it. And therefore, "Just as the dream-time is continuous and neverending, so is the task of the poets." In fact he had seen the Jindyworobaks as a stimulus to poetry, but not in themselves —himself among them—as creators of a major Australian poetical renaissance. This was not an inaccurate summing-up.

But he had not always taken so judicious a line. In his earlier and more boisterous Jindyworobak days he could well be seen as the most vocal—most belligerent, most assertive, most obdurate, and certainly the most crusading—Jindyworobak of them all. He preached a noisy sermon, usually more vigorous than subtle; what never failed him was energy. There are isolated moments and phrases of striking poetic insight in what he wrote, but he was always a talker first and a poet after that. The sound of his voice, his resonant accent, penetrated all his writing and still the echo of it rings in memory. In his later days he wrote less and with increasing care; not long before his death in 1976 he produced several poems in a much mellowed tone which hinted at a greater measure of thoughtful reflection in what was to come. But undoubtedly it will be for his early gusto that he will be remembered.

He did not appear in the 1938 *Anthology* and his "As Are the Gums" in 1939 is still rather tentative, speaking of "the gums that grow as we should grow,/ roots in our land . . ." But there he articulates his "land" symbolism, already a Jindyworobak orthodoxy.[8] Again more boldly in the 1940 *Anthology* he says in "This Land":

> Give me a harsh land to ring music from;
> brown hills and dust, with dead grass,
> straw to my bricks.

This, incidentally, was not the desert interior: it was the Adelaide hills in summer. The rest of the poem is plangent and lusty-lunged:

> Give me words that are cutting harsh
> as wattle-bird notes in dusty gums
> crying at noon . . .

His appeal is for "strength and austerity/ that this land has". Music and harshness, power and beauty, aridity and opulence, the Australian paradox of the hard and the tender together. He says much the same thing in "Corroboree to the Sun" in the same issue, but spoils it with moralizing.

For all three of the early Jindyworobaks the temptation to moralize was nigh to irresistible, and their style was apt to glide from that point into political nagging. Of the three, Mudie nagged most insistently, perhaps it is also fair to say most persuasively. As a political nationalist he was the closest of them in affinities to the outspoken P.R. Stephensen, and sympathetic towards Stephensen's Australia First movement of which the official eye of the day took a dimly hostile view. Stephensen and some of his associates were interned during the war and Mudie himself was questioned, as also was Ingamells. Mudie solved the problem simply enough by joining the army and seems to have enjoyed the years he spent in the service. He distinguished himself in Army Education, was connected with the journal *Salt* and assembled a lively anthology of *Poets at War*, 1944, issued under the Jindyworobak *imprimatur*.

It seems to me there are really three Ian Mudies, and none of them wholly dependent on Jindyworobak theory yet none incompatible. The first and most characteristic—the most idiosyncratic style—is the lusty talker, superbly captured in "They'll Tell You About Me" 1952:

> Me, I'm the man that dug the Murray for Sturt
> to sail down,
> I am the one that rode beside the man from
> Snowy River . . .

The second is the political preacher, nationalist and propagandist, seen at his most aggressive in "The Australian Dream" (substantially represented here); or in "This is Australia", reprinted complete. The third and rarer Mudie is the reflective lyrical poet, capable very occasionally of a vivid image and a quiet mood, as in a poem like "The Blue Crane". In all three the style is rational rather than intuitive, and social rather than introspective.

WILLIAM HART-SMITH

With Ingamells, Hudson and Mudie the first and primary phase of the Jindyworobak movement was complete. It is the more innovatively aggressive, more original and controversial part of it; also the cruder. But still relatively impersonal in the Aboriginal sense. It is lyrical, but lyrical within limits; plain and not as a rule rhapsodic. In the two Jindyworobaks who are to follow, something nearer to a rhapsodic style becomes possible. I am not thinking of Shelleian rhapsody, or odic or dithyrambic verse, but simply verse in which personal sensitivity is given freedom to develop. In Hart-Smith there is a good deal of scope for what I think may be called wit—not in the merely clever sense, but conceptual thinking shaped so as to exhibit itself in idiosyncratic forms: "I think so", "This is my considered way of seeing it" poetry. For Hart-Smith being a Jindyworobak amounted to thinking carefully about Jindyworobak subjects and using Jindyworobak images, but not actively preaching doctrine; simply being himself and choosing, for the time being, to express himself in that mode. Robinson was different: he needed a large design to lose himself in and the Dreamtime vision supplied it. Had he undertaken, in other circumstances, to encompass the wanderings of Oisin, he still would have found his way. The individuality that comes out in him is a passionate obsession. Still there is a restriction placed upon him by his Jindyworobak allegiance and it keeps his imagination within bounds: it is a discipline of a sort. Self-indulgent as his emotions sometimes are, the Jindyworobak element keeps them sufficiently under control to render them valid for all men as well as for the restless ego that struggles continually inside the forms. This denotes more control—more Jindyworobak, or in effect more Aboriginal reticence—than is commonly credited to him. These two poets have not the kind of crusading Jindyworobak spirit we find in the early three. They fit and belong much more comfortably into the European continuity of poetry than do Ingamells, Hudson and Mudie. But they are Jindyworobaks still. Perhaps this could be said in another way. They are able to *join* without first needing absolutely to *let go*.

"To me," William Hart-smith remarked in a private letter in February 1977, "the only legitimate aim of a poet, or any other artist for that matter, was to produce a work of art." As a comment made long after the heady excitement of his earlier Jindyworobakism had cooled (and not only his own, but largely also that of the movement itself), this was a backward glance at a dissatisfaction which had always been there. Time was required, though, to render it clear. Of course it is not enough to say that the whole aim of an artist is to produce works of art; any kind of art needs to acquire meaning in a context, whether in tradition or history or social acceptance or whatever—something in the nature of a background, or to use Mudie's other metaphor, a *tribal* hinterland. During the 1930s Hart-Smith was aware of a strong poetic gift, but at a loss to find speech for it. The "tribal background" of the Jindyworobak programme provided a practical stimulus towards articulation. But at the same time there was also an uncertainty. Was there a realizable purpose beyond the Jindyworobak propaganda? There the doubt lingered.

Hart-Smith had no inborn conviction of the Great Australian Uniqueness to build his poetical projections upon. He was of an age with the other Jindyworobaks, but of "alien" birth. In 1923, at the age of twelve, his family moved from England to New Zealand, with which country he developed a first identity; but he moved on to Sydney in the thirties and there found himself, a little like D.H. Lawrence, surrendering rapidly to the mood of Australia, perhaps simply because he was of an age to feel a need of some such support, and because the sensations were vivid. I draw a little further, with permission, upon the letter just quoted. "I'd been writing poetry for some time," it continued, "and pretty awful stuff it was . . ." Two or three pieces had been published, not much satisfying his sense of self-achievement, when

> In the stacks at the Mitchell I came across some typescript MSS by David Unaipon, an Aboriginal—pastor, I think.[9] His retelling of his people's legends fired something in me. This sort of fused with my delight in, how shall I put it?—the Australianness of Australia. I began to write . . .

It would appear, then, that if he became a Jindyworobak, it was by an independent original approach and not after proselytization by the Adelaide group. Among the poems which then "just came out, *fell out*," were three which, before I had heard from him, I had already selected as representative: "We Are the Elders", "La Perouse" and "The Fishing Lubra", all reprinted here. When these pieces were shown to Ingamells they were welcomed, understandably, as "just the kind of thing he was looking for". They were printed in the *Jindyworobak Anthologies* of 1940, 1941 and 1942. It was not, however, until 1942 that Hart-Smith and Ingamells met. "We had a long talk," Hart-Smith remembered, "continuing it the following day . . . He outlined his Jindy ideas. I agreed with most of what he said, keeping my disagreement to myself." He was a little inclined to be wary of Ingamells's appearance of fanaticism, and accordingly cautious; but interested enough to go along.

Ingamells professed that in selecting verse for publication in the *Anthologies* he held to two (not necessarily incompatible) criteria: it might recommend itself as simply "good poetry", or more hopefully, "good Jindyworobak poetry". A poem like "Summer Day" (see p. 99) may well have caused him a little difficulty and gone in, finally, under the first category; it is not ostensibly Jindyworobak. And yet it is developed upon a symbol of intense "Australianness", if not of the Dreamtime, then warmly related to it: an image of heat and cicadas. The modulation at the end, when the stridency of the day is over, is however subtly different. It is as though when the noise drops away, suddenly we are hearing the music of Debussy. So, too, "La Perouse" is not pure, uncompromised Jindyworobakism, but, like most of Hart-Smith's writing, possesses softer overtones. The poem is not concerned with the famous French navigator, unless by ironic inference; it is about the place named after him, a comment on modern reality in contrast with mythical romance:

> Here the tram crashes to a stop
> coughs once and dies . . .

Briefly the lyric brings together images of present and past, including a "sloe-eyed" local half-caste girl, "with her print frock, permanent wave", who is "off to the pictures". (Ingamells would surely not have cared for "sloe-eyed"!)

Hart-Smith became a sincere Jindyworobak, but never exclusively. Among the work he published in the same active years were a number of lyrics which perhaps had some sympathetic affinity with Ingamells's sea-heroes but beyond that no Jindyworobak content whatever: these were his Columbus poems—isolated pieces in *Columbus Goes West* 1943, enlarged to a sequence in *Christopher Columbus* 1948 and again extended in *Poems of Discovery* 1959. In 1945 Hart-Smith returned for a period of several years to New Zealand. In 1941 Ingamells printed a poem of Hart-Smith's entitled "Hinemoa" which was an attempt to see a New Zealand subject in Jindyworobak terms—a pleasant lyric, but I do not reprint it—and ten years later an attempt was made to bring out a "Trans-Tasman" edition of the *Anthology*, which Hart-Smith edited with Gloria Rawlinson. However, these were attempts to join and annex elements which refused to knit. Thereafter Hart-Smith's work, without any violent change or wrenching, inclined increasingly towards "good poetry" and away from "good Jindyworobak poetry". But the Jindyworobak strain left its traces. It would never be correct to call it a misdirection of his talent; the use he made of it was constructive, creative as long as the impulse survived. As late as *The Talking Clothes* 1966 there are still Jindyworobak subjects and sentiments in recollection, though nothing programmatic. Even in *Minipoems* 1974 there remains a little Jindyworobak nostalgia: I quote here two entire poems:

> Fire can't take me by the throat.
> I wear a charcoal overcoat.
>
> "Blackboy"

(a wittier and more succinct treatment of the same grass-tree image-subject than my lyric with the same title which is also reprinted in this volume)

> In this forty-degree heat
> when each bit of raw, red meat
> I flick to a pair of magpies
> sticks to the concrete,
> how is it the ants can stand it
> on their little bare feet.
>
> "Ants"

If Jindyworobakism is about adaptation to environment, what could illustrate it better than these ants? Here Hart-Smith is laughing, which Ingamells could seldom do; but the point is equally well made.

A little more must be said of Hart-Smith's Jindyworobak years, though the reprinted selections cover the ground reasonably well. A number of the poems which appeared in the *Anthologies* were collected in his volumes *Harvest* 1945 and *The Unceasing Ground* 1946. His closest tie with the movement was in 1944 when he edited the *Anthology*. There are still Jindyworobak poems in *On the Level*, published in New Zealand in 1950. Back in Australia he published *Poems of Discovery* 1950; this collection contains only seven "Australian Poems" but all have a strong Jindyworobak colour. It is interesting, though, to make a comparison. I take the poem "Willie Wagtail" from *The Unceasing Ground* (reprinted, p. 115) and "King of the Castle" from *Poems of Discovery*. It is necessary to recall the Aboriginal reputation of the wagtail as a mischievous gossip of a bird before whom it was unsafe to expose secrets, though he has an insidious wheedling charm. The earlier piece begins descriptively, with birdlike rhythms:

> Then Willie Wagtail hopped along the branch . . .
> So close I could see the whiskers bristling
> At the root of his beak
> And the little black beads that are his perky eyes . . .

Deereeree is the blacks' name for this downy bird. I quote the second poem complete:

> Hidden away in the wilga-tree
> is a prickly person called Deereeree,
> King of the Castle, a glittering mound
> of leaves in the moonlight
> and a lit space around.
>
> Birds that mimic the feudal state
> must take it further and feel irate
> when from trees diminished in size
> by tricks of perspective
> come counterclaims and challenges.
>
> Bird calls to bird. They whistle and wait
> for the call to return. Faintly, "I'm here, mate!"
> And some so far, not a thing is seen
> of the trees where they chirrup.
> And the moon as big as it's ever been.

Two wagtail portraits, the first by day and in a bright humour, close enough to the bird's totem-character to be clearly Jindy in impact and fancy; the second pure nature-poetry, by night —a nocturne—quieter, richer, more melodious, and quite un-Jindy. The movement is away yet not unfriendly.

The poem "Nullarbor" puts Hart-Smith's Jindyworobak phase into an interesting light. Most of the time the Jindyworobaks in general pursued the Aboriginal interest for symbolistic reasons, not significantly for practical ones. "Nullarbor" recalls the poet's brief encounter with a young Aborigine during a train stop in the desert. It was a vivid reminder of the difference between fantasy and reality, wholly human in its impact. And as such it almost bursts the bonds of Jindyworobak fantasy. Can poetry really be written to a programme? Hart-Smith had always doubted it. In the end he was sure.

ROLAND ROBINSON

Roland Robinson may yet be considered the best, the most naturally gifted of the Jindyworobak poets, his *opus* the most highly textured and unified of all of them. But that judgment has not with any deep certainty yet been made. What makes him harder than the others to evaluate is a certain awkwardness in . . . how might one put it? his poetical valency. He was born in Ireland; and although he was only nine years old when he was taken away, in a sense he carried the twilight with him. He has the Irish richness, imagination, the Irish ear for words and language, and a good deal of sheer Irish temperament and passion. Did his Australian education—such education as he had, it was little in the way of schooling—merely substitute the Dreamland for what should have been his Dark Rosaleen? It is interesting to suppose it could effect such a substitution. I think it did. If it did, the change-about was complete. The Dreamtime became his world of romance.

After a not very happy childhood Robinson left school at fifteen and took a job in the bush, as a rouseabout in a woolshed. From then on he followed a great diversity of occupations, in which the one traceable line of continuity has been his profession of poetry. In practice he has been a labourer, house-boy, ballet dancer, artist's model, greensman at a golf course . . . and much else. There is no need to follow this career of miscellanies; he tells it all, in any case, in his two autobiographical books *The Drift of Things* 1973 and *The Shift of Sands* 1976. It is of interest to learn that, very early in his life, he came across a copy of the *Intimate Journal* of Amiel, which became his *vade mecum*. It was that, or something even more deeply inevitable, which turned his thoughts to poetry. But he never had any inclination to toe the standard literary line, and to an early criticism retorted "Did they expect the Irish–Pommy–Australian that was me to write as though all my stimulation came from England or America?" (*Drift of Things* p. 370). There were conflicts and contradictions in the man from the beginning, but also a spirit that had to find its way out. He had the imaginative opulence of a Yeats or a Joyce—an equal abundance, at least, of poetical impulse. Abundance is not dimension, discipline too is another matter. But the discipline in Robinson's poetry may not be as lax as some of his critics have supposed. He is not yet read as he is entitled to be read; he is not yet fully accepted in his Australian and Dreamtime context, and therefore not fully understood.

As to that, time will tell; but time has not yet done so, and cannot be hurried along. I can only take Robinson as I find him; the future may have another way of seeing him and revalue him accordingly.

He tells a story in *The Drift of Things* (p. 476) which amounts to a vivid, brief portrait-impression. He had sent some poems to the *Bulletin*, which accepted them. Douglas Stewart was then the Red Page editor and poetical arbiter. Robinson went to see him on some matter. As he was leaving, Stewart remarked, "By the way, I particularly liked that poem on the Rock-lily you sent me".

> This was a great compliment. It was, to me, in those days. And I reckon such a remark would be a great compliment to me today.

When Douglas Stewart said this to me, I blurted out "You did?
Do you know the price one has to pay to write poems?" I think
that Douglas Stewart said something like, "Well, I've a pretty fair
idea." "Well," I told him, "on the day that I 'got' that poem, I'd
tried to drown myself." I remember well Douglas Stewart's reaction
to this. He jolted me back to sanity. He said, "I'm glad you wrote
the poem before you did."

The anecdote vignettes both men. It is characteristic of the
impulsive Robinson that he must go on after this to relate the
incident; but no less so that he can also compel us to listen.

On the day that I "found" the Rock-lily poem, I had set out
with my pack from Bundeena. In those days I might camp in a
cave, and, as the fire died down, and the light of the last flames
no longer lit up and played on the wall of the cave, I would feel
sleep coming over me. I did not want to ever leave that cave. I
did not want the night, or my sleep, to end. I prayed that I might
not waken from my sleep.

When I came to Wattamolla, the creek coming over the cliff
into the lagoon was in full spate. Wattamolla was then a deserted,
untouched place. I crossed the rushing, narrow outlet of the lagoon
where it ran through the rocks and little beach to the sea. I stood
at the edge of the deep lagoon. I resolved to put my "death-wish"
to the test. I slipped off my pack and stripped off. I stood a long
while on the rocky edge of the lagoon. Then, like someone making
the snap decision to jump from a cliff before reason found some
reason not to act, I dived in and swam to the middle of the lagoon
where I reckoned it was deepest.

I dived and swam down and down. I resolved to swim so far
down that I would not have breath left ever to swim back up again.
The water became colder, darker as I swam down and down. And
then came the decision. I could not do it. I turned and began to
swim as hard as I could upwards. How far did I have to go? How
far had I swum down? I swam upwards with all my strength. I
thought I could hold my breath no longer. Like a madman I swam
upwards. When, when, would I break the surface?

And then, it was like being born, my head broke through the
surface of the water. I must have gulped in air, but what I
remember is the day, the sunlight glancing, glittering on the
surface. I saw the treees, the rocks, the scrub in the sunlight. I
swam slowly to the shore.

I am standing near the shore knee deep in water. I keep cupping
my hands and dashing water into my face, trying to shock myself
back, to wake myself from my insane act. And yet I am shaking
from the cold of the water and from the insanity of what I had
tried to do.

I was telling myself, "So, you want to live. You do not want
to die. You have decided. Go and live then. And never whine and
moan to me again."

Self-dramatizing, self-critical, abandoned to his own subjectivity, all this seems out of pitch with the clear, bright message of Ingamells's shining innocence. But it is merely a different kind of vision, a different kind of concern.

Robinson visited Adelaide in 1944 while he was a member of the Kirsova Ballet. It was an opportunity to meet and consult with Rex Ingamells. Ingamells asked him for samples of his writing and Robinson—the only Australian poet ever, perhaps, to carry the whole of his repertoire in his head; he has always scorned poets who could not remember and speak their verses as well as print them—sat down and wrote off the poem "But this sea will not die":

> But this sea will not die, this sea that brims
> Beyond the grass-tree spears and the low close scrub,
> Or lies at evening limitless after rain,
> Or breaks in creaming lines to the long golden beach
> That the blacks called Gera before the white man came.

The lines containing the title of his earliest volume, *Beyond the Grass-Tree Spears*, which was to reach print that same year, were pre-Jindyworobak in invention but Ingamells approved them. "But," he demurred, "we can't have the word 'creaming'. That's English." Hart-Smith, who edited the *Anthology* in 1944, did print it, but in the published volume it is altered to "curving". Robinson considered it as "my best poem" and Ingamells's criticism evidently stunned him, though he recounts the incident lightly (*The Drift of Things* pp. 238-9). In the reprint in *Altjeringa* 1970 the whole line is altered. The story is trivial but it illustrates two points: Ingamells's pigheadedness in regard to the "debunking of much (English) nonsense", though the word was surely not offensive; and Robinson's sensitive (over-sensitive? thin-skinned?) reaction to criticism.

It is not imperative to trace Robinson step by step through his publications, since in the end the whole of his work—the major part of it, at any rate—coheres in a single total design. This fact may not at once be grasped; the manner in which the poems were issued, some with titles, the titles afterwards removed and the pieces merely numbered, may cause confusion. The explanation is simple enough. He composed upon impulse (or inspiration) at periods of heightened imaginative activity, and the poems produced formed natural groups and sequences, though the plan was never really narrative; he was always a lyrical rather than a narrative poet, invariably so when he wrote subjectively and autobiographically. When he first wrote them down the poems were given titles; when later their

relativity and coherence began to seem more important than
their separate status, they were grouped and numbered. The
volume *Beyond the Grass-Tree Spears* 1944 was later absorbed
into *Language of the Sand* 1949. *Tumult of the Swans* 1953
adds more that is quite new, but all are reassembled in the
volume *Deep Well* 1962.[10] *Altjeringa* 1970 contains some
retreated material and adds more that is fresh, but is of a
different kind. *The Hooded Lamp* followed in 1976; it added
nothing of particular value. There are a few Jindyworobak
lyrics but they stand isolated and indeed the volume lacks
something that the others have from their thematic continuity.

Deep Well is the definitive volume. The chronology of the
poems is not to be assumed from their printed order. The book
may be read as an intensive autobiography, but the order of
the constituent poems is emotional rather than temporal. The
work as a whole is also, in the full Jindyworobak sense, "land"-
oriented. It is passionately contained within its own site-magic.
Robinson does not incessantly preach the Dreamtime message.
But he lives it.

This can be said even literally; he has actually dwelt with
it. Among poets some few are by disposition tramps and bums,
swagmen, rovers and wanderers. Lawson was one. So, at times,
in spirit more often than fact, was Mudie. Robinson could not
have been the poet he was in his younger days unless the roving
spirit had been in him too. He has lived, for most of his life,
a settled existence, but there was also another side to him.
When he was young he tramped south from Sydney to find
peace and asylum from the rat-race in the bush and at the
coast. In his wanderings then he met occasionally men of
deeper and lonelier misfortune than his own, wanderers who
were also Aborigines. They were long detribalized, yet, when
questioned sympathetically, had memories. It was from them
and from the Aboriginal bush itself that he had his first insights
into Aboriginal reality. So in effect when he joined forces with
Ingamells the main change was merely that he acquired a
bright banner to walk under and a formula to help put his
thoughts in order. He kept up those early Aboriginal contacts
for years, meeting the same people many times but sometimes
only after long intervals. During the war he worked in the
north in the Civil Construction Corps—this was the situation
which provided material for much of his inland poetry
including *Deep Well*. He also joined Eric Worrall, the natural-
ist, in outback excursions looking for museum and zoological
specimens. These varied experiences brought him into close
contact with both semi-tribal and tribal Aboriginal com-

munities and he camped among them as much as he could, becoming a collector of myths and legends for preservation and publication. He had no training in anthropology, but recorded vividly, imaginatively and with a good measure of system what material came his way. Naturally the result was of literary, or quasi-literary—legendary—interest rather than strictly or elaborately scientific; but all was of valuable, traditional Dreamtime substance. Most of it emerged in prose form: his *Legend and Dreaming* 1952, *The Feathered Serpent* 1956, *Aboriginal Myths and Legends*[11] 1966 and the volume of stories, *Black-feller White-feller* 1958. In the course of this field-work he met and took encouragement from that almost legendary Territorian and authority on native life and tribal affairs, W.E. Harney. In fact he proudly claims a part in the naming of one of Bill Harney's most successful books about Territory life, *Brimming Billabongs*.

The prose collections, though they are an important part of Robinson's work, can only be mentioned briefly. But some of this collected material also emerges as verse, and among it a good deal that is remarkable. A typical example is "Mapooram". He was "given" this piece by a detribalized New South Wales native, Fred Biggs; it appears first in *Aboriginal Myths and Legends*, where it is set out in the language and form in which he received it:

> You go out and camp somewhere. You might be lying down and a little bit of wind comes. You hear this "mapooram". "What's that?" you say. Why, that's a "mapooram". You go and find that tree rubbing itself. It calls out, "mapooram, mapooram". That's two tree boughs rubbing together in the wind.

Fascinated with the Aboriginal talk, he tried to make it into poetry; but changed it very little. The piece appeared among a dozen others in the volume *Deep Well*, forming part of a sequence called "The Wandering Tribes" (no. 16):

> Go out and camp somewhere. You're lying down.
> A wind comes, and you hear this "Ma-poor-am".
> "What's that?" you say. Why, that's a Ma-poor-am . . .

Some of these reappear in the volume *Altjeringa*, "Mapooram" without further change but others altered in form while still retaining the same content. The names of the speakers who gave him the stories are in each case preserved, and Robinson does not claim authorship. Fred Biggs (whom he met at Menindie) also gave him "The Child Who Had No Father", which occurs first in *Deep Well* (No. 27):

> Before the white man came here with his sheep
> the plains were covered with all kinds of flowers.
> And once two sisters, who lived in a cave,
> would go out walking through the flowers at evening
> looking for any food that they could find . . .

In the version which I reprint from *Altjeringa* there is a metrical change which seems quite versatile, yet the words themselves largely remain as they were. The narrative continues:

> And when those sisters walked
> among the flowers;
> there were no mai, no men,
> in all the world. . . .

The versions reprinted here are all from the later volume, but comparisons may be made with interest. There is some difficulty in deciding where to place and how to value these pieces. I think in the end they must be accepted as poems and not merely as records and documentaries; and if they are poems, they are surely Robinson's as much as they belong to the Aboriginal speakers.

This dilemma brings to mind once again the question that has been continually before us while we have been reading all the Jindyworobaks. What are the proportions, in all their work, which mark the black and the white Dreamtimes? What is truth and what is mythology in all that they say? And where does the truth, or the mythology, of the one end, and that of the other begin? Do they, or do they not, overlap? We need to know these limits and understand them and digest them better than the nation has yet done, before we can attempt a final judgment of the Jindyworobak achievement.

THE ANTHOLOGIES

The best years of the *Jindyworobak Anthologies* were those covered in the 1938–1948 *Review*. Only the first four issues and one other, the tenth in 1947, were edited by Rex Ingamells but his personality pervaded them—not oppressively; he did not attempt to dominate the other editors, but occasional notes and messages included by their courtesy served as reminders of his leadership. In any case the early issues provided the opportunity for the general Jindyworobak idea to sink in. Hence the main missionary work was done while his was still the controlling hand. In later issues and especially after 1948 a few mild changes were admitted but none were radical.

The early contributions were of necessity concerned largely with policy and propaganda. Whether missionary verse can ever be good verse depends a good deal, no doubt, upon the mission. The worst of the Jindyworobak weaknesses was that, in such a cause, faith was almost bound from the first to prevail over works. The Jindyworobak sense of the power of their zeal was above the capacity of most of the followers to express it. They were a community of small but earnest talents whose gifts were often less than their goodwill; their industry and sincerity made up in the long run for what they lacked in quality as individual poets. Hence they built up to a collective effect which was impressive even when their individual contributions were less so. One of the effects of such a process is likely to be some wavering in definition; another is the prevalence of a certain amount of repetition. Among the selections reprinted here I include two pieces of my own which may be regarded in this light and kicked about; I shall mention them again later. Rather than discuss them immediately I refer to two contributions by another experimentalist, Wolfe Fairbridge. His "The Banksia" in the 1938 *Anthology* used local and familiar bush trees and plants to create the Jindyworobak-Aboriginal sense of "joining" that was exactly what Ingamells was preaching.[12] But in another piece, "Alf", he attempted an impressionistic style which was aimed at but perhaps did not quite successfully reach the post-Aboriginal Dreamtime. Alf is a farmer in the West Australian wheat belt:

> From parrot-morn to magpie-night
> He gathers in the wheat for all the world.

Closer to the propagandist Jindyworobak image was Ian Tilbrook's "Gums":

> Aboriginal . . .
> grey-brown and old . . . so old beside the river reaches;
> aged and bent like a white-haired black
> whose hunting days are at an end.

Here already a stereotype had appeared, of a kind that can wither with much iteration. Emblematic repetition is not necessarily bad; it may be a sign of vigour. But these Aboriginal gum trees were to grow tiresome. On the other hand, a word or a phrase which breaks the expected pattern may equally be disconcerting. Victor Kennedy described an Aboriginal child:

> Queer little deep brown almond eyes
> turned to me now with grave surprise.
>
> "Queer Little Almond Eyes"

Expressive as they are, those "almond" eyes are out of Jindyworobak keeping and one wonders how they appealed to the Ingamells who could not accept "creaming" in Robinson's poem. But Fairbridge's farmer and this Aboriginal child were not the only instances of poems and details which strained at the Jindyworobak leash. Paul Grano's "Out Samford Way" has its own kind of site-magic, but simply as poetry of the country; I reprint it as an example of Jindyworobak border-hopping. Flexmore Hudson's Whitmanesque poems also seem to me boldly to cross a border; but they came later. In the 1938 *Anthology* he is represented by two Mallee-country descriptions (three if one includes "The Farmer"), three love-lyrics (a little, at least, out of Jindyworobak context) and the more germane and expansive "Song of an Australian". Ingamells gives himself three pages in 1938, including the excellent "Garchooka". There are also five pieces, all short, by Max Harris, which attempt the Jindyworobak mood but not very comfortably; his "Dead Gums at Night" imitates a model which hardly seems very congruous:

> Pray the cool unreality
> Pray the cool
> Pray

The piece ends with a whimper:

> I cannot understand.

Russel Ward's formal sonnet, "Kangaroo", on the other hand, might be described as a model Jindyworobak contribution; it commits no formal fault.

The 1938 *Anthology* successfully launched the movement. It had sixteen contributers. The second in 1939 had twenty-eight and the third, 1940, had thirty. Numbers meant something to Ingamells. He said in an editorial note in 1940: "Twenty-three people submitted work for the *Jindyworobak Anthology* in 1938, sixty-three in 1939, and ninety-eight this year. The proportion of rubbish submitted has risen in three years from about fifteen to about fifty per cent . . ." If progress could be measured in terms of what the movement could afford to reject, that was progress indeed. "At the same time," the editor added, "the wider field of good verse has enabled me to indulge my tastes (and prejudices) more freely." He was convinced there was "a great deal of literary talent in Australia cherishing a sense of national direction". "National direction" was the important element, but Ingamells now found an inclination slightly to shift—or perhaps only to clarify—his aims. This was his distinction between "good verse" and "Jindyworobak verse", declaring himself ready to accept either, but hoping, naturally, to discover them as often as possible together.

A number of somewhat improbable Jindyworobaks contributed from time to time—for instance, both A.D. Hope and James McAuley. Hope's early poem "Australia" would certainly have been welcomed had it been offered; it was not, however, and what he did send must be accounted "good verse" and not "good Jindyworobak verse". McAuley's is a different case. He contributed twice, and in both instances with distinguished and now well-known poems that the editor could have no hesitation in placing in the last category. They were his "Envoi for a Book of Poems" (1940) and "Terra Australis" (1943). "Envoi", with its emblematic images of the continental map, the desert landscape and the gush of artesian waters makes a strikingly intellectual and highly controlled use of what can fairly be described as stock Jindyworobak material, and its emphasis on the Australian aridity, whether of the landscape or the spirit, accords precisely with much that Ingamells himself wished to convey. Similarly "Terra Australis" implied the same kind of search for a Great South Land of the spirit as that which motivated Ingamells:

> Voyage within you on the fabled ocean
> And you will find that Southern Continent,
> De Quiros' vision—his hidalgo heart
> And mythical Australia . . .

It is of some interest to remark that in his *A Map of Australian Verse* (Melbourne, 1975) McAuley does not reprint among his own verses these very impressive early pieces, though in his title he keeps the image of the map.

A number of other poets of distinction who were not attached programmatically to the Jindyworobak movement nevertheless contributed. Their names appear among the reprinted selections, though no effort has been made to drag them in without Jindyworobak relevance. Judith Wright had a certain sympathy for the Jindyworobaks though she would never consent to be regarded as one of them. R.G. Howarth, who was certainly not one, published with them (on a "good verse" basis) and was interested enough in a detached way to accept the editorship of one of the *Anthologies* (1949). Douglas Stewart, on the other hand, for a long time stood out against them on principle, as lax in their poetic standards. As a result Rex Ingamells for some years regarded the *Bulletin* as his natural enemy. But in the end, through the good offices of their mutual friend Miles Franklin, the two poets met and the differences were healed; Stewart contributed to the *Anthologies* in 1951 and 1952 and, without bending his own characteristic style, the pieces he sent were pleasantly congenial to a Jindyworobak outlook. By the fifties, however, as far as the receiving public was concerned, the vogue of the Jindyworobaks had begun to lag and was practically over. The campaigning phase was complete; the *Anthologies* had served their purpose. The last was issued in 1953. A fourth, to be edited by Colin Thiele, was announced for 1954 but it never appeared, and after Ingamells's death in 1955 the prospect was no longer to be entertained. Judith Wright's comment in the 1938–1948 *Review* makes a fair summing up:

> It seems to me that the Jindy movement was essentially an effort to get the problem into perspective. . . . The regional, the national outlook *has* a value . . . It may be that because of the Jindy movement, even those most fiercely opposed or most indifferent to it know themselves a little better.

CODA ON A PERSONAL NOTE

I ask an indulgence here to include a few pages purely on my own account; the reader is welcome to ignore them. So far as I have personally had any part in the Jindyworobak movement, and it was slight, I feel the impulse to obtrude a brief explanation. That my views have modified will be obvious. All I can claim is that when the movement was forming I was near enough to the scene to form a few impressions. I was a friend and admirer of Ingamells at that time, though I was not after the end of 1937 in Adelaide, hence no longer intimately involved.

In the 1938–1948 *Review* Leonard Mann had this to say:

> It is significant that the originators were mostly young writers who were teachers and students in Adelaide, not a large city. It was their own particular and narrower environment that angered them . . . The Jindyworobaks must have felt both physically and spiritually isolated . . . They seemed at first to be unaware that an Australian tradition of letters had been established for a number of years.

What "Australian tradition" he meant seems uncertain: whether the *Bulletin* school, of which everybody was aware, or some other more "literary". The young writers in Ultima Thule were, on the other hand, distrustful of the "Australian" literary principles of those others in the "large" eastern cities. They were at the time inclined to regard them as the menacing supermen of a dubious Sydney–Melbourne literary axis, joined, if in nothing else, in a dangerous collaboration designed to overrun and defeat the "real" and homelier Australia, which lay undefended. They feared the threatening onslaught of an overseas-inspired literary sophistication. No doubt the embryonic Jindyworobaks were in a parish-pump situation. But by the same token they were innocent and uncorrupted, though dissatisfied. If they turned, not to London, Paris and New York, but to the Arunta for stimulus, it was because there too was what they conceived to be an innocent and undefiled waterhole of inspiration. Mann added with some generosity, "In Adelaide they were much closer to the lands where the Aborigines still live", the implication being that they only had to make a short excursion in order to encounter the afflatus. That too was an extremely naive view. In point of fact, though several of them (including Ingamells) did make the pilgrimage, and were enriched by it, in the first instance the Jindyworobak initiative could not be described as anything but bookish. It was an idea before it became an ideal. We all listened avidly when Rex Ingamells expounded the Dreamtime; we all dipped, albeit lightly, into *The Arunta*. Ingamells began to publish and others gathered round. After *Chapbook* died in its second issue, 1936, Ingamells himself produced a magazine, *Venture*, 1937, and to this I contributed an undistinguished short story, of which the best that could be said was that it was "environmental" as a scrap of nostalgic colonial history, based on a family anecdote. I then, in 1938, became a very junior and insignificant young academic in Perth, and so was not on the scene as the Jindyworobak plan rose to practical shape. Ingamells formed and became the centre of a "Jindyworobak Club", which gave the movement a certain social, or sociable, *raison d'être* at its beginning. But when the first *Anthology* was mooted I was already away, and I knew of it only from letters. However I responded with enthusiasm (tempered by a new-found academic reticence) and even succeeded in recruiting a couple of young Western Australian contributors, among them Fairbridge. I have mentioned two contributions of my own: one appeared in the 1938 issue and I was rather pleased with it, smugly satisfied with the image of the grass-tree or xanthorrhea (called in the West "blackboy") as an emblem of the departed tribes. How artificial this stroke of genius was I blush to remember; I had at that time scarcely ever seen an Aborigine, let alone had any acquaintance with one, and never heard one speak until later in that same year when I visited New Norcia. There were no Aborigines to be seen in Adelaide or other southern cities. (There are many now, but not then.) My second Jindyworobak poem in 1943 did not cling to the tribal archetype but was constructed about an image of the sun. I believe I hoped and expected it would be interpreted as an Aboriginal sun and the bird (the poem was called "The Golden Eagle") as an Australian eagle, though the symbolism was that of the halcyon, and Greek: a somewhat more exacting effort at Aboriginal "joining" than the other. If this was not obvious, at least it was meant. The point I am straining to make is that these were attempts to make poetry to accommodate the theory; and I believe others made similar, and equally earnest, efforts to do the same kind of thing.

An indiscretion of which I am inclined to be less tenderly defensive was my contribution to the 1938–48 *Review*. After ten years of slow academic incrustation it took the form of an arrogant outburst of criticism with the title "Jindydämmerung", which at the time I thought rather clever. It was true that the movement had entered as it were a twilight of its energy, but the implication that it was petering out without having achieved anything at all was ridiculous and offensive. Ingamells, I belive more in sorrow than in anger, very generously published it—though not without a gentle rebuke. "There is in Mr Elliott," he remarks mildly, "a strong disposition to pontificate." I had by this time so far retreated into Academe as to refer to the Dreamtime as an exotic dogma. " . . . But his course," Ingamells added, "is fixed at present in the universities, and he seems to have cast about for conclusions such as would be acceptable to entrenched diehards." It was a fair thrust. Faith had decayed in the heart of one who ought to have sustained it more courageously. From that time forth I began to re-think my critical attitudes. The result was this reappraisal, tempered by a long period of re-examination and reflection, of the real value and effect of the Jindyworobak poetical institutions. My conclusion is not that they were a product of exceptional genius, but that the movement was spontaneous, natural and inevitable, and that it had an effect upon the nation—upon the national literature, but also upon the nation itself—that went beyond what was obvious in the poetry. In Judith Wright's words, the Jindyworobaks have taught us all to know ourselves a little better.

NOTES TO INTRODUCTION

1. Spencer and Gillen refer to this tribe as Arunta, the Strehlows as Aranda. There is no standard spelling.
2. "The change that has thus taken place" (that is in the past ten years) "has inevitably altered—and invigorated—Australian poetic diction, and in a lesser degree, Australian prose diction. A man who looks at an Australian paddock as an Australian paddock . . . is incapable of referring to that paddock as a field. He *must* call it by its correct name." Mudie, *Jindyworobak Review 1938-1948*, p. 63.
3. Sydney, Angus and Robertson, 1971.
4. See *Songs of Central Australia*, pp. 658-9.
5. From "The Old Innerah" (*Sun-Freedom* 1938). Innerah: solitary woman; kombora: wild berry. Ingamells inadvertently omits to gloss "mooloona", which remains baffling. "Allinga" denotes the sun and implies a fine diffusion of sunset colours.
6. A paraphrase of "Moorawathimeering" may be found helpful:
    Into sanctuary in the land of the lost (a place of the dead, whose sacrosanct borders the tribesmen may not safely cross) you have fled, O outcast (victim of a punishment party sent to revenge a murder). But there you shall have no hut to take shelter in, only some comfortless cave. Murderer! our curses (that is, of the avengers) shall go with you, even if we ourselves may not violate the border to follow in the footsteps of our one-time leader. Far away in that land of ghosts, outlaw and fugitive, you shall wander, safe from the punishment of ritual law but in silence for ever. Nothing but your shadow may ever walk beside you, but the voice of the north wind will wail and the wings of scavenging crows hover in the air above you.
7. Mary Gilmore's gloss: "Cowal: a coolamon-hole or small lake".
8. In this poem he repudiates certain "alien gods", continuing, "Kill them, O Land", preferring to be "Of you, and of your totem-gods of stone and tree". An unhappy devil in the composing room misprinted "gods" as "goods". Mudie winced but laughed and subsequently emended the word to "dreams".
9. David Unaipon, *Native Legends*, Adelaide, 1932.
10. At the end of the volume *Deep Well* (p. 79) Robinson supplies an "Index to Titles" which relates titles to the numbered sequences and is useful as a guide to the structure of the work as a whole. In this Portable one sequence, seven poems from *Deep Well*, is reprinted entire.
11. Mostly his own but the book includes some items received from other collectors.
12. There is a reference in this poem to xamia palms, unfortunately misprinted "xamais", which ruins the sense and spoils the rhythm.

PART 1

Major Jindyworobak Poets

Rex Ingamells

EDITOR'S NOTE

Rex Ingamells was born at Ororoo, South Australia, in 1913, the son of a country minister. He attended school at Prince Alfred College and afterwards read honours history at Adelaide University. He became a teacher but later gave it up to work for a Melbourne publisher. He founded the Jindyworobak Club in Adelaide in 1938, and this developed into the Jindyworobak movement. His death occurred as the result of a car accident, 31 December 1955.

His books include: verse, *Gumtops* 1935, *Forgotten People* 1936, *Sun-Freedom* 1938, *Memory of Hills* 1940, *Content Are the Quiet Ranges* 1943, *Selected Poems* 1944, *The Great South Land* 1951; prose, *Conditional Culture* (with Ian Tillbrook) 1938, *Of Us Now Living* (novel) 1952, *Aranda Boy* (children's fiction) 1953. He was general editor of *The Jindyworobak Anthologies* 1938–1953 and editor of *The Jindyworobak Review 1938–1948* (one issue).

LUIS DE TORRES

Luis de Torres, on the *almiranta*,
whose canvas was a wave-hugged sunset cloud,
looking back beheld,
beyond the glowing beauty of the *zabra*,
the sea-track darken,
and sorrowed for de Quiros.

"This broken quest I would he could have mended.
I doubt he'll ever, after this, be given
command of ships for seeking the Unknown."
He moved a quick hand in gesture, and went below.

With sails and rigging changing from colour to colour,
the *almiranta* and *zabra* went swinging on,
sweeping along the tropics to Manila,
while, beyond the port horizon all unseen,
in unfound glory lay the Great South Land,
her sombre sandhills brightening in the glare
of a parrot sunset, then glowing under stars.

BOOMERANG

This piece of hardwood, cunningly shaped,
Was curved so evenly while piccaninnies gaped
At a warrior who chipped at it with pieces of flint,
And formed it by meticulous dint upon dint.
Outside his wurly he sat beside a tree
And chipped at it patiently for hours—not for me,
But to kill the wallaby in the rocky pass,
To kill the fat wild-turkey hiding in the grass.

THE AFGHANS

Four Afghans sit in evening light,
With features dusked by turbans white,

But eyes like sun-glow I've seen smoulder
On a lonely desert boulder.

In circle, cross-legged, they converse,
With accents guttural and terse.

Unknowable are nomad faces
Till you haunt all desert places:

The same pent dreams glint there unknown
As on the eve-lit boulder-stone.

Earth brother, I must stranger be
To such fierce taciturnity.

FORLORN BEAUTY

O I have seen one flaming peak at dawn
Across a sea of sand. Alone it stood,
And bare of all but colour; no great wood
Had up its sides a shaggy mantle drawn.
Sered by the desert winds, by hot suns shorn
Of Nature's tenderest gifts, it seemed to brood,
As if it knew its beauty never could
Bring joy, forever mighty and forlorn.
There was naught else in that vast lonely place
To breathe of Beauty; and I gazed in awe,
To think that even there she held her sway;
To think that, her staunch slave, with such fierce grace
That peak at dawn blazed centuries before,
And so blazed now, and so should blaze for aye.

EVENING IN THE MACDONNELLS

Look at the rocky range, wallowing in the sun's glow.
The fierce white sun sinks, regretted by the black crow.
The black crows are calling, forlornly crying out,
For they like not the radiance of evening spread about.

The black crows like not the hues and the hazes
Of the valleys, but the fire where a last peak blazes.
The guttering colours and the desert's smoky smoulderings
Lead them into darkness jetter than their black wings.

The darkness will come when the colours glide away;
The darkness will come and the darkness will stay,
With points of mocking silver, the stars and the dew,
And the cold bitter winds till day break through.

Now before the stars burn, Evening brings her beauty here
To walk on the rocky range and on the stony plains near.
Evening sucks the venom of the day's distress,
And all the tortured land takes on new loveliness.

I will stand and watch the beauty of the desert, though the
                                                           crows
Let me not forget the harshness the long day knows,
The heat that has vanished, the mirage that has gone,
I will stand and watch the beauty till night come on.

THE BULLOCKY

A bullocky came at noon,
    With his lumbering team and slow,
Leaving behind a heavy cloud
    Of red-dust hanging low.

Up over the ridge he came,
    In worn-out, dusty clothes,
Cracking his long, lithe, greenhide whip,
    And lustily shouting oaths.

He heard from the country school
    Young voices singing come;
"Wo-a!" he cried, and stopped his beasts
    Beneath the Leaning Gum.

He listened awhile; the smoke
    From his old black pipe curled up;
Then, when the singing ceased, he called
    To his blowing team—"Gerrup!"

EXCITED CROWS

In the MacDonnells once I saw,
Where gums stood stark
Against the first stars in the purpling dark,
A noisy concourse of excited crows
Burst from the glooming clouds of silent leaves,
Shattering all solemnity
With their devilish "Kark-kark!"
Then soundlessly these wheeled above the rows
Of gumtree tops,
Then settled again . . . .
And night surged in uneasily.

GARCHOOKA, THE COCKATOO

Though the waters, wind-stirred and red-glowing,
shadowed by the evening-gloom of gums,
bend in their banks the way the day is going,
while a dusk-gold haze of insects comes
over the ripples in their coloured flowing,
Garchooka, beating from high branches, screeches
discord up and down the river-reaches.

GARRAKEEN

Garrakeen, the parakeet, is slim and swift.
Like a spear of green and red he flashes through
the cumbered branches by the river-bank.
Watch him, brighter than the clouds, before the day is done;
watch him in the morning, when the gums are bathed with
dew,
rivalling the spears of the sun.

When dawn flamed on the Murray I watched for Garrakeen. . .
Opaline purple and crimson was the river . . .
He came from the west with blood on his breast,
and the colours of the water were sluggish in sheen
compared with his fire in the air;

the voice of the water was shattered by one
shrill from the spear-bird hurrying there,
flying with the light of the east in his sight,
rivalling the spears of the sun.

RIVERS AND MOUNTAINS

1

Yarra and Murray,
Murrumbidgee and Darling,
Lachlan and Derwent,
Swan River and Hawkesbury River . . .
By your old or your new names;
And all your brothers and sisters,
Numberless rivers, creeks, and billabongs
What can you not all tell me
Of the days gone by?

Do not your waters,
Yellow and crimson in the dawn,
Whisper, whisper round your banks?
And cannot I pry out the age-old secrets
That they whisper?

Secrets of
 The days gone by—
Of blacks' camp
 And coo-ee cry.

Do not your gumtrees,
Ringed with the marks of many floods,
Seared and blackened by many fires,
Fling grotesque shadows on your waters?
And cannot I read
Those strange hieroglyphs?
They are wed so with the movement of the water
And the movement of the trees,
And with the sound of the water,
With wind-ripples and reed-ripples,
And with the patient sound
Of the wind in the trees,

And with the quiet drifting
Of leaves and bark
On the surface of the water.
What do they spell,
Those strange hieroglyphs?

Secrets of
   The days gone by—
Of blacks' camp
   And coo-ee cry.

2

All you ranges,
Blue Mountains, Dandenongs, Plenty,
Flinders, Barossa, MacDonnell,
By your old or your new names,
And all your numberless brothers and sisters,
Ranges and ridges, cuestas and monadnocks,
Fertile and beckoning or craggy and forbidding,
What can you not all tell me
Of the days gone by?

Know you not the secrets of the totems?
Are you not great ancestors yourselves,
Or, some of you—
Like the furrow of Ilbumeraka—
Dragged and scooped and tortured from the plains
By the swishing tnatantja?
Were not some of you
Formed by the writhings of a hideous snake,
Like that of Emianga,
Or made as by the digging of Lukara
Among the roots of the acacias
For the prized and juicy tjameta worms?

When dawn is kindling along your crests,
Or when your flames die into darkness,
Or while you stand boldly or cloud-hidden
Through the main time of daylight,
You still have your secrets about you,
And shall have ever.

Secrets of
   The days gone by—
Of blacks' camp
   And coo-ee cry.

BLACK CHILDREN

Where now uninterrupted sun
   Is shrivelling the sheaves,
Black children leap and laugh and run
   Beneath a sky of leaves;
And where the farmer thrashes wheat
   With steel machinery,
Go glimmerings of their little feet,
   If he could only see.

LONG AGO

Corroboree . . .
Corroboree . . .
Red fires all night:
Men in the firelight,
Twisting and turning
Under contorted gums.

Coo-ee . . .
Coo-ee . . .
Echoing over
The calling of the plover,
And the far-ringing notes
Of magpies at dawn.

Boomerang . . .
Swift-hurled boomerang . . .
Glinting with sun,
Killing the emu
On the run;
Felling the proud old
Kangaroo,
In dawn-dim grasses,
Cold
With dew.

MOORAWATHIMEERING

Into moorawathimeering,
where atninga dare not tread,
leaving wurly for a wilban,
tallabilla, you have fled.

Wombalunga curses, waitjurk—
though we cannot break the ban,
and follow tchidna any further
after one-time karaman.

Far in moorawathimeering,
safe from wallan darenderong,
tallabilla waitjurk, wander
silently the whole day long.

Go with only lilliri
to walk along beside you there,
while douran-douran voices wail
and Karaworo beats the air.

FORGOTTEN PEOPLE

1

As the sun leaps up behind the range and throws
    His radiance round the gums upon the crest,
All earth, it seems, remembers—all earth knows
    A pang whose bitterness cannot be guessed.

As the sun swings up and over in the sky,
    Each moment bears the smart of memories,
Although the creeks go brimming, brimming by,
    And the cockatoos fly, screeching, in the trees.

Though magpies in the bush call all the day,
    From dawn until the sunset hills are gold,
Their ringing beauty does not charm away
    A pang whose tenderness cannot be told.

How can a stranger hope to understand?
Dark ghosts go with me all about the land.

2

With half-closed eyes, I saw by an old gum
  Black, gleaming-bodied men stalk shadowily
To trap the kangaroo—and others come
  Loud with the zest of wild corroboree.

I saw men flashing in the fire's weird glow,
  Painted and decked with the white down of birds,
Stooping and crawling and leaping, row on row,
  Shattering the night with charmed fantastic words.

Under that gum I saw bark wurlies stand:
  Beside them, in the noon, the lubras sat,
While piccaninnies tumbled on the sand,
  And warriors hunted wildfowl on the flat.

I caught the echo of faint coo-ee crying;
I glimpsed a vision of a people dying.

3

Before white men made wurlies out of stone
  To loom like tnatantjas against the sky,
The wandering black, in bushlands all his own,
  Rubbed fire, speared fish, and watched the eagle fly.

After the white man came, the black man lost
  His hunting-grounds and camping-grounds. He went,
Lonelier and lonelier, pitilessly tossed,
  By fates he knew not, into banishment.

His waterholes were stolen or defiled,
  And all his sacred tjurungas were tainted:
He went not stalking when the wan dawn smiled,
  And came not to corroboree, weird-painted.

He lived not in reality but dreams,
A stranger to his tribal lands and streams.

4

Long strips of bark are hanging from the gums,
  Long strips of bark . . . And on sun-withered grass
Long strips of bark are trailing . . . A bee-swarm hums
  On an old mossed-over stump . . . Bees pass and pass.

How keen and sweet is the wild honey smell!
    With wary glee the black folk robbed the bees,
Oh, long ago . . . And their delight how tell?
    Delights like that were theirs for centuries.

I see a well-timed spear glint in the sun,
    And the small rock-wallaby killed on the jump,
Then hear the laughter, watch the white-teethed fun
    Of black folk feasting by that wattle-clump . . .

The magpies in the leaves above my head
Sing joy to-day, but the black folk are dead.

5

No more the smoke-wisp signal climbs; no more
    The boomerang glints, arching, in the sky;
The bush hears not the swinging-stick's low roar,
    Nor mountainsides the echoing coo-ee cry.

Things one with a forgotten people these.
    Where black men roamed, our towns and cities stand:
Disrupted are their tribal mysteries;
    Wheat, wool, and grapes are produce of their land.

How can a stranger tell the way they felt?
    At best, sincere imaginings are mine.
I find the old bark places where they dwelt,
    See stars above an empty bushland shine.

I can but guess their pain, and guess the white
And exquisite laughter of their lost delight.

6

Though to the west—where once the bushland plain
    Stretched primal from these ranges to the sea—
The white man's city has, in spreading, slain
    Nature and hardly left a memory,

This hill is just as rugged now as when
    No white man's eye had seen it; these gaunt gums
And rooted rocks look seaward now as then;
    And still the magpie's ringing beauty comes.

Yet spirits of lost laughter and distress
   Seem here to change even this spot of the ranges,
Lending trees, rocks, and song a wistfulness
   For vanished folk; but nothing else here changes.

The young leaves of the gums burn like real flame—
And so it was before the white man came.

SUN-FREEDOM

I have not known sun-freedom for so long
that I go carrying hatred in my heart
for streets and trams and limousines . . . the song
of birds about the bush seems so apart . . .
When shall I tread brown bark beneath my feet,
and, through grey branches, hear the magpie's call
ring down a valley in the midday heat,
like the cool, strong voice of a waterfall?
when shall I walk neck-open to the breeze,
and know again the friendliness of trees?

For it is in my heart to fare and find
the beauty of earth, content no more with dreams.
The sun will be the comrade for my mind,
and, like a lad, may beckon by old streams,
and, like a farmer, lead through yellow sheaves.
The sun and I, forgetting whence I came,
may gaze for hours, like natives, into leaves,
where gumtree flowers burn to scarlet flame . . .
Certain it is I will go forth, imbued
for days on end with some sun-given mood.

A thousand little unimportant things
will enter my attention on each day,
and in my soul evoke such marvellings
as broaden out life's meaning every way:
a tiny bird a-twitter in its flight—
a strip of golden bark upon a gum—
a cowman's mongrel yelping in delight—
a haywain driver, pipe upon his thumb . . .
Such little trifles make a magic string
that binds sheer gladness into everything.

SHIFTING CAMP

Glint of gumtrees in the dawn,
so million-coloured; bush-wind-borne
magpie-music, rising, falling;
and voices of the stockmen calling.

Bellowing of cattle; stamping,
impatient of the place of camping;
barks of dogs; and the crack-crack-crack
of stockwhips as we take the track.

Neighing of night-rested mounts . . .
This is a day that really counts:
a day to ride with a hundred head,
and a roll of canvas—That's my bed.

OUTBACK

All the unhallowed beauty I have found;
all free-discordant shrills
and form-defying wonders above ground,
like writhen trees with draggled foliage
straggling along the courses of wayback creeks;
scarlet-and-green
sky-streaking parrot-fires, with parrot-shrieks
echo-shattering the shoulders of the hills;
and desert-sunset-rage:
Rage for my mind, be clamant, do not cease;
you are my holiest habitat of peace.

EARTH-COLOURS

Earth-colours, rich, primeval, blaze and smoulder
on claypan-flat and river-cliff and cuesta-boulder.
My heart should burn to praise yet fear gripes, cold and colder.

Blood blinds the world: in war-zones blood is running.
Where Ethiopian lizards scuttled, sunning,
all the air is filled with smoke of gunning.

Death's keen minstrels
ping like rain
through the pleasant
land of Spain.

Death's engined angels
range the sky
where China's smouldering
temples lie.

I watch the streaks of sunset metafusing:
my heart should burn to praise but it rebels, refusing . . .
I see the wake-waves of dark carnage-squadrons cruising.

Dare you now behold the new day dawning?
There comes no radiant goddess to your fawning—
Smoke-clouded Mars, blood-hungry, cavernously yawning.

NGATHUNGI

This bone, the flesh of which has been
eaten by my enemy,
I cover with grease and human hair
and clay from the roots of a river tree.

See how I gut it firmly now
to the leg-bone of a kangaroo
for burning, so that the man I hate,
one-souled with it, may perish too.

It spits and sputters in the fire;
it cracks and crumbles to blackened bone.
Never again shall they name his name,
and I shall delight in my deed alone.

BOOLEE

The dark moon grins.
That must be Boolee up there,
because the clouds fly
all the same as the heavy brown dust
he loves to whirl
over the plains and pretty quick into our camps.

BLACK MARY

Mary, the lubra,
walks wonderfully.
She came along the dust-track,
swinging her body freely, stepping
lithely and with perfect measure.
The beautiful rhythm of her body
flooded my heart with joy as do leaf-calls
in a place of many birdsongs,
flooded my heart with joy
such as must be
to apprehend perfection.

Superbly swung her supple form
along the dust-track,
for she walks wonderfully.

But she saw Tommy, and
her resentment of yesterday
rose, instant,
to tear all harmony to harsh-edged coarseness.
Suddenly all rhythm died
and in its place
was jarring discord of a nagging voice,
disrupting all the
vision of her I had.
Tommy, her husband, fled like a bush-rat
from her ugly, angular gesticulations.

MEMORY OF HILLS

There are rock-rooted ranges to dominate
the ways of man with peace, enforced but healing;
there are crows settling on the boundary gate,
or poised in the sky, or wheeling.

Slowly the sun moves over the red land, slowly
over the dust-puff silence that never changes
except for crow caws that suddenly, wholly
envelop those random ranges.

The flowering of sunset is riotous, wrought of fire
and rock-smoke drifted through sere foliage, higher
and higher into the opal sky
till the night heaves with stars and the colours go by.

The old hills are obstinate in my mind,
and I thank them now for the long familiarity.
Merely I shut my eyes to find
their reflex of moonlight, their kind
wrinkled acknowledgment of the moon's clarity.

Keenly the wind blows from the scrub-tufts and rocks
of the obstinate old hills in my heart;
and the stars, night's nomad friends,
press, as the moon ascends,
their steps a little apart.

Yet seeking no smug beatitude
from me the dark hills brood:
I have hard faith to keep in midst of sham
because suburban tritenesses would damn
the human spirit, and defeatist breath
fails under load of bitter pang
in cramped backyards of memory-death
where moon-pale mists of washing hang.

FROM A DYING PEOPLE

The sun shall wound with flickering fang
night-weary ridge and shadowy plain
and send the blood of evening down
the western gorges time again.

Though we depart from camp and soak,
from gidgi-shade and waterhole,
each night shall speak the desert-oak,
in season shall the thunder roll.

Spirits shall haunt this land. O we
shall roam a dim Alcheringa.
Our gods shall show us mystery
and you not know it, Waruntha.

BLACK BOULDER

Black boulder,
gust-chilled,
dew-filmed for starlight . . .
you show me only a mood
which makes you
stolid-silent, sombre.
I know you are
a raging-red coal of the sun
earth-flung
to set this mountain on fire,
its scrub
flaming each dawn.

DESERT DAWN

It is a ghost that walks before birth.
As a faithful promise it comes.
To have known it is to yearn with heart and eyes
for the long hush,
for the long, long hush
under starlight in the desert with the winds,
waiting the sun's rise.

DARK CRY

Dark cry, claim the dark-shored lake.
Quicken your echoes round the hills. Dwell
in, possessing, earth and sky. Take
farewell . . .

Engined with knowledge, as fast
that very way the confident mind must push,
cry of a winging wild duck cast
to the insatiable hush of the bush.

THE SWAGMAN

(To John)

Green valleys for white flocks of sheep;
red deserts for black crows;
dark billabongs for light of stars . . .
and me for all of those.

Raggedy trees for kookaburras;
ridge-rocks for the close
of day with colours; roads for tramping . . .
me for all of those.

FROM THE GANGRENED PEOPLE

Those who would have poets delight,
in the present age,
are not devotees of beauty:
they fear the true page,
encourage fools to sing
for a poor pittance
lest they should sting
for nothing.

I desire no praise
for loving beauty
from those
who do not love beauty:
the patronizing inclination of the head
while the hand files credit
convinces me
beauty requires
murder.

BILLAI

She bound dheal twigs to neck and knees;
she cut her arms for blood to pour:
that fellow Gubbee could not seize
what was no woman any more.

A green bird gashed with crimson wings
into the darkness . . . . Billai! . . . . Billai!
Echoes alone of her sorrowings
came from the star-camps of the sky.

YARAANDOO

Now the hunger-perished fool
and Yowee glare by Warrumbool,
where Yowee carries Yaraan high,
a tree of darkness in the sky.

Ever the white-winged Mouyi screech
for nests in branches out of reach,
and ever the far eyes, blazing through
those branches, make up Yaraandoo.

FROM UNKNOWN LAND

We who are called Australians have no country;
no country holds us native heart and soul:
our boast that Federation made a nation;
our boast that Anzac proved it with our blood
are tragic fictions. Our standards are fictitious:
we dwell in the limbo of a harsh deception,
a criminal betrayal, guaranteeing
the selfish satisfaction of the cunning,
exploiting us for money, money, money,
spreading the itch to purchase every day,
filling our hearts with fatal loyalties
to notions not our own, nor suited to us.

Australia is a land that has no people,
for those that were hers we have torn away,
we who are not hers nor can be till love
shall make us so and fill our hearts with her.
Australia waits a people who will woo her
and win her for heart and mind, not money only.
Can we awaken, leave our evil limbo,
look on Australia's face and clear our hearts
of self with one another and the world?
Or shall we deservedly give place to others—
failing to right ourselves, let others love her?
Australia waits a race whose active bone
will mutter the white light of her limestone rocks,
whose blood will riot with the unreserved
rage of the red light of her sandstone ridges,
whose minds will know the cleansing strong communion
of midday hush, of tree-entangled stars,
of raucous cries on dimming lakes at evening
and all her timeless mystery of dreams.

AUSTRALIA

1

This is the oldest Land,
wisest, most stoic,
where rock-hearted ranges stand,
Archeozoic.

Around raves the ocean . . .
above stream the stars,
wed to Earth's motion
with her tjurungas.

Moons of her dream-time,
guardian still,
rove over scrub, climb
cliff-scarp and hill.

Ruthless, the sun spites
skeletal mallee,
and, fierce in the blue, smites
legended valley.

Day bleeds on shingle
and billabong,
while solitudes tingle
to shrill parrot song.

Where ghostly the tribes go,
dwindled and few,
Alcheringa dusks know
didgeridoo.

In gunyah and windbreak,
by desert and sea,
the lubra sings heart-ache
for birrahlee.

And, lest the camp-embers
turn ashen in dark,
the bush-wind remembers
and coaxes a spark.

Whenever a gust
wakes a spark in the night,
dream figures in dust
frenzy, ochre-and-white.

The past for the morrow
has ample employ:
and waters of sorrow
bear echoes of joy.

Though tribesmen must grieve
and camp-fires depart,
no wonder can leave
Australia's heart,

while the Wet brings the sound
of thunder and rain . . .
while kangaroos pound
in the night on the plain . . .

while stars in the dim
dusk shimmer and quiver . . .
while waterhen skim
on a reach of a river . . .

This is the oldest Land,
wisest, most stoic,
where rock-hearted ranges stand,
Archeozoic.

2

Here were the sails furled,
under the blue,
where, older than Old World,
glittered the New.

No cottage by willow
where sweet swallows dipt . . .
but camp and hard pillow
by gaunt eucalypt.

Instead of the pale greys
over the lawn . . .
rocks rampant with red rays
scarred heaven with dawn.

No cuckoo-calls reaching
the ear from the sky . . .
but cockatoos screeching,
galahs spearing by.

No owl from the steeple,
no snow on the moor . . .
but sweat for the people
and ants at the door.

3

Could no generation,
renouncing derision,
sow seed of a Nation,
and show men a vision?

Mere dominant strangers
made domicile here,
malevolent dangers
accruing at rear.

Taught to cajole,
but not to invoke,
we still limp in soul
from nostalgia yoke.

Our Race, that should stride
on a sun-facing ridge,
is drugged, without pride,
is a monetary midge.

Here in Australia
an introvert race
travesties beauty
and high human grace.

Here in Australia
the rich have their thumbs
on dynamic of labour
in suburbs and slums.

But, over the gidyea
and billabong,
solitudes tingle
to shrill parrot song.

This is the oldest Land,
wisest, most stoic,
where rock-hearted ranges dawn,
Archeozoic.

TO MIRRABOOKA

Mirrabooka, across the still branches
of trees that are older than settlement and now dark,
but bright with Alcheringa, my spirit calls to you . . .
Lacking artificial daylight
to help them imagine
the immense night inferior,
now may my people,
walking in black-out,
expelled from their neon-niche,
find you, Mirrabooka.

Let your pinnaroo branches
sinew the heart,
your ancient hills
hallow the soul,
as once in starry hours when Earth
grew big and heavy with Alcheringa
and the vast beauty of little fires swung
a master constellation,
announcing the spirit.

MARTIN'S PUB

The front wall stands, with a board so bare
you may just read "Martin's Pub".
The rest is rubble, entangled there
with the sure returning scrub.

The Martins built by a billabong,
where wild duck still make cry
and magpies still make sun-up song
and parrots still screech by.

Blue shimmer of faraway razorbacks
and bright blue overhead
and the crow's call brood at noon on tracks
the drover's horse would tread.

The sheep are travelled by railroad now;
the drovers pass no more;
no swagman pauses to wipe his brow
and enter the Martins' door.

The station-hand at mustering
rides with uncaring face,
where rouseabouts of old would sing,
and hardly sees the place.

But, with light of stars on the billabong
and winds far out in the scrub,
a rough-and-tumble of ghosts belong
to the rubble of Martin's Pub.

MACQUARIE HARBOUR

Macquarie Harbour jailers lock
the sullen gates no more . . .
but lash-strokes sound in every shock
of ocean on the dismal rock
along that barren shore.

No more the bolters hear the hound
that bays upon the wind,
and terror-spurred keep onward-bound
until they drop upon the ground,
starved and terror-pinned . . .

but gales that whine among the hills
sniff at the savage tracks
the hopeless took. The snowfall fills
bleak ranges; then the moonlight spills
broad arrows on their backs.

CAPTAIN WILLIAM BLIGH

Look for an iron soul to bear the piled
anathema of time, to take, without
abjectness, scorn of every human rout,
colossal though by all the world defiled!

Discovering such in Bligh, instruct your child
in burning shame that one man, walled about
with rigid purpose, so should feel the flout
of History's rogues through Legend running wild.

The suffering soul of Bligh bends not to shame,
but, as sand-heavy hills wait greening grass.
hoists high the lie till truth shall square the score.

His soul is innocent. Watch! It will flame,
superb, when gritty storms of falsehood pass,
and, by humanity, will tower the more.

THE TOURIST DUMP

I found and lost Alcheringa;
I lost it by the bend;
I came too far, a chain too far,
to where it has an end.

On lofty bough and blackened stump
the kookaburras din—
but one is cock of the tourist dump
on a rusty kero tin.

Green and yellow reeds are here,
drinking the stream and sun;
overhead the parrots veer,
fifty that cry as one;
here, in the sleepy summer noon,
all frogs and crickets are—
but not till dimness of the moon
will be Alcheringa.

SLIGHT AUTOBIOGRAPHY

When I was ten at Burra I would speak
with waterhen beside the reedy creek.
I was a Copper Miner after school,
taking it easy down there in the cool.

At lunch-time I would wander on the flat
beside the School, some notion in my hat
that Gordon's dying stockman went that way;
and there he goes for me until this day.

Down Murray reaches in a frail canoe—
though all the world should doubt me, this is true—
went Captain Sturt eleven years ago.
I tell you I was there and ought to know.

And any day in our King William Street,
if you would come with me, perhaps you'd meet
Deakin and Cook, just dropped along to see
if anyone has them in memory.

Lawson steps round a corner now and then,
flipping a wisp of rhyme from off his pen,
and that goes singing through my head as though
it holds a truth which everyone should know.

FROM **THE GREAT SOUTH LAND**

COLUMBUS AND BALBOA

The Genoese, Columbus, taking service
with Isabella and Ferdinand of Spain,
found in the waters of America
illusion of the waters of Cathay.

The knights of Spain found otherwise, observed
huge Terra Firma, barrier athwart
their sea-route to the marvellous Moluccas.

Exploiting this New World, they yet sought passage,
through or around it, fit for galleons.

And Vasco Nunez de Balboa heard,
while weighing Indian gold at Panama,
rumours of lands to West where gold was thick,
so thick his scales would be ridiculous
for computation of it.

              So Balboa
ventured in exploration, and beheld
the sparkling Southern Sea, and, reaching this,
rushed in it, fully clothed, in ecstasy
of patriotic and religious fervour.
Shouting, and brandishing his sword, he claimed
for God and the Castilian King, that Sea
with all of Kingdom and Glory that might be in it.

So Spain looked out upon the Southern Sea,
and Alonso Martin launched a frail canoe,
first European navigating waters
where later fair and tired Armadas rode.

The Spaniards, clad in mail, with pennants flying,
with sword and cannon, oaths and pious words,
bestrode the New World and subdued its Kings.

THE *TRYAL*

When the Indian Ocean was a Dutch reserve,
with purposeful captains, strong in powder and steel,
trading to the Moluccas, come from the Cape
with favourable winds, beside the verge
of wild, O wild, New Holland, mysterious region . . .
how came the *Tryal* there, first English ship
recorded on that Coast?

                    So scant the record,
the *Tryal* comes swaying into wondering minds
suddenly, unannounced, at the end of a voyage,
the beginning and purpose only dimly guessed.

Behold the end of a voyage—an English ship,
the first recorded wreck on a Coast of Wrecks . . .

The men were superstitious,
fearing they knew not what of evil spirits
in waters strange to them.

The bosun said, "I 'eard
fr'm one old seaman as knowed Cap'n Drake
thet there be dragons in the calmest waters
outside Atlantic . . ."

Point Cloates was thought to be
an island. It hazed, south-east,
into the blue horizon as the ship—
the *Tryal* brought by Britons near New Holland
years before Dampier—
made northward for the spicy Isle of Java.

On May the twenty-fifth the sunset turned
the sky into a great red lily flower,
the sea into a green mauve-mottled leaf.

The waves were gentle then in crowding darkness.
the boisterous fo'c's'le settled down to silence.
The helmsman's task was easy.

Dreamed Thomas Bright, Chief Officer, on deck:
"This minds me of all the quiet nights of stars
I've known upon the sea made into one . . ."

The helmsman held belief
in mermaids, and his eyes
were keen upon the sea.

The crash,
rip-and-long-shudder, as the *Tryal* struck,
woke Captain Brooke,
hurled and bruised him into wide-awakeness
against the reeling porthole, through which showed
the dim, untroubled, star-reflecting sea.

There was no land-loom, reef-flash, break
of wave; but jagged fangs
of monstrous underwater rocks held, splintering,
the good ship *Tryal*, whose hull was swamped
and fore-part fell away,
while, in the glinting dark
shark-fins split the drowsy sea.

There were some who made a hard escape
in little open boats, while others stayed,
perched perilously on wreckage
out of sight of land, where no sail came
and shark-fins split the water.

The lucky made for Java . . . It is not likely
those left behind lived, any of them, beyond
some horrible hours of torture and defeat,
with the waters beginning to growl and gnash white teeth,
and the sharks impatient . . .

                It is not likely
that human ingenuity could contrive,
in that predicament, the waters leaping
for sure from unwonted calm, rafts for retreat—
retreat to what? . . . the sharks pursuing . . . to harsh
and inhospitable sandhills of New Holland?

THE PENSIONER

The celebrated Mr Barrington,
retired Superintendent of Convicts, pensioned
on twenty-five pounds of Government pay a year,
is very comfortably settled at Parramatta

—except that he is visibly declining:
through that old wound and the grim solace of grog,
come early to dusk of an eventful life.

He looks at his convict, remembers those other women,
Egerton . . . West . . . his wife . . . and Yeariana,
with tribute thought for Egerton's beauty drowned . . .
West's loyalty that surely led her through
fatal jail-fever to the very angels . . .
his wife and child, though tenderly he loved them,
left unfarewelled and never seen again . . .
and the glimmering dark girl, vanished into the bush.

He looks where his window frames a warmth of blue.

Once Dublin . . . London . . . the *Justitia* . . .
Newgate . . . the transports . . . So to New South Wales.

Violent coughing takes him sometimes. Then
he spits pitifully, while accepting the facts:
It's that damned self-inflicted stab that brings
increasing reminder of his worst despair.

He has mental utterances that make no sound
to the ears of his convict housekeeper and visitors.

Memory is a strong stream, with eddies and whirlpools,
dashing by rocks of his present infirmity,
bearing the flotsam and jetsam of his past
experience into habitual stoic awareness.

A far, far cry—casually he rotates
the glass in his hand—from those days when he moved,
flash rogue, in presses of gentility.

The nerve-ends of his fingers tell afresh
the dexterous slitting of pocket-linings, the swift
extraction of valuables for transference
to the waiting accomplice . . .

                                The nerve-ends feel
the glass to be the smooth wood of the dock.
The brain repeats the brilliant self-defences.

His lips purse with the knowledge: Lies, all lies

—all but the ingenuous plea he made to the Baron,
who, disconcerted, ordered: *Take him away!*

Good men, he thinks, have done him grievous wrong,
though better, like Phillip and Hunter, have been his friends.

It was that scoundrel, Price, led him to ruin—
but would not let him die, paid hospital expenses.
George Barrington can harbour no harsh blame.

A long, long way he travelled over the ocean
to be a diligent, sober, impartial defender
of law and order in a Land of Thieves.

He chuckles audibly; and the housekeeper smiles,
for his sense of humour is proverbial
and infectious. However, she cannot guess
he savours the epithet "sober" Phillip allowed him:
Sober I was, though not so sober now.

Aloud: "I do declare, I've spilt my rum!" The woman
is quick to wipe it up. "Sorry," he says.

She doesn't mind at all. He's a good master,
as assignees on both his farms agree.

EXTRACTS FROM ULURU

AN APOSTROPHE TO AYERS ROCK

Uluru, Katatjuta and Atila are the native names for Ayers Rock, Mt Olga and Mt Conner. Ayers Rock is the largest monolith in the world, measuring seven miles around at the base and reaching a height of eleven hundred feet. The three formations stand in a straight line, east to west, the Rock being situated between the other two, at a distance sixty miles west of Mt Conner and twenty east of Mt Olga.

> Uluru of the eagles, standing between
> Atila, the flat-topped mountain,
> and Katatjuta's thirty conglomerate pillars . . .

I have known the dawn
one shattering voice of birds to celebrate
the magnificent beauty of the Rock, Uluru;
I have known the Sun
assume her hair-string veil to hide her face
from the evening dazzle of the Rock, Uluru;

I have known the night
one radiance of moon, cicadas chanting
the astounding history of the Rock, Uluru.

Surely I have proved elision of Time,
gone more than distance to drink at the springs of wonder!

. . . . .

Mulga after mulga, mallee after mallee,
ridge-top after ridge-top, valley after valley . . .
The distance-traversing sandhills throng:
the saltbush spinifex
spinifex bluebush
bluebush, saltbush
sandhills throng . . .

Lizard and snake,
whisper across the ground,
whisper by gibber and stick, or make
no slightest sound . . .

Casuarinas preen on the red sand-plain
through the heat-heavy noon . . .

Myriad tufts of silvergrass
are ground mist to the moon.

. . . . .

It would not be enough to walk,
footsore, a thousand miles to you, Uluru,
Rock, Uluru, over the dry and harsh
expanses of sand and gibber, ridge and valley,
saltbush, bluebush, spinifex, mulga,
casuarina,
beneath the unblinking blue.

Arrival is more than physical: it is
the dreaming at the inner shrine,
with sun and star, sun and star,
moon after moon,
message-stick and tjurunga,
rock-hole and dune.

Approach, Uluru, must
be with eyes clear for taking
the great red contours or black buttress of stars,
and mind staunch for making
the incredible journey that still
remains to be made
beyond sight, touch and hearing.

Approach, Uluru, must
be from a Past so distant
that Man is but a perilous dream of Nature,
instinct of Being,
and suns and storms are furiously beating on
a vast, unshatterable stone diprotodon.

Approach must be naked of Knowledge, except
what is relevant.

Here the red euro has lept
the jumble of boulders at the west base;
here the sun smites and the ages go by;
here the moon's
a male hunter, with bright woomera, spear and boomerang,
striding scarps where, in the world's dawn, the winds sang
the same chants as now,
intoning awesome Dreamtime corroborees
here, vast Rock,
through your caves and your crowding trees.

. . . .

As I stepped out from one of your Caves of Paintings,
I knew myself forever part of you,
inspirited through ochre, charcoal and pipeclay,
through aeons of ochre, charcoal and pipeclay,
into your colourful darkness of timeless Being—
yesterday, today and ever after
eternal Dreaming in your heart, Uluru.

As I stepped out from one of your Caves of Paintings,
you and the wedge-tailed eagle soared together
high in the battering blue;
and I, in your vibrant shade, Uluru, knew
life-strength that wells alone
from your stupendous quietness of stone.

W. Flexmore Hudson

EDITOR'S NOTE

Wilfred Flexmore Hudson was born at Charters Towers, Queensland, in 1913, but as a child moved to Adelaide, South Australia. He attended the Adelaide High School and the University of Adelaide and became a school teacher, at first in the Mallee, for a time at Scotch College, afterwards at the Adelaide Boys' High School. His career also included a period of service on local ships in the coastal trade.

His books (all verse) include: *Ashes and Sparks* 1937, *In the Wind's Teeth* 1940, *With the First Soft Rain* 1943, *Indelible Voices* 1943, *As Iron Hills* 1944, *Pools of the Cinnabar Range* 1959. He was editor of *Poetry* (magazine) 1941–1947, and wrote many uncollected short stories.

SONG

I sing thee, sweet, my heart was the barest
desert; then love digged a well.
Now the wind runs over the fairest
blossoms, thy hid springs to tell.
  But pierce its hard soil, and unsought,
where one will,
thy waters reach up to my thought,
give it life till
derision the rose in her burning
flings to the stars above,
and the dark of that desert is waning,
lit with oases of love.

THE POET AND THE WORLD TODAY

My heart is a last year's nest in a broken bough;
a dried-up well, the clay sides crumbling;
a dream of fair smiling faces, a long time now sour-festered
                             in the sod;
the embers of a home where once child voices rang;
a withered hand insensate that once made love's caress;
a forest of gaunt dead trees in crucifixion on an ashen sky;
my heart is such; my heart is driftwood,
flotsam and jetsam on the ocean's rim;
the love that is hopeless; the skeleton moon
that a callous sun bleaches in the desert of night.

SONNET, 1935

Slaves, you are slaves, my people, to the lust
and greed of thieves who mock your wretched lot,
who starve you while machines stand still and rust,
and crops are burnt, food dumped, and cattle shot.
While tax-gorged states waste wealth preparing guns
and tanks and poison gas to blot out life,
disease feeds on your daughters and your sons;

beauty is scoffed at, pity scorned in strife.
In swarming cities millions now are born
to small fame-thirsty powers who see elsewhere
vast empty fields. You wake at each sad dawn
to threats of war and death, day's long despair.
Yet love your mad disorder has defied.
Woe if to you, as me, love were denied!

THE FARMER

Star-mist was on the hills; the cows had been fed:
It was twilight, soft and windless,
and the trees in the west tipped with red.
I walked with the farmer through the brown ploughed field,
while the dogs drove the sheep ahead.
We had to shout in that babble of lambs bleating
in long bursts of hunger that fell into hushes,
while the ewes ran from lamb to lamb frenziedly sniffing,
searching with strange rushes,
and the rams turned to stamp at the dogs.
And though I had lived with the man in his home,
seen him a thousand times with his children and wife,
I had not known before such tenderness to come
into his face as he raised a sick lamb from its rest
and, folding its forelegs gently, carried it close to his breast.

TO A BOY ON HIS ELEVENTH BIRTHDAY

1

When I think of him and his boyish love for me
my heart is grateful and at peace;
the sun stands overhead, the wheat-crops ripening;
my vines are laden with the purple grapes;
my sheep grow heavy with wool on the grass-covered hills.
    And when I see his eyes so trustfully search my face
believing that I can explain the mysteries of life
I am a little downcast, knowing my insufficiency.
    When I see how he strives to act and speak for my approval
I would be nobler for his sake.

2

    Watching him at play with his schoolmates
or racing his pony
I admire his slim eleven-years-old limbs,
the supple small-hipped frame, the slender neck,
the finely-balanced head, the firm tanned face,
the innocent enquiring eyes that life's injustices will hurt.
    And I see that he is perfect and lament that he must change—
that spring must cease and the blossom perish
the sun descend at noon
the moon-flower petals fade.
I am afraid for him. My heart is sore
that he must come to manhood in such troublous, dangerous
                                    years
when the few are fabulously rich, the many poor and hungry
and brooding on rebellion;
when oppression and hatred are so rife,
so many nations vast armed camps.

3

   Strange that these young lips must pale with passion,
these eyes speak want, this shrill voice sound with pleading,
these limbs strain the limbs of a lover.
Strange that a man's consuming loves and hates
must play upon that smooth, unblemished face,
transforming it with wrinkle fold and line.
Strange that this serene young heart
must wake to anger, be humiliated, scorned, embittered,
perhaps betrayed by friends, its love go unrequited.

4

And oh I hope he, too, will be a lover of mankind,
imposing no distinctions of race or class or colour,
eager to help all peoples reap the riches of science and art.
And I hope he will fight to abolish poverty
which is so shameful in a world so rich!
Such hope is sunrise over spring-clad hills,
the flash of silver wing in a clear summer sky;
my heart is light and I exult
as one who has this moment paid an impoverishing debt,
as one who after years of the blind-darkened sickroom
walks in the sun at last.

And oh I hope he can be ever fiercely honest,
unrelenting in proud integrity—
never constrained to prostitute his soul . . .
never be a teacher believing in love yet having to preach
                                      imperialism,
or an artist who smutches the face of beauty
to please the vulgar who hate what is finer than themselves;
may he never have to profit by injustice,
never have to sweat the helpless unenlightened poor,
never a soldier deceived by empty words into fighting those
                                      whom he does not hate.

But often when I think how men are beaten—
the flower of their nobility despoiled
by the wind of poverty
or by the too-hot sun of sudden riches
or by the chill of enslaving passions,
I am afraid for him . . .
    And in the hours when men as self-directing creatures
seem merely contemptible,
capable only of contriving mischief
and the wanton destruction of their kind,
when I am apprehensive of the downfall
of our too-haughty, machine-tortured civilization;
a dark tide beats on my crumbling cliffs,
my hope is scattered as the desert sand,
a blight is on my leaves,
the rank roots of despair
suck at the skeleton that is my heart,
the sunk floor and the sagging beam
that is my heart.

MALLEE FARM AT DUSK

The ringing flight of a startled bird
and the thud of my horse's hoofs
were the only sunset sounds I heard
on the track that wound through the mallee plain
to the squat pug-huts with the sun-tinged roofs
in the stony straw-blown clearing.
    But at the gate, as I drew rein,
an eager bird burst into song
and, without dismounting,

I listened there so long
that now the memories of that strain
to every golden dusk belong
with a rabbit's cry and a plover swooping,
drowsy clouds stretching themselves for rest,
and the full-blown petals of a windmill drooping
stirless in the lonely west.

DROUGHT

Midsummer noon; and the timbered walls
start in the heat,
and the children sag listlessly over the desks
with bloodless faces oozing sweat
sipped by the stinging flies.
Outside the tall sun fades the shabby mallee,
and drives the ants deep underground;
the stony driftsand shrivels
the drab sparse plants:
there's not a cloud in all the sky to cast
a shadow on the tremulous plain.
Stirless the windmills, thirsty cattle standing
despondently about the empty tanks
stamping and tossing their heads
in torment of the flies from dawn to dark.
For ten parched days it has been like this
and, although I love the desert, I
have found myself

                dreaming
of upright gums by a mountain creek
where the red boronia blooms,
where bell-birds chime through the morning mists,
and greenness can hide from the sun;
of rock-holes where the brumbies slink
like swift cloud-shadows from the gidgi-scrub
to drink when the moon is low.
        And as I stoop to drink, I too,
just as I raise my cupped hands to my lips,
I am recalled to this drought-stricken plain
by the petulant question
of a summer-wearied child.

AS THE FUGITIVE GRASS

My sole ambition was to leave my race
some landmark for those travellers who turn
bewildered to and fro at dusk
in this place of multitudinous cross-roads
and contradictory sign-posts.
I dreamed of fame and in my folly went
near to neglecting love.
But I am prouder now to shape for you
poems of thankfulness
as delicate and unpretentious
as the fugitive grass that the first rains bring
to the naked clearings of the mallee.

MALLEE SCENE

On the death-still plain
two steel rails glare.
Then a lame scorched train
limps from the cutting's golden flare
as if each slow pant hurts,
and a sorry flock
of crows go up with a shiver of air,
and a faint hare spurts
from his squat on jerky limbs;
while thin clouds pass and pitilessly mock
the thirsting mallee scrub that the drift-sand rims.

MALLEE COURAGE

Have in me the silent courage of this mallee plain
that still bears brittle leaves
beneath the haggard skies
in time of drought
when driftsand buries the hard-bitten boughs
and birds have flown,

the courage that unflinchingly endures
the angry years
till the winds hiss the rain on new grass
and the crickets in the scrub
and the birds
wake the sun with their singing.

MAIL NIGHT; MALLEE STORE

The sun sets, the parrots fly screeching from the stacks,
the schoolboys leave their play and canter past;
the windless afterglow turns gray, while down the rooty tracks
the wagons rattle home. We light the lamp at last;
and, just as the moon from the drift draws near,
sit down to dinner and a long swig of beer.

ANDREW

Andrew and I used to ride on the hills
and swim in the warm lagoon
and listen together to parrot-shrills
and larks that soared with the moon;
and we laughed and sang and took every chance
of a kiss on the long drive home from a dance.

But now the hills are very very far away.
The Bank has the farm; the homestead's leased;
and I am cooped in a room all day,
while Andrew's gone to be a priest.
And I wonder if still when he kneels to pray
he dreams in the silent dark of his cell
of bronzy hills, and parrots and the hack he rode so well.

PRAYER

To Alexander Constantinovitch Platonov

When an ulcerous anger, lit
by the cruel shams and greed
of the many men I hate,
burns into my desert-hardy soul
I would there might be given, then as now,
a glimpse of the eternal
rhythms of the universe, and love
vast as the skies that ring this mallee plain with dawn,
and the patience of the thirsting mallee soil
that keeps its seeds without once failing
through the fires and frosts of drought.

SONG OF AN AUSTRALIAN

1

I have travelled my land, my heart big with pride,
coming on many a township drowsed in the sun,
riding for hundreds of miles through the sheep-clotted plains
that tremble at noon like the bed of a running stream,
watching with lazy eyes the blue mirage
recede before me through a sunburnt day,
stopping at homesteads that nestle in the gums.
I have crossed our mountains, amazed at the hues
of sunset and sunrise on timber-lit slopes,
drawing rein in rapture on many a spur.
I have swum across our creeks and forded them on horse.
I have seen the almond and the apple picked,
the cherry, the olive, the mango and the grape.
I have watched the red sun float upon our tropic seas
and set the sails of pearling fleets on fire.
    And I have wandered through our coastal cities,
gazing on the people, the traffic and the shops,
gladder to stroke a broken-winded carthorse
than goggle at ingenious machines.
I know the cities' splendour and their wealth. I know their
                              slums.

So I have learnt to love the mallee more and the blue salt-
bush,
and the desert, and the little ports where wheat-ships
load at jarrah jetties.

2

I am proud to be Australian and I love
all trees Australian, birds and beasts,
all ranges and their rivers, yearn for them
as the stars that reach their hands
to our still lagoons must yearn.

3

I know, Australians, most of you go poor
in the richest land on earth
and I am angry: yet I still exult
you have the courage of our desert trees
that heave green leaves from famished sands
undauntedly surviving drought
and fire and flood. I love you, I am by
in all your sorrows, feel your setbacks, share
your pioneering pride. I promise I shall ever
sing your land's beauty and the greatness of your soul.

GUM TREE

Its trunk is a shadowy track across the plain;
its branches hug a snoring mountain close;
toptwigs clutch the clouds that sunrise climbs.

TO MYRLE: AND THEN YOU SANG

And then you sang; and all at once the night
—the warm moon low to the roofs and the purple hills
beyond your face—took on a beauty
I had missed before. And then I understood
my need of you, my long, unutterable need.
I knew at once we had to make a perilous journey down the
                                                                  years,
not staying long in orchard-gullies, towns or ports, but making
                                                                  tracks
across the furthest ranges and the gibber plains,
risking all the deserts, the bushfires and the treacherous creeks
                                                                  in flood.
I knew at once our love would heal the sores of money,
relieve the cureless ache of sorrow,
and forever find new beauty
in the loneliest bare and stony places.

MAGPIES

From every gum in the gully creek
came sweeter songs than moonlight ever fetched
as sunrise blazed on the coldest peak
and wakening shadows stretched.

BLACK COCKATOOS

Black cockatoos, high in the gold of sunrise,
swooping down past gum trees upon an alien pine.

SUNDOWN

Galahs going home to the creek gums circle
above me, breasts aflame,
drowning the magpies' warbles with their cries;
piled high with sandalwood, a squeaky cart
slowly lazily lumbers up the road;
one by one the windows in the little township glow:
but I stay a long time trying to distinguish
the purple plain from the purple mountains,
the purple mountains from the purple clouds.

TO EDGAR H. MERCER

From SONNETS ON THE WAR

If sometimes I forgot you or lightly bore your going,
it was before this bitterness, before this sleepless pain
made me fear your memories of our friendship would be
                                                          growing
faint with despair we should ever meet again.
But now when the range is purple and the magpie sings
and the horses jog to water through a dust of gold,
each galah coming home to our creek gums brings
a longing to share with you this beauty as of old.
So often I'm sad, sad even nights when her breath
sleeps on my cheek and a moon shows lips to kiss
—wanting for you a peace no war can mar.
Wanting you too to love, and outwit death,
I'm sad all I can do is never miss
to wish you good-luck daily wherever you are.

GALAHS

Cherry blossoms fell from the skeleton boughs
    of a mallee, and returned.
        And lo! They were galahs!

WAR

I can appreciate the satisfaction of preserving traditions of
>   Empire and of providing opportunities of promotion
>   for the army,
doubtless without these our civilization would not be what it
>   is—
but what of the low-browed slum lad who is tricked into hate
>   by lies, what of the girl turned nun to escape from
>   the world, and lost to love? . . .

I can appreciate the satisfaction of statesmen making
>   grandiloquent gestures, safe, full in the limelight, tipsy
>   with pride and power—
but what of the young wife who dares not have a child for
>   fear of unemployment, conscription, invasion, poverty
>   and worry?

I can appreciate the satisfaction of armament-firms, steel-
>   cartels, oil-combines and all their investors—
doubtless their wealth is the keystone of our culture—
but what of the student who turns away from his microscope,
>   the poet from his song, heartsick, unsettled, asking
>   what good is their work in a world that mocks at their
>   dreams? . . .

AS SEEDS THROUGH YEARS OF DROUGHT

CONCLUSION*

Now it is cooling; lank shadows inch towards the east, more
>   birds are busy in the pepper-tree, the gray gums now
>   look cold.
On the hills they're burning off, thin smoke mounts like a tree
>   to a cloud . . .
Over in Europe smoke hangs high over a burning, shattered
>   land. Millions there are dying, and glad to die because
>   of pain. Planes sow bombs in cities crowded as hives;

---

* From *The Jindyworobak Anthology* 1941. This poem forms Part IV of "With the First Soft Rain", 1943.

> children insane with fear dig at the earth with their
> hands and their teeth to hide. Tanks make jam of
> wounded men. Flame-throwers roast the tank-crews.
> Men shoot, gas, choke, bayonet, crush, drown, bury
> one another.

But worst of all, in every land men are beginning to believe
> evil of their own soul, beginning to lose heart and fear
> that wars and suffering are as remote from our control
> as the rotation of a spiral nebula!

And against this sad despair I raise my cry.

A mere poet, sprawling in the sun, I laugh defeatists down.

If there is evil now, it was determined by the injustice and
> ignorant cruelty of the past. Knowing this, we need
> not betray the future to evil.

Beauty is our spirit's lasting hunger. So we shall ever strive
> (since beauty is born of love) to build a world that
> we can love. (All acts, all thought will in that world
> be beautiful.)

Empires may tumble; generations be poisoned by hatred, fall;
> whole nations slip back into darkness.

Here now we need not despair.

That noble act, that plain-vast thought, that song—they are
> not lost;

they are enregistered!

We have felt their beauty, time

can promise no greater discovery, not even death.

We must be like our desert grass—

endure as seeds through years of drought

to race green shoots

to rapid flowers

with the first soft rain.

You and I are sufficient to prove the nobility of man . . .

When I see you bitter and disheartened,

I can no longer bother to rhyme a pretty song.

I want to help you climb the mountain of my courage.

I tell you that our sun is young in astronomic time—

there are many million years for man to shape his life

by the truths we poets know,

many million years to discover that Beauty

is the dearest dower of life, to be bought without money or
> power.

Millions of years!

Long before that some race will end

the tragic misery of our disordered days . . .

Now it is sundown; not a bee or an ant can be seen, not a
> starling shakes the pepper-tree, the late galah going

home to the creek is black against blue ranges. Soon
the eastern hills will be red with afterglow.
Far out on the plain a young bull is blorting his want;
there is no mistaking what he means.
We too, poets, must blort what we want;
men must not mistake what we mean . . .
One low star shows red in the west . . .
I am happy still . . .
I have sent up this shout, this blorting,
before I too am poisoned by horror or hate,
before misery sends me mad or withers thought,
while I am happy still . . .

Extracts from INDELIBLE VOICES

I sing for a generation given
early to hunger and shame,
fed from childhood on lies and dreams,
befooled, but not to blame.

Filled with a horror of war and made
incapable of hate,
now we must fight, and we wonder
have our eyes been opened too late

To the truth no cause was ever won
by a battle of thoughts in the brain,
but only by blood and sweat and toil
and sacrifice and pain?

.   .   .

We are no refugees from Eden,
nor angels under ban;
hell is our past, and but for love,
hellish the nature of man.

.   .   .

We had built upon the heritage
of thought and song and science,
but overlooked the longer past
that snarled a red defiance.

We had overlooked the vanity
and the cruel and jealous rage
sleeping lightly in our blood
from a primitive heritage.

And now the long-frustrated instincts
riot in drunken revel,
and the lusts and hate we caged and hid
loose the tiger and the devil.

And this is the doom of all nations
till love is honoured and freed,
and Beauty can sleep all day in the sun
unafraid of Greed.

Young as we are, in love with the sun
blue range, mirage and plain;
Young as we are, in love with the moon
and stars and snow and rain;

Yet we have wished primeval night
would smother our sun and earth,
and the solar chaos engulf our festering
cities of shame and dearth.

Though Art could give our night the beauty
of desert afterglows,
though love and friendship warmed our hearts
while round us winter froze,

Still we have prayed some star would sweep
the ashes of our guilt
into the nebulous dark from which
clean worlds may yet be built.

. . . . .

What can the future hold for *us?*
The peace that we are after?
Work we love, a wife, and a home
and friends, and children's laughter?

Shall *we* arrive with dignity
at an age when we can make
long meditation in a singing orchard
or by a secret lake?

No, you and I will most likely be crushed
like a snail, or burnt, or shot,
or drowned in poison-gas, and left
on some foreign shore to rot.

Or return worn-out to a shadow land
where reason is forlorn
and the spirit whines for the dark of the womb
as a baby newly-born.

. . . . .

For I have loved my fellow-men
and earth and sky and sea;
even as a child, the waves, the clouds
and the hills confided in me.

Beauty has set my heart of a sudden
dancing, again and again,
dancing, making of no effect
the despair of learned men.

I have seen the wattle on indigo scarps,
I have come on waratahs
by a mountain-stream with a coral bed
and camped there with the stars.

I have ridden down the sun all day,
and galloped down the moon,
through virgin scrub, by desert beach
and glittering salt-lagoon.

Drought, rain, dust-storm, flood and fire,
mountains hushed by snow,
desert-scrub in spring, hot jungles:
all have been good to know.

For me the brumbies frisked in frost,
in heat cicadas dinned;
the magpie over the mallee sailed
sideways down the wind.

For me the swans and the pelicans mustered
noisily on the lagoon;
For me the kangaroos came from the scrub
silently under the moon.

A subterranean river feeding
roots deep under sand,
friendship has kept my branches green
in the glare of a droughty land.

Our nature is a battlefield
where implacable instincts clash;
even the hidden forts of dream
their suicide-raiders smash.

Yes, we are the heirs of brutes that murdered
tortured, and gloated on tears,
destroyed, burned, raped, betrayed for greed,
pale with irrational fears.

But in our brain, indelible voices
sing too of love, as old
as the first cave-fire, from camp and village
and cities now in mould.

What in our life is as sure as Death?
Perception, electrons, pain?
Thought, or will, or the urge of sex?
I answer Beauty and Pain.

To worship Beauty is to love
Humanity and Truth;
therefore this worship does not bid us
dream away our youth,

Does not command,"*Make love your drug,
or hide in desert-caves,
far from the brawling noisy mobs
machinery enslaves.*"

But, *"Work as those slaves to set them free*
in a world that men can love,
where bench and machine will move the heart
as lagoons with stars above."

For as premature scrap in the knackers' yards
our ships of dream will end,
till the engine sings, and the lathes bloom
and the spade has the grip of a friend.

HARE IN SUMMER

In the little strip of shade
that a strainer-post has made,
squats a weakly panting hare.
All day he has squatted there.
Only with the shade he shifts.
As I approach he slowly lifts
his goggling eyes, but will not run,
fearing me less than the naked sun.

WORDS

Just a few words she said:
   And on the Pacific back of my mind
   Just as their island loomed ahead
   a hurricane scattered the migrant fleet
   and drove them, shook them, till men lay
   shivering, hungering, half-blind
   —and every coconut washed away.
   Then, bearing down with thirst and heat,
   a red sun with a heart of stone
   discovered one canoe alone . . .
   Just a few words she said.

Just a few words she said:
   And high in a winter sky back of my mind
   just as the flare-path shone ahead
   one's engine failed and lit a wing,
   and a dive but set the tail alight.

Hating death, unresigned,
he struggled out and clutched the night.
Then, caught by his harness, like a stone in a sling,
he swung, as the plane spun, round and round;
and the flames reached him before the ground . . .
Just a few words she said.

KIRSOVA

(Written after a ballet performance in Melbourne during the New Guinea Campaign)

Kirsova danced—
and I dreamed how the fall of a leaf on a waterhole woke
                                                        a gum
and tossed a hovering hawk, when a flame
of crimson turned to a lory and flew from a silver wattle;
and the grace of her was music, rainbow music crying
for a boy, in a lost freedom, who watched the golden gorse
running with delicate steps down to the windy sea.

Kirsova danced—
and soon young lads who watched her will bleed away her
                                                        beauty
in the jungle shadows, in the sea;
then will their white cry against the pain and dark,
calling for the lost light, be a call for Kirsova.
Her they will reach for, in reaching for the loving hands of
                                                   the earth . . .
And the waves unloosing their fingers will be unloosing . . .
                                                 Kirsova.

GIOVANNI RINALDO, P.O.W.

He had heard in a wind cooling his wounds of fire,
in the whisper of the mango to the moon that climbed the
                                                      wire,

Maria, his wife, and Nino, the son of their tears,
calling more sweetly than Death, all through the years.

Nearer now and surer they sound, so he ploughs
the frosty fallow singing and, fetching our cows

home through the yaccas that burn on the misty flats,
he sings as the sundown dislodges the owls and the bats.

At school my youngster Billy boasts of the size
of the stones by our swamp that his friend the prisoner shies,

so Giovanni is coaxed into feats of strength and tussles
by little boys brought home to admire his bulging muscles.

And my wife and daughters go humming unawares,
I, too, the saddest of Sicilian airs,

Last night his laughter surrendered the outposts of pride,
and, moaning, he rushed from the table to his room outside;

and the crumpled paper told us our troops were bombarding
the town his sleepless prayers had long been guarding.

"Dio buono!" he moaned—and his wife's name—
sending his heart to an orchard dissolved in flame;

while the little photos he had often shown us streamed
blood down our minds as we listened, and then as we dreamed.

Cutting chaff this morning, I heard the birds,
the sheep, and the engine itself, dinning the words,
"Dio buono!"

And they told me that Billy, staring wide-eyed
while the rest of the class were writing, suddenly sighed,
"Dio buono!"

NOSTALGIA

I caught my tram and took my seat
in Swanston Street, in Swanston Street,
and I was then a water-hole
staring up at a sorrel foal
and two galahs, with wings full spread,
on a red-gum branch above his head.

At Prince's bridge, at Prince's Bridge,
I had become a quartzy ridge
watching the sheep on the plain below,
purple sheep in the afterglow,
and horses racing to drink at a trough
and frightening gusts of magpies off.

I barely noticed the windows glowed
as the sundown lit Commercial Road,
for I had turned to an eagle gliding
deep down gullies where hares were hiding;
and my shadow cast a quiet that stayed
a long while after my kill was made.

Before we had rattled through Prahran,
my starry night as a scree began,
with snow on my scarp, and falling rock,
the gully holding its breath for the shock,
while a rabbit gave a warning thump
and a wallaby peered from a wattle clump.

A frog dived, and the soak went plop!
at the Gardiner stop, at the Gardiner stop,
for I was a wind that swayed the reeds
and rolled the pods of the salt-bush seeds;
and so I reached my gate—too soon,
waving a she-oak across the moon.

THE KISS

(For little Bronnie Norman)

Because my lips construed her cheek
as parrot light on a wattle creek

today I learnt that soursobs meant
distant thrushes by their scent,

while cicada chirrs, to my listening eyes,
were a rippling heat-haze in disguise.

And since her laughter shook again
almond blossom down the rain,

the gannet stitching the silver swell
rang on my tongue a muscat bell,

while the purr of the reef where the surf broke
was a kitten wind my hand could stroke.

BASHŌ

Bashō, the ragged poet, the wanderer Bashō,
astride a sleepy horse at the edge of a rustling pond
where teal, at the splash of a salmon, sail for clumps of bamboo.

High on the opposite bank, a gusty pine is waving
across the noon-white snow of distant Fujisan,
pouring cascades of gold-dust, luminous, gentle as mist,
on blue sky, blue ripples, and morning glory bells.

And his horse is drowsing, drowsing—a dragonfly close to its
ears!—
while Bashō, brushing the gold from its glossy mane, is smiling
that such a little thing as pollen clouding a wind
should outweigh the fifty sorrows, the disillusioned years.

MALLEE IN OCTOBER

When clear October suns unfold
mallee tips of red and gold,

children on their way to school
discover tadpoles in a pool,

iceplants sheathed in beaded glass,
spider orchids and shivery grass,

webs with globes of dew alight,
budgerigahs on their first flight,

tottery lambs and a stilty foal,
a papery slough that a snake shed whole,

and a bronzewing's nest of twigs so few
that both the sky and the eggs show through.

A HYMN FOR THE DARK AGE

Jesus, when I was a child I was taught and believed
no one had ever suffered such agonies as you;
stronger even than my horror that your heavenly father
had allowed you to redeem mankind
by so terrible a way of blood and pain,
stronger even than my gratitude for my eternal life,
was sorrow for your suffering.
So that sometimes, alone in my room,
in the sanctuary of night,
reading the Gospels, I wept.

And through the day I bore my little griefs and hurts
with fortitude
and looked upon the heaving sea of Time that I must travel,
with steady, innocent eyes,
believing the anguish of any man was paltry
when weighed against your death
and that your love upheld me like a father's hand.

But now—my childhood faith destroyed—
I know that you were lucky
to have perished in a Roman province
and not in Hitler's Germany:
I know the obscure and ordinary Jew
endured in my own days
agonies your tormentors never would have sanctioned.

The *German Jew* was seized by the guards
in the timid hours before dawn,
hooked from a sleep of fear
and flung, like refuse, into a prison van.
He did not will his death to fulfil prophecy;
no words that *he* could utter
could snap the fetters on his wrists.

You were taken in the fragrance of the evening starlight,
by the brook of Kedron, in Gethsemane;
to temper the menace of the envious priests
and the jibes of the rabble,
you had the solace of disciples ready to defend you,
a sense of purpose in your choice of death.

And what was a slap in the face from a fool—
the contumelious captain in the hall of Annas?
what was the derision of tipsy soldiers
in the praetorium, what even the crown of thorns,
the reed for a sceptre, the gobbets of spittle on your face,
what even the scourging?

Was there not compassion, respect, in the looks and words of
                                                    Pilate?
And did the Sanhedrin ever deny you were human?
Did Pilate torture Mary your mother, in your presence,
till she screamed, insane, broken words of betrayal
to faces as empty of human kindness
as the frozen scarps of Himalayan peaks?

And then, dear Jesus, your final agony was mercifully short:
A strong man carried your cross up Golgotha hill;
not long after the driving of the nails
and the shudder of the stepping of the cross,
the customary analgesic
was pressed on a sponge to your quivering lips;
a quick spear pierced your side while you hung insensible.
And there was comfort, deep though mixed with bitterness,
that there at your feet wept Mary your mother,
and Mary Magdalenĕ, and Mary the mother of James,
and sweet Salome;
and you could see love and grief in the eyes
of your intimidated followers
standing afar off
till you sank into the mercy of the dark waves,
mourning your spent mortality
in those most piteous words of disillusion:
"Eloi, Eloi, lama sabacthani!"

But, gentle Jesus, you never suffered scientific torture;
never dehumanizing drugs, nor mutilating surgical
                                           experiments;
never, for you, the loneliness of herding in a concentration
                                           camp;
never starvation corroding courage as lime a corpse;
your daughter was never conscripted as a prostitute for the
                                           guards;
you never watched the oven chimneys vomit smoke,
knowing one puff was the kissing flesh of your own wife;
you never ate with your daily bread

the fear that evil, a universal Sahara,
had possessed the fruitful heart of man . . .
O Jesus, I am glad you did not die in Buchenwald.

But this, magnanimous Jesus, I believe:
if, from your cross of blood in the earthquake dark,
you could a moment speak to our unhappy world,
with prescience of the epic of our shame,
you would cry out in horror, *"Pity me not;*
but comfort the Jews my people,
comfort my desolate people,
the most wronged of time.
Compared unto the burning mountain of their pain,
these nails are a night-fire of sticks in the desert.
These tears, my ultimate tears, entreat you,
comfort my people!"

COACH IN TRAINING CAMP

(For Richard Chinner)

The year we broke the record
for the Head-of-the-River boatrace
a dozen of us camped in the Murray Bridge shed;
and we rowed about a hundred miles a week.

One morning the early light on the veranda
woke me before the peewees had called up the sun.
I stretched myself, drowsily grinning
at the sight of the sleeping boys
tangled in mosquito nets.
The river sounded choppy,
as if the wind were high;
and yet the willow leaves were stiller than the sleepers.
Curious, I got up to look . . .

What I had heard were little splashes
made by thousands of fish
leaping into the insect-filmy light:
the wide water from bank to bank
was splashed into silver wavelets,
silver desquamations
like white clay peeling on the bed of an inland dam.

"Wake up, Stroke," I whispered,
"here's something we'll never forget!"

And together we watched the fish
arching into the blue dawn
I remember they fell with a sound
of corks being pulled from little bottles.

Then over the ridge of the opposite bank
the summer sunrise poured
and lit a comet-tail of dust
behind a speeding car,
and flooded down the hazy reaches
between the green willows,
turning the fish and the splashes to fire,
and revealing cormorants hunched on stakes,
and a white dinghy adrift.

And a silent flight of black duck
flew downstream so low
they sprinkled the water with dark shadows;
and, just like the tail of a kite rippling in the wind,
a string of fluting swans came over the butter factory
and, one after another, climbed and dived
to miss the surges of the smoke.

And we watched . . . and the golden splashing died away.

Then, till our piper roused the camp,
we talked in whispers of the Eight,
glad we were ready at last
to put up our rating and make our maximum swing.

Ian Mudie

EDITOR'S NOTE

Ian Mayelston Mudie was born at Adelaide, South Australia, in 1911. He was educated at Scotch College, Adelaide, and later worked as a journalist, real estate salesman, and publisher's editor. Although mainly associated with Adelaide, he managed to move about a good deal. During the war he served in Army Education. In his youth he lived for a time in London, and it was on a return visit to London that he died suddenly in 1976.

His books include: verse, *Corroboree to the Sun* 1940, *This Is Australia* 1941, *The Australian Dream* 1943, *Their Seven Stars Unseen* 1943, *Poems 1934-44* (collected edition) 1945, *The Blue Crane* 1959, *The North-Bound Rider* 1963, *Selected Poems 1934-1974*, 1976; prose, *Riverboats* 1961, *The Wreck of the Admella* 1966, *Rivers of Australia* 1966, *The Heroic Journey of John McDouall Stuart* 1968; anthology, *Poets at War* 1944 (editor).

AS ARE THE GUMS

Not of bodies are we born but of the earth—
as are the gums that grow as we should grow,
roots in our land, branches that take from air
and give to it, the measure of their nature.

Not "land-tamers" should we be, taming the wild
to petty yardsticks of an alien growth,
but of the land, letting our measure be
what measure shall the bush-wed land decree.

Once, alien gods, Odin, Osiris, Pan,
came crowding in upon our entering heels.
Kill them, oh Land, free us and let us be
of you, and of your totem-gods of stone and tree.

THIS LAND

Give me a harsh land to ring music from;
brown hills, and dust, with dead grass
straw to my bricks.

Give me words that are cutting harsh
as wattle-bird notes in dusty gums
crying at noon.

Give me a harsh land, a land that
swings, like heart and blood
from heat to mist.

Give me a land that like my heart
scorches its flowers of spring,
then floods upon its summer ardour.

Give me a land where rain
is rain that would beat high heads low.
Where the wind howls at the windows
and patters dust on tin roofs,
while it hides the summer sun
in a mud-red shirt.

Give my words sun and rain,
desert and heat and mist,
spring flowers and dead grass,
blue sea and dusty sky,
song-birds and harsh cries,
strength and austerity,
that this land has.

STREET VISION

One night of mist the bush came back again
into the city street, I saw
glint of gum-sapling, rough trunk of blackwood
and the twist of mallee; there
the sheoak mourning for the dead, long dead,
red-gums that stood along the river,
shut out the neon lights and let the glare
of moon creep down the mist, and shine
to white the gums long gone.

That night of mist the bush came back again
into the city streets, I saw
a yacca pointing to the stars, near where
the great 'roo slept, undreaming of
the boomerang and spear; that night I heard
the mopoke call the hours where but
a dream before the clock-tower stood.—And then
the bush flowed back again; an English tree
drooped lifeless in the soggy square.

CORROBOREE TO THE SUN

And shall a million dull tomorrows roll
with naught but bright sun-worship sleep beside the surf,
while fuddled mediocrity creeps in and out
among the seats the mighty should command?
Shall this clear sun that beats be only half
welcomed and comprehended, shall we grasp
only its ease, its blessing, and not heed
its burning-glass of energy that calls
trees, grass, mountains, and plains to beauty?

Shall we thus sleep and let our heritage be swept
by white and pudgy hands into a crawling net
in which no flame, no genius may live,
but only little souls that are too damp and meek
even to smoulder? Let us, oh sun, take fire
from your bright heat, let bushfires rage
about the scrub and ranges of our hearts;
let all the dross be burned, and, as the wattle seeds
that crack and sprout not till a fire has passed,
let then our hearts, our minds, burgeon at last
in growth too strong for little minds
and little men ever to cramp again.

EARTH

Earth is our fire, our meat, our beauty,
from earth comes the matter of our minds;
all things we love are earth,
earth moulds us, from earth
we spring, and from the earth
we gather knowledge.

We eat, and we eat earth,
we drink, and the flavour of the wine
is made by earth.

Is it not good to love
the earth we know? The vine that grows
beneath the gum makes wine of flavour
foreign to northern vintage.

Earth then is in our blood;
And shall we twist our minds
as if they fed on alien soil?
Earth in our blood.
Our earth.
This earth.

UNDERGROUND

Deep flows the flood,
deep under the land.
Dark is it, and blood
and eucalypt colour and scent it.
Deep flows the stream,
feeding the totem-roots,
deep through the time of dream
in Alcheringa.
Deep flows the river,
deep as our roots reach for it;
feeding us, angry and striving
against the blindness
ship-fed seas bring us
from colder waters.

MORIALTA MEMORY

Morialta, "the ever-flowing"
between her steep gully-sides
echoes the days that should be our dream-time.
Here, where the sheoaks sway their green and comely hair,
once the spear sped.
In the high walls, above grassed earth-screes,
hero of older time his dream made.
Under overhanging rock with its yacca
was bone pointed.
Beside these ever-flowing falls were spears fashioned.
Beside the tall gum were the songs sung.
Up that track went dark traders
with flints and ochre for barter;
and went those with sacred head-dress
of mission to the distant sacred sites.

If mind drifts from the formal beds
and from shelters with bush-fire warnings,
from the picnic papers,
and the gardener's rake,
and imported plants,

and from *To First Fall ½ Mile*,
it hears the talk of old men,
the deep chuckle of lubras,
the noise of the camp,
in the voice of the creek.

GALAH

High in the wind, high against
clouds coloured as ash of vanished fires,
flies the galah.
Pink and grey, colours gilded by the last rays
of sun setting in unseen salt water,
beats slowly over.
His caged brothers, sensing him, shriek;
wings beat against the straight bars,
calling him.

Next year he will come again,
bringing a hundred others,
knowing it is time to return
to repossess the ancient
tribal grounds.

HAVE ANGER

Wail for them, wail for the lost totems,
for the tribes beaten under by the destroyer—
rubbed out beneath the wheels of his desire
for the profit that profits not your virility.
Wail for them, burn wurleys of the dead,
and where your tribal grounds hold gypsum
make of it mourning helmets for the widowed land.
Wail, but let not your wailing be weakness,
keep from it pity and self-pity,
and the tears that are neither of men nor of women
but of monsters created in you by alien gods.
Wail, but let your wailing have anger,
the strong lust of men and of women
to kill the things that would destroy them.

Have anger, strong anger that rends,
anger that lifts spear, aye, and yam-stick,
at the destroyers of totems, at murderers of our hearts,
to patterned tameness of other gods.
Have anger against those that,
throwing our gods to darkness,
breaking the tjurungas,
tearing down totem-trees,
slay all our wilderness.

BELONG

They're trying to convince you you don't belong
where the wireless drowns your corroboree song;
they're trying to kick you out of the city;
they talk of your whole dark race as a "pity".
They seem to forget that it all is yours
as long as their "home" land drags and draws,
that while old Europe's the whole of their song
—damn it, Jacky, *they* don't belong.

Damn it, Jacky, you know it too;
the whole damn country belongs to you;
they never belong for even a day,
for Europe is only a dream away.

Damn it, Jacky, it's not Adelaide
—it's Europe, that's the way they're made;
they see it all as gothic spires,
they never notice your signal fires

that leap and curl a wreath of smoke
from one black bloke to the next black bloke,
signalling far across the range
"I met an Australian, just for a change".

THIS IS AUSTRALIA

This is Australia, this is the wide continent
that holds the gate of the world for men and warmth
against icy immensities of emptiness
—cold light and great darkness—of the southern seas.
This is Australia, this is the new-old land
where conflict breeds, where even now (as always
since de Quiros gilded its image in men's thoughts)
man has his choice to make between the high
banner-flame of allegiance to his land
and the shop-sign of rabbit-burrowing blindness
that gnaws at roots, and, plague-like, kills
all that will never fill his purse nor stretch his bellyskin.

This is Australia, this is each one's earth
that is Australian, this soil is sacred
now and forever for each one for whom
the vision of this land resurgent ever stirs
in every landscape, for each one that sees
in every town and township, every house
and paddock, every street and track
each patch of untouched bush, each wasted acre
that the greed of sheep or wheat or axe
has furrowed and scarred and swept
and ploughed to barrenness, for each that sees
as his own body and as mighty all this land.

This is Australia, not even the close slums
which greed, transplanting with itself—and them—
from colder earths the huddling timid minds
of driven sheep, has set like cankerous disease
close to each city's heart, can stint or limit
the wide magnificence of this land's vision,
that men—slum-minded all, in city or in vastness—
seek in their living death of mind to cramp and set
in pocket-handkerchief-size dreams of northern lands,
each one afraid, knowing himself too small
to see as one, forever unified and great,
this mighty land that seeks its dedicated sons.

This is Australia, each tree and bush, each hill,
each mountain, each vast plain where dust-storms
ride the ancient beds of ancient seas,
each headland set to face the surf,
each creek, long dry, that thunders when the rains
break their all-feeding benediction on the earth,
each rock that carving bears or tribal myth explains,
each billabong the heron's grey reflection shows,
each jungle-patch along the north-east shores,
each valley and each gully where the euro runs,
each foot of earth, each stick, each grain of dust,
makes, and is ever part of, each Australian.

This is Australia, this is the land
whose sons and daughters are forever blind
and deaf to all its mystery; this is the land
barren of lovers; this is the land defiled
by those whose flesh is quarried from its earth;
this is the land whose sons and daughters turn
their faces from it, holding always
vain dreams in their small minds of their own greatness
greater than it; this is the land whose children
fear it, being so small and petty-mean
that never in their hearts is courage great enough
for them to love its beauty and immensity.

This is Australia. This is the land
now raising new the spirit of its earth;
this is the land that now a few do love
fiercely and fearlessly; this is the land
that now has found a few to call
its vision from the cupboard of neglect
and set it up for every man to see.
This is the land preparing for those sons
who shall acknowledge their full fellowship
with every fistful of its soil, sons who shall hold
that soil as their own flesh, sons who shall be
fanatic and consecrated in their loyalty.

I WOULD NOT GO

I would not go to a far land where days are grey and green,
nor to the land of ancientness, where greatness once was seen;
I would not go to Africa, where lions roam the land;
nor yet to Asian cities, with mystery at each hand.
No; I would roam the hot plains, and dream in mountain ease
in this vast land, this strong land, that lies in its own seas.

THE YOUNG WARRIORS

Buds on boughs of the hacked trees,
fresh suckering from sand-hidden roots
of the felled mallee, long dormant
seeds germinating, the young saplings
leaping to the sun, the strong sap
running, the leaves
breaking and flaunting
in the gale.
Soon, soon,
the time of National
flowering.

And the new growth
the young warriors.

They stand at the head
of the gully of dawn,
unsensed kylies in their hands,
forward-looking, yet still unseeing,
blinded by mists.
Soon shall they know
the strength of their magic,
soon shall they go
forward to battle
leaving woe
to alien dreamers their minds
no more shall know.

GLORY OF THE SUN

These are my people, these the nationless
caught between blackness and the undreamt dawn;
these are my people, their stars unseen
bright-burning in unfound Alcheringa.
Yet these my people fight and ride
from the nearest shore to the furthest tide.

These are my people, their souls possessed
by myths that slaver from Europa's bull
while Europe rides her lover-beast through mire
of all her thousand years of infamy.
Yet—these my people—their wild vitality
ploughed upwards in one page of history.

These are my people, who unknowing starve
for all that strength with which their country's breasts
stretch taut and full; dry tongues and parching lips
thirst for the milk of loveliness which she
holds for their mouths that scorn to touch her flesh.
Yet these my people when they wander far
dream of the wattle and the waratah.

These are my people, each one idly drifts
on his own creek or his own billabong
heading nowhere; the Murray's single flow
points no swift moral for meandering hearts
nor marches its strong vigour through their verse.
Yet these my people, unity their dream,
once flowed one instant in a single stream.

These are my people, who let vision slip
back to the stubble-land of last year's crop;
glory they let slip for gold, wisdom for ease
and self-reliance for dull luxury's pursuit;
making this land a vassal, they proclaimed
culture subservient to alien trade.
Yet these my people have produced such sons
as history shall remember while it runs.

These are my people, only by the earth
that seeks to suckle them shall they attain
to nationhood, only by living dreams
built of the air they breathe shall they escape

the trap between the blackness and the dawn;
only by following their seven stars
shall these my people reach Alcheringas.

These are my people, these the nationless
caught between blackness and the undreamt dawn;
these are my people, their stars unseen
bright-burning in unfound Alcheringa.
These are my people, how many years shall run
before they drink the glory of the sun?

IF THIS BE TREASON*

So this is treason, that a love of land
strengthen and circle in our hearts
through every hour of every day?
So this is treason, that our minds
should stir to none but native breeze,
that we should dream of unity
and our land's high purpose,
that we should see
a national future
triumphant in our song,
that we should be
willing servants
of Australia's dream?

If this be treason, then let every tree
fall to the axe, let all brave flowers
wither in traitorous disgrace.
If this be treason, then the very earth
offends against the state,
and every stick and stone
plots order's overthrow,
assassination breeds
in every waratah, the wattle's sabotage
broods on each golden hill.

If love of land a dastard treason be,
then black glows the sun and solid is the sea.

---

* This poem refers to the internment of a group of writers associated with P.R. Stephensen and the Australia First movement. See also "Written for Ian Mudie" by John T. Kirtley, 1947, in Part 2.

From **THE AUSTRALIAN DREAM**

PART 2   PIONEERS

Dawn after coloured dawn rolled by to sweep
the great lakes dry and make the rivers run
backwards upon themselves until there crept
the great diprotodons to the last mile
of mud, where until then the jungle grew,
to die and leave a legend memory
in sons of men that even then
chipped emu tracks and alligator heads
at Moolooloo and Panaramitee.
Noon after sand-swept noon blew through the land;
Nurunduree and Byamee tracked far,
making their tales and songs for men to hear
about the fires, until each stone, each tree
sang with its meaning and its rich intent
in tribal lore and sacred mystery.
Night after velvet night across the sky
drew its dark smoke; the shining star-world camps
reflected fires beneath the eucalypts
and in the mangrove swamps. The great land slept,
with its dark sons and daughters well content
to leave its soil unraped, and cherish it
as mother-goddess of their hero-gods.
The dingo howl went echoing the plains,
and year by year came drought and came the rains.
Then in far woods a ragged Yankee mob
turned to an army under their far stars,
and closed their ports to clank of ball and chain.
While Cook dreamed homewards of his Yorkshire moors
and of the cushioned ease of glass and pipe,
smug Banks knew not he was to father soon
new home for sons of England's rotting hulks
and stinking courts, and sightless, lightless gaols.
The yacca's spear still stood upon the hill;
the land still failed to know its rock-brown sons
soon, as blown ash, would scatter to the dark.
Behind the prows the weary sentries paced
the oozing pitch, and watched their cargoes sweat.
Then eucalyptine shores descried arrive
unwilling future lovers, conquering captives
—England's convict sons, torn, full of protest,
from their most mighty and most callous dam.

Huddled about the Cove's sweet stream they lived,
gaoler and gaoled, together in affright
at this vast land and its strange mystery
of sight and sound and smell, a giant land
that to their green-fed English eyes blasphemed
by its wild splendour and virility.
Not till first paler sons to cornstalk grew
did eager fingers stretch in from the coast
to grasp at acres of a continent.
Then avid men followed the tracks; and greed
led the white wash to all the ship-fed ports,
and hunger pecked the continent's one shore
from Brisbane to the Swan. Life was now on;
a land to rape lay spread beneath the sun,
with chase of good land further out begun.
West, west, west, west, shrieked wheels across the plains,
and, *north, to the north,* from Adelaide-side,
east, ever east and north, the West replied.
Shirts took colour from earth, rotted from sweat;
the earth took imprint from the passing hooves,
and idly echoed to the whip's demands.
All the wild while the reckless timid men
hated, from fear, the land they quartered up
and hacked and razed and spurned and slew and broke.
So, when they rested from the team or plough,
they found the ever-present beauty sparse,
or else nostalgic eyes envisioned it
as green and cultured fields and rounded hills,
painted the scrub as coppice or as wood,
and pictured casuarinas as the oak or beech.
Yet all the while their songs and thoughts and speech
drained through the sands and lost their alien burr;
acorns gave birth to gum trees, wattles grew
from their small homesick sprouts of English elm,
and kookaburra hatched from alien eggs
poached from the squire and parson in far village woods.
But still they talked of *Home,* and in their dreams
they wandered by their distant meadowy streams.
Their poor and petty slum and hedgerow minds
strove hard to cramp Australia's loveliness
to ancient fogs and old ancestral ways,
but she by flood and fire and wild fertility
survived the hurt and broke the hedges down
from round their hearts, and caught a few full hard
in her embrace; soon she had browned their flesh,
and slowed their speech to Murray's easy pace,

and set their minds to Darling's easy days,
and tuned their voice in prelude to her praise.
But stolid minds kept to their ancient track,
and hated her, and leered into her face,
and, finding her deep love and her strange power,
became enflamed, but were too dull for love.
Like bushfires ran their lusts from end to end
of this our land, consuming fertile earth
in one eroding rape, burning the growth
with all the torrid heat of cheap desire.
Down fell the trees, down fell the sacred sites,
and many a place was sown with Europe's salt
so it would never bloom again. The land
untamable must be made desolate;
sprinkle her face with cold and foreign names,
let kings and queens, their pimps and parasites,
degenerate cities, old and slum-sick towns,
the names of these and of mean villages,
eat the sweet music of her ancient names,
wipe the sweet imprint of the vanished tribes.
—But yet the tide runs on and ever on,
and all her foam-white coasts take up her song—
So went the rape, but gold, and gold again,
brought thousands roaring to her many fields,
until life's gusto met her fate for one
rich moment in Eureka's unity.
Then rose her flag, to fall for many years
while her true sons were hot with angry tears
as back in colonial courses ran the game
and still a continent remained unloved.
The iron rails shone as they clattered
around the fertile pattern of her coast.
And here a one and there another
welded her music to his songs and made
a love of her the symbol of his trade;
and still far strangers at their conferences
nodded wise heads, sprinkled our hopes with smiles
and gave our manhood their incessant nay.
Then roared the spirit for the single stream
and turned the tide towards Australia's dream.
But Federation's cold confusions came
to further sever hopes of unity.
Humbly, like starving peasants, cap in hand,
we gaped at Europe, aped its alien ways
and filled our blue and gold Australian days
with sycophancies. Next flowed Australian blood
to red the veldt and rich the Flanders mud

and feed virility to blundering plans
that made a beacon of Gallipoli.
Then homesick hearts that dreamed of our blue skies
died in their thousands on far foreign fields,
and cradleless the lone Australian homes
while Europe's war prepared fresh villainies.
Back to the slack days of easy peace
we slid; once more we drowsed and drooled
in slave-like luxury of apron-strings
—colonials, worshipping all alien things.
To-fro our ports there shuttled greedy ships
that carried off our wealth to all the world
and drained our pockets and suppressed initiative.
Dumb went the shipyards, dusty the machines
in interest of Imperial debts; Murray boats
rotted and sank; no more their paddle-wheels
gave their rich sound to the Australian air.
The world's demands filched all our flooding wealth
and fed us with unneeded luxuries.
At Lombard's shining desks the debt-mad pens
scribbled and wrote, and on their signs and words
depended sustenance from day to day.
Fat with his orders from across the sea,
the proud and strutting bailiff smiling came
to knot our belts. The international game
battledored Australians into penury.
Then cradleless and visionless the more,
things of the spirit diced into discard,
our sturdy people drooped, soft ease their dream.
But still our virile earth conquered more hearts,
and by its strength defeated Europe's arts.
The few that loved Australia saw her strength
in her own cloudless skies; true patriots,
they dreamed our shores all ringed with singing planes.
—But still there came the drought and came the rains.

Now, with Australia's sons at the defence
of many a shore beside her sacred own,
war crept close, the bombs sang crashing down.
Anger, love, hope, impel the eager pen,
and turn the words to the Australian dream,
the brush to the Australian idiom,
until a song of 'Loo's shrill, uphill streets
or painting of a gum-lit landscape shouts
a national spear-thrust at all enemies.
Forward, the pen commands, the brush shouts *On*,
and all our days echo the swagman's song.

NEW GUINEA CAMPAIGN

Are you there, Peter Lalor, are you there,
ghost with gold-dust in your hair;
and lean Stuart do you ride
to seek your northern tide
where in greens they're slowly swinging
through the mud, too tired for singing,
where the poison of New Guinea fills the air?

Are you there, untiring Eyre, are you there,
with your heart beyond compare;
are you there, you brave wild Kellys
where heroes on their bellies
through the jungle now are creeping
—may their women have no weeping—
where snipers from their tree-tops coldly stare?

You ghosts that walk beside
them, do you watch them now with pride
as through green hell and glory
they carry on your story
where in mud their feet are sinking
and in dreams they're always thinking
of their homes and of the cobbers that have died?

UNABATED SPRING

My heart has no bleak winters of bare limbs
and stripped boughs where birds cry
more mournful than the mopoke in such
nakedness. My sap is never still, my spring
lasts year-long; buds ever strain
at flesh of my desires, and burst to green
fired red all seasons through. My limbs
are root-fed all the year, no frosts
nor snows nip at my verdure.
My heart . . .

But so, fed by a year-long sun, I boast.
And sometimes, "Come in Spinner", laugh the gods.

Yet the felled tree ever
sprouts from the lowly butt.

And, "Come in Spinner", laugh the gods again.

"Well, who'd believe it . . . tails!" my empty pocket cries.
But still there blooms my unabated spring.

NO PHOENIX AUSTRALIS

The stillness stirs, a metallic rustle
clashes the leaves edge-turning to the sun,
birds gape in the choking shade,
a willy-willy races through the clearing
snatching at dead leaves and the hot dust,
then is gone, racing on, or suddenly expires.
A bird calls, then is silent, and far down the road
a horse moves in the mirage, and then is still.
A truck passes, bumping and whining and grinding,
then the dust hangs and drifts among the branches,
scatters and settles and disappears.

And you, murderer with the matchbox,
pigmy prometheus,
bare black branches will point accusing fingers.
Remember, there is no phoenix
in our mythology.

THEY'LL TELL YOU ABOUT ME

Me, I'm the man that dug the Murray for Sturt to sail down,
I am the one that rode beside the man from Snowy River,
and I'm Ned Kelly's surviving brother (or did I marry his sister?
I forget which), and it was my thumbnail that wrote that
                    Clancy
had gone a-droving, and when wood was scarce I set the grass
                    on fire
and ran with it three miles to boil my billy, only to find
I'd left the tea and sugar back with my tucker-bag,

and it was me, and only me, that shot through with the padre's
                                                        daughter,
shot through with her on the original Bondi tram.
But it's a lie that I died hanging from a parrot's nest
with my arm in the hollow limb when my horse moved from
                                                    under me;
I never die, I'm like the Leichhardt survivor I discovered
fifty years after the party had disappeared; I never die,
I'm Lasseter and Leichhardt both; I joined the wires of the
                                                        O.T.
so that Todd could send the first message from Adelaide to
                                                    Darwin;
I settled everywhere long before the explorers arrived;
my tracks criss-cross the Simpson Desert like city streets,
and I've hung my hat on Poeppel's Peg a thousand times.
It was me who boiled my billy under the coolabah,
told the bloke in the flash car to open his own flamin' gates,
put the goldfields pipe-line through where the experts said
                                                nobody could,
wanted to know "Who's robbing this coach, you or Ned
                                                    Kelly?",
had the dog sit on my tucker-box outside of Gundagai,
yarned with Tom Collins while we fished for a cod someone'd
                                            caught years before,
and gave Henry Lawson the plots to make his stories from.
Me, I've found a hundred wrecked galleons on the Queensland
                                                        coast,
dripping with doubloons, moidores and golden Inca swords,
and dug a dozen piles of guilders from a Westralian beach;
I was the one that invented the hollow wood-heap,
and I built the Transcontinental, despite heat, dust, death,
                                            thirst, and flies.
I led the ragged thirteen; I fought at Eureka and Gallipoli and
                                                        Lae;
and I was a day too early (or was it too late?) to discover
                                                    Coolgardie,
lost my original Broken Hill share in a hand of cribbage,
had the old man kangaroo pinch my coat and wallet,
threw fifty heads in a row in the big game at Kal,
took a paddle-steamer seventy miles out of the Darling on a
                                                    heavy dew,
then tamed a Gippsland bunyip and sooled him on
to capture the Tantanoola Tiger and Fisher's Ghost
and become Billy Hughes's secretary for a couple of weeks.
Me, I outshore Jacky Howe, gave Buckley his chance,
and have had more lonely drinks than Jimmy Woods;

I jumped across Govett's Leap and wore an overcoat in Marble
                                    Bar,
seem to remember riding the white bull through the streets
                                    of Wagga,
sailed a cutter down the Kindur to the Inland Sea,
and never travelled until I went to Moonta.
Me, I was the first man ever to climb to the top of Ayers Rock,
pinched one of the Devil's Marbles for the kids to play with,
drained the mud from the Yarra, sold the Coathanger for a
                                    gold brick,
and asked for beer off the ice at Innamincka.

Me, yesterday I was rumour,
today I am legend,
tomorrow, history.
If you'd like to know more of me
inquire at the pub at Tennant Creek
or at any drover's camp
or shearing-shed,
or shout any bloke in any bar a drink,
or yarn to any bloke asleep on any beach;
they'll tell you about me,
they'll tell you more than I know myself.
After all, they were the ones that created me,
even though I'm bigger than any of them now
—in fact, I'm all of them rolled into one.
For anyone to kill me he'd have to kill
every single Australian,
every single one of them,
every single one.

THE O.T.

Be still, and listen,
the wires are faintly humming
above the saltbush that shines faintly
in starlight, cold at nights
in this inland expanse that sleeps
with no such soft blanket of sea-air
as wraps the coast-lands.

Be still, and listen . . .
You will hear only the faint hum of wires,
only the faint humming above you, nothing more,
until a dingo howls far off, like an echo,
and then with slow padded thud
a kangaroo passes unseen in the darkness.

Look hard; despite the torches of the stars
you will see only
the faint shine of the saltbush,
and almost indistinguishable outlines
of black beheaded crucifixes
carrying the faint humming of the wires above you,
carrying it away into darkness, into the distance,
away to be lost in sodium-lighted cities
where the mystery of darkness, of silence, of starlight,
has been swallowed in noise,
has disappeared into the roar of traffic,
has been burned away for ever,
like the sticks that boiled the quartpot
at the midday camp-fire.

Be still, be very still and listen;
there is so much to hear in such small noises.
. . . Be very still, for now that you have heard
the faint corroboree of sound made by these wires
the memory will echo for you always,
and the darkness, the starlight, the silence
will never completely forsake you,
will never, even in the roar of the cities,
completely forsake you.

THE WRECK OF THE *ETHEL*, LOW TIDE

Between waves there is only the hiss of the undertow,
the shrillness of whistling eagles, the cries of the gulls,
and once a month or so the sound of voices
and of a stone scratching on forty years of rust
a name the next tide's violence will erase.

Sluggish and silent each wave rolls in,
poises, while a green light from the sun shines through,

then crashes down, hundreds of tons of sound,
sucks back in a hiss of foam, is gone,
and in its place falls down a new green wall.

And up on the sand the hull rusts slowly,
rudder twisted, deck and masts and shrouds all gone,
forecastle empty of shanties, all rigging rotted,
nothing loose left to clank or rattle or flap,
waiting to withstand the crash of the coming tide.

Better thus, lying in state on yellow sand,
with tall cliffs for mutes and gulls for mourners
(corpse of an age of gracefulness and sweat),
than as coal-hulk or lighter, dirty and spat upon,
floating in the scummy backwater of some busy port.

ONE DAY, PERHAPS IN SPRING

Don't make rules for us, don't shake your fingers at us,
don't tell us what we shall do or what we shall think,
what we shall wear or how we should talk,
for we only go the way you think we should
for as long as it suits us. Today, tomorrow,
or perhaps the day after that,
we'll burn your dictionaries, tear up your textbooks,
and use your editorials for undignified purposes;
for we are the people, we are the tide of humanity,
and every now and then we take a right or a left turn
without anyone telling us to,
us, the despised people, the rabble, the unintellectuals,
and you're left as followerless leaders, going nowhere
—editors, politicians, "nice people", union bosses,
planners, agitators, union bosses, pacificists, war-mongers,
pedants, professors, chairmen of this that or the other,
the whole mob of you who get a cut out of organizing us,
who swell your profits or egos by marching ahead of us,
all the self-elected leaders, magging your heads off—
you're suddenly out on a limb with no tree to it;
and you find we're not listening to you,
that we don't speak the same language as you do,
and that we're not going anywhere you intended us to.
Whatever blueprints you've made for the future
are suddenly split wide apart, with our fists through them,
and all your signposts are chopped up for firewood.

So if you see us going somewhere we shouldn't
—or somewhere you don't think we should—
don't stand in front of us like johns on point duty,
with your hands up to stop us, or waving us
down a side street. Don't try that.
We won't even see you. We won't
even know you're there; we'll come straight on.
And one morning when you wake up as usual
there won't be anyone reading your newspapers,
listening to your radios, or obeying your laws;
no one to preserve your *status quo*, fight your wars,
keep the peace for you, or carry on your revolutions
—no one at all.
We'll all have gone off fishing, or to the pub,
or just have stayed in our gardens or our beds.
You'll discover
we've only bothered to build your cities,
punch your clocks, listen to your talking,
and helped you tear down governments or support them,
because we couldn't be fagged changing it all,
never got up enough energy to tell you to go to hell,
and because after all a circus is fun for a while,
especially if the management thinks that you
are one of the clowns, or perhaps a performing seal.
But that morning the sun will be shining,
or it will have been raining or something,
and we'll just down tools and let your civilization
roll away into a dusty corner like a chipped alley,
and go off to do just whatever we feel like.

And then perhaps you'll realize
that we, the rabble, the people, the mob you've all despised,
haven't been listening to you,
haven't been listening,
haven't been listening
for a thousand years.

THE BLUE CRANE

> I am no poet of the fellowship of man,
> I sing no universal brotherhood,
> no oneness with all mankind
> from furthest land to furthest land

—I sing only of the solitude,
the inner secret loneliness,
each one hugs happily unto his heart.

No graceful gregarious brolga I,
no flock-flying spadger, starling,
only a blue ungainly crane
stalking round muddy waterholes,
along the edges of tree-shadowed dams,
or fishing for thoughts
in swamps where none else seems to live,
only my ghost-like, tussock-crumpled reflection.

SITTING-ROOM, STRZELECKI HOMESTEAD

No one passes now, the track leads nowhere
anymore, for this was the last homestead
to hold men's voices along the Strzelecki Track.
When it was closed the sand crept to the windows,
leant its shoulder against the glass,
crashed through, and trickled slowly in
upon the carpet (bought for a city bride)
until the pattern was hidden, and the chairs
were set paddling in its sterile anonymity,
and muted were the sounds of the feet
of the ghosts that once laughed there,
mated on the other side of the wall,
planned vast flocks, with fruit-trees
near the bore, and vegetables beside the overflow.
Higher the sand crept in the deserted room,
up into the chair seats and into sofa springs
broken by festive and cheerful buttocks
at sweaty and songful Christmases long ago
when paper hats laughed at the lack of feed,
champagne washed dust from throats,
and cigar smoke strove to neutralize
the drought-thick smell of cattle corpses
scattered over the pavement-bare countryside.
Over the table the sand sprawled next,
for ever erasing all marks on time
of letters once written upon it
to go down to the country inside the fences,
to go down past Monte-Collina

carried by the mailman's trotting donkeys,
fording belly-deep through flooded creeks, swimming rivers,
and always struggling up and over the Cobbler,
last and most difficult sandhill of all,
named from the cobbler of the shearers,
the worst sheep to shear, left until last.
From the table the sand climbed higher,
over the rest of the furniture,
hiding the scars made when Ali Mahomet's camels
went mad, broke their nose-ropes,
and fought fully laden at Mulowortina;
then up the sand crept to for ever silence memories
of Chopin, Strauss, and Do You Remember Black Alice
among the snapped wires of the piano.
Higher still, until above its surface showed
only the nail and wire supporting someone's photograph
hanging on the discoloured wall, someone
who once told tall tales of Leichhardt relics
out towards the border where the dead men lie
and the living are often liars,
someone who also told over and over
tall stories of mustering in mirages,
of whipping the bubbles at Lake Eyre Crossing,
of hearing the kuddimukra cry at night on desolate lakes,
and about how Kidman made his fortune.
And there it stopped, the invading sand,
stopped with no ghost's head left above its surface,
but with over it the iron pyramid of roof
still protruding from the hand-smooth sandhill,
a pyramid that the wind will soon blow down
and scatter across the devastation
where once dreams saw great flocks grazing,
but where now the only living moving objects
are the fluid mirage, the flowing, blowing sand,
and a sad and stunted rabbit racing to nowhere,
pursued into the mirage by a dingo shadow.

BUSHFIRE

The shy buds in the shadowed bush . . .
the young man's dreams of fame.

The ground-lark running between tussocks . . .
the young girl's thoughts of love.

The silence among the trees at midday . . .
the quiet thoughts of solitude.

The bushfire roaring across the hills . . .
the years burning at our heels.

I WOULDN'T BE LORD MAYOR

A chap I was talking to in a pub was telling me
it costs a fortune to be Lord Mayor of a city like ours.

He was saying there's so much entertaining to be done
and having visiting bigwigs to stay with you
and giving a fiver here and a fiver there for charity
—which is something apparently no mayor can get out of—
that in the end a bloke's hundreds of quid out of pocket
just through being Lord Mayor of the city for a year.
Of course, the salary seems a fortune to the rest of us,
and everyone treats a Lord Mayor as a sort of tin god,
and he has flash cars to drive round in whenever he likes,
and his picture in the paper whenever he opens his mouth,
but it really seems that the job's not much chop after all.

Then there's the expenses for his wife, the Lady Mayoress:
She has to get most of her dresses straight from Paris
to keep up what they call the dignity of her position,
and she has to wear pearls, and sometimes even a tiara,
so that at a ball everyone can spot who she is;
and if the Mayor happens to be owner of a sheep station
they have to ask the Governor up to stay with them sometimes.
—Think of all the wads of dough the poor cow has to spend
just because the people insist that he becomes Lord Mayor.

I'm sure I wouldn't care to be Lord Mayor of a city like ours,
even though a man could take the expenses off his income tax,
and although he might even finish up with a knighthood
and being made director of half a dozen companies.
I feel real sorry for the poor cows who're made Lord Mayor,
and I wish that now and then the whole mob of the people
would insist that for at least a year or two
no one should be forced to take the rotten job.

IN NEON PASTURES

Once again it is a wet Saturday night,
And city streets will all be paved
With neon signs.
We will drive down Rundle Street
over upside down advertisements
—red, purple, white, green, blue—
for talkies, underwear, tobacco and nylons.
Across them our tyres
will draw black lines
that will disappear in an instant.

The city is never so lovely
as on wet Saturday nights
when roadways blossom
into shining paddocks of neon lights
where petrol-blooded monsters
graze on electric flowers.

TO ME
THE POEM

To me the poem
should be
as spare and bare
as the pruned tree.

Let the reader
dress in the flesh
of perception
dry bones of words.

RIVER PORT

Once the shipwrights' mallets sounded up from the river
like frogs in a swamp, the slips were busy,
the agents scribbled and shouted, and the sun and the moon
heard the sound of singing and fighting from bar-rooms
where bare-footed men drew fingers through spilt beer,

making charts of voyages described in detail
(reef by reef, bend by bend, and snag by snag),
told tales of palms bleeding through heaving across shoals,
of steering by tree-tops in the 'ninety floods,
stories of barmaids and an up-river whore,
and girls in dancing halls along the Echuca shore.
(Ghostly paddles turn, and ghostly whistles sound,
calling to a hundred skippers long since underground.)

Wool from the Darling, bale upon thousand bales,
flour, salt, and sleepers, tallow, hides, and stock,
all came here once, barge behind loaded barge,
steamer following after throbbing steamer,
down from the Darling, the 'Bidgee, the Edward,
unload, and on down to the Lakes and Goolwa,
out through the roar of the Mouth to the ocean,
and load load load again while the rivers were up,
and on again to the back of beyond, almost to Gundagai,
shouting and sweating, to Walgett and Mungindi.
(Ghostly paddles turn, ghostly steamers sound;
do you hear them skippers, lying underground?)

The mallets are stilled, the agents' signs have fallen,
the pub windows are empty, the lift-span of the bridge
creaks with disuse, the high-heeled girls have gone,
no trains carry away tallow and hides and wool,
the deck of the wharf frets and splinters and cracks,
the last abandoned steamer settles in the mud,
the barges swing empty, the winches idly rust,
and the last old-timers draw sadly in the dust
charts of voyages to Narrandera, Menindie, and Moul'mein,
where once they went, but never shall again.
(Ghostly paddles turn, and ghostly whistles sound;
few today can hear them who are not underground.)

THE CRAB OR THE TREE

The crab or the tree
losing one limb
grows another.

The tiny lizard also
its severed tail
sprouts anew.

Can I be sure
my human mind
has the same power?

Losing faith and doubts
can I my doubts and faiths
ever renew?

As an experiment
let me lop off one finger
of thought.

You try it, too.

THE DAY THE RAIN CAME

Always, I don't know why,
when I was about ten the summer seemed to end
on a hot afternoon.
    My mother
always wore an apron at the time; therefore
it would be after four o'clock, or perhaps even five.
She must have risen an hour or two before
from her after-luncheon nap, and now
would be preparing the evening meal, and so
surely there would have been the warm thick smells
of cooking and of the hot oven coming out
into the rest of the house through the kitchen
doorway.
    Probably it was late March,
or even early April. There were squashed grapes
outside the back door, pecked down by birds.
Also, a few leaves were turning dirty yellow
in pale autumnal example of the untidy habits
the vines and fruit-trees had inherited
from their northern ancestors.
    I remember it
as always being a steamy day of humid heat.
Sweaty clothes and drowsy schoolrooms where

blowflies buzzed and banged against the window-panes
had made our lessons even duller than they usually were.
On the way home we—my friend Rusty and I—
had piped to other boys, in imitation of our elders, of how
it seemed like rain, and that summer should soon end,
but had thought no more about it.
                                 In the garden
many of the softer plants were lying flat upon the earth,
and the garden-hose was hanging on a peg within the shed.
(For reservoirs were low; a bent adult knuckle
rapped on the iron tank gave back a hollow sound
of emptiness.) The thirsty soil was pale brown, still scoured
from February winds, so that even on ungravelled paths
a faint grittiness made games unpleasant.
                                         Games!
Rusty had gone home early; we were too listless
to find anything worth playing at; trains
and motor-cars and chasey all seemed too tame;
it was too hot to climb trees or to chase the fowls;
gum-leaf cigarettes bit too sharply at the tongue;
and even seeing which of us could swear the harder,
and wondering vaguely about the so-called facts of life
and details of the private lives of little girls
had lost their especial fascination.
                                        Now
I mooched round, chewing a dry stick.
Nothing seemed worth the doing.
                           My sister
started to practise her music. She played a few pieces,
then banged the piano-lid down and was silent.
                                              I
went and sat on a box and watched the parrot,
waiting for him to shriek out when he heard
(and first of us all, too, he was always the first to hear)
my father's neat staccato boot-heels
that he had polished so carefully that morning
come quickly rapping down the street from the tram-stop
as if he were still a young athlete, and not
the white-headed gentleman with the neat paunch. But
the parrot just sat with his eyes half closed,
and his beak a little open, holding out his wings
as if they were too heavy for his body.
                                       There
was no excitement anywhere. I prayed
that by next morning I would be twenty-one, and past
the cares of youth. But not even that usual anodyne

for the pains of life was any use today. So
I just sat and wished that I were someone else
—a missionary, or a lawyer, or a train-driver—
but that didn't work either.
                      Then, suddenly,
I noticed the sky. The high grey clouds
with a faint tinge of dust about them
had concluded their display. A new set,
purplish-black like a stale bruise, were being dragged
across the ceiling of the world.
                      I felt
something exciting was about to happen.
                            Someone
(perhaps I thought it was God) beat a drum of thunder
away in the distance. A trio of magpies
went hoarsely cawing across the disturbed sky.
The sugar-gums thrashed in a sudden explosion of wind,
and then were as silent as before. Thunder again.
                                Then,
beating quickly in from the dark south-west,
there was a sound as if a thousand or so boys
were running sticks along an iron fence. The rain
was coming, marching over the iron roofs
of street after street, house after house,
suburb after suburb.
                  I ran inside
just as it arrived.
                  First just one or two drops
plopping singly in splashes the size of two-bob bits,
then it roared down upon the house.
                          Out on the veranda
my sister and I shouted to each other beneath the sound
on the corrugated-iron roof above us; and I
held out cupped hands to catch a dozen drops or so
to lick into my mouth. And the smell of it!
Rolling and running in sparrow-powdered patches of dirt,
streaking and washing the summer-dusted leaves
—the cool, for-months-forgotten, sweet smell of it—
to sniff it was like taking a drink on a hot night
from the waterbag under the vines, only better.
                              And then
I realized I had no more need of prayers to be twenty-one,
or wishes to be somebody different. Life
had become an adventure again.
                            The rain had come.

INTRUDER

When I walk
I do not know
what ancient sacred place
my foot may desecrate
of if my tread shall fall
where some cult-hero bled,
or shed blood,
or gave fire to man
in the far dreamtime.

Vanished elders
of the long-dead tribe,
forgive
my taboo-breaking,
my uncicatrised intrusion;
and do not send
kadaitcha men
to haunt my dreams.

Surely you can guess
my conscience
is uneasy enough
already.

William Hart-Smith

EDITOR'S NOTE

William Hart-Smith was born in England, at Tunbridge Wells, in 1911. At the age of twelve he was taken to New Zealand, and since then has had periods of residence in both Australia and New Zealand, though, over a lifetime, more in Australia.

His books (all verse) include: *Columbus Goes West* 1943, *Harvest*, 1945, *The Unceasing Ground* 1946, *Christopher Columbus* 1948, *On the Level* (Canterbury Poems) 1950, *Poems in Doggerel* 1955, *Poems of Discovery* 1959, *The Talking Clothes* 1966.

AVENGER

It is he who had a name but yesterday,
This presence in the night that fills me so with dread.
Those are his eyes which peep
Down through the swaying branches;
Those are his feet
Which softly tread the leaves among the stones,
Breaking a stick, a brittle stick,
Brittle as bones.

He it is who is not yet buried,
Whose body is not yet put away,
Whose breath is in the leaves of all the trees.

Though he is wrapped in bark and bound with reeds,
Though his eyes are sunken and see no more,
Though his mouth is dumb,
And though his limbs are like the joint of a throwing stick
That none may bend without breaking.
He walks in the night
And sleep I dare not.

I would take comfort from the shelter of the cave,
I would take comfort in my loneliness
From the fire at my feet,
Yet am I filled with dread.

His spears were true,
Yet my shield was swift as a darting bird,
Swift as the spear which struck when his shield faltered,
Faltered as the wings of a bird which is struck in the air.

I hear him sigh
High in the leaves of the forest.
His breath is in the fire as it leaps at my feet
And his eyes look from the glowing ashes.
I am afraid of him.

I dare not sleep,
I dare not close my eyes
Thinking I see him in the shadows everywhere.
I dare not rise
And go out among the shadows.

Do I turn on my side
All my back is cold with dread;
Do I lie on my back
His eyes look down through the swaying branches.

It is as if the night will never go,
It is as if he has bound the night with reeds
That it cannot escape.

LA PEROUSE

Here the tram crashes to a stop
coughs once and dies
yet another of its innumerable deaths

I shall not call shades
this night
of two or more venerable gentlemen
for picturesqueness' sake
though I should like to have them haunt
for contrasting of

this palpitating monstrosity on wheels
and

boulders above
a white new-moon of beach
a breaking foam of cloud

Goonooween after successful
fish-spearing, feeling weary, lying
down to dream of incredible fish,
in his mia-mia

and this sloe-eyed child of mis-mating
with her print frock, permanent-wave,
off to the pictures

SUMMER DAY

All this is past:
The pale surprise of morning,
The soaking up to throbbing saturation, sponge-greedy,
Drinking, drinking, until the most persistent, high,
Piercing cicada shrill spirals wearily into oblivion.
The hot sap at bursting-point at noon,
Tight-shimmering all through the long afternoon,
Earth's hands pressed to her aching, aching, head.
               Then,
Like taut strings snapping one by one
The spell is broken;
A ragged scrap of blotting-paper wind puts filaments
Into the golden flood and drinks.

There is exquisite relief in the forest's re-surrender.

How suddenly all grows cold!

THE FISHING LUBRA

If that awful moment could come back again
And take the place of other memories,
A little ghost would haunt in other guise
Sobbing a silent agony to trees.

But the shades are kind to her; she haunts the bay
Crouched in a frail canoe, clasping her cord,
While dancing wavelets lap the shores
Disporting silver moon-flakes on their backs,

Slapping and washing, drubbing the darkness clean.
If she could but remember she would dip
Cold hands into the sea and paddle home;
But the waves have washed her sorrow all away.

She heeds not time nor giant-strided day
As softly she sings of lovers she has known,
Dusky of limb and lean, and as she dreams
The waves tug at the bark cord all night long.

WE ARE THE ELDERS

We are the elders,
Sapient, aromatic, sardonic.

We are the wise old fellows
Who chuckle in our beards,
Who flaunt gnarled limbs,
Who would have you think we are decrepit
And utterly devoid of humour.

Old joints bulge,
Lean calves shrink . . .
Consider only, making a friend of patience,
Time must have his fun,
Finds us so willingly obedient that we twist
With pleasure underneath the aeons heaped upon us.

Even our children are born old,
Young old men with dry tongues,
And with us
Clutch fantastically.

Dry skin flakes . . .

Time sleeps
Waiting for sinewy grip to relax
And let us topple over into night.

APRIL 28TH, 1770

I stood as my father before me,
allowing my limbs to claim the stillness of trees,
stood while the waves dashed themselves at my feet,
and my spear was raised to strike.

I fought my amazement
and held it silent and still,
as I hold my spear to strike at the fish
that are swift shadows in the flurry of foam.

I fought my fear
and spoke to it as I speak to myself,
nor would I lift my look again
as It came floating.

And when we saw they were white of skin,
fear conquered and we hid away from them,
who came and took our spears,
made toeless footprints in the white sand,
shouted and beckoned to us,
then went away from the land and were seen no more.

Before That came bearing them,
before this new thing happened,
day followed night without question,
tide followed tide and wave followed wave,
breaking at my feet,
and I made the waves' voices say what they would.

Now they are asking the question,
and turning over the question,
breaking up the question,

and bringing to me all complete again
the question, that is also in the wind,
in the whispering voices of the night,
in the eyes of all who saw them come and go.

MOONDEEN

Moondeen, the oldest man of the river tribe,
Too old for the council of the elders.
Thin as the meanest desert myall
Felt something happening within him.

As he chipped at the throwing-stick
Fixed between his old knees,
He watched the little rock-lizards that gleamed and shone
Going over his feet sometimes,
Quick and cold as a drop of rain.
And he thought a long time about that.

As he worked the euro fat into the wood:
Rubbing fiercely till it came smooth
Like the black stones in the river,
Then pushed it into the hot ashes again
And rubbed, and went on rubbing,
He remembered that the wood had once been a tree;
He thought about the trees,
And made one name for them all,
One name which would be for one tree
Yet all of them together,
And he muttered it over and over to himself.

He thought about the throwing-stick he was making
And who would hunt with it, and lose it, and where,
And where it would lie one day lost forever,
And how long was forever;
And he dreamed adventures about it whilst he was still awake.

He thought about the river,
Where it started, right down to where it ended,
Pouring into the great water that stretches away forever;
He thought about it all day long,
Until the men came back from their hunting
And the dogs and women went out to meet them
With a dust and a hullalooing,
Which made him forget the word he had almost made for
                      the river,
And a rage took fire within him over nothing at all.

Nobody knew why Moondeen was always angry and short-
                              tempered,
Spat like a lizard when disturbed.

BLACK COCKATOOS

> Look, going for water, going down there,
> to water somewhere in the salt marshes,
> birds all black, crying harshly;
> urgent with all day's thirst they
> sideslip above the yellow wheat-stubble
> into the strong wind, calling up stragglers.

Wings wind-ragged, coal-black cockatoos;
blunt of head, ponderous of beat they drive
into the wind, borne up and carried sideways
in a long sideslip, wing-tips open like fingers,
coming up and over the hill in labouring flocks
until only their cry and calling
is heard as they dwindle
fainter, fainter to silence.

PROLOGUE TO CHRISTOPHER COLUMBUS

Said Bishop Cosmas,
The world is flat,
and that's that!
The Holy Word is explicit
that Christ will come and visit it
again, when all mankind shall be
illumined by the Light will shine
from His Countenance Divine;
and if the Light touch on a ball,
the heathen will not see at all!

That is not so,
said Augustine,
the world is round,
for I have seen
from my tower above the sea
the ocean of infinity,
and watched the far horizon sweep
in one great arc from deep to deep.
And Christ His Word has this great merit:
the things of spirit are seen by spirit!

SPACE*

Columbus looks towards the New World,
The sea is flat and nothing breaks the rim
of the world's disc;
He takes the sphere with him.

Day into night the same, the only change
The living variation at the core
Of this man's universe;
And silent on the silver ship he broods.

Red gouts of weed, and skimming fish, to crack
The stupefying emptiness of sea:
Night, and the unimpassioned gaze of stars . . .

And God be praised for the compass, oaths
Bawled in the fo'c'sle,
Broken heads, and wine,
Song and guitars,

The tramp of boots,
The wash and whip of brine.

THE PEAR-SHAPED EARTH

Therefore much that has been marked
substantial on our maps
must vanish, as it were,
in a bright effulgence, a dazzling flare;
because the earth is rounded like a pear
with an apex lifted, swelling into realms
Celestial. The Earthly Paradise is there;
and where the great fruit's stalk should be,
if 'twere a fruit, and not the Universe
which God created, is a spring
that pours a flood of crystal water down
to press upon the salt tides of the sea,
shaping these islands lengthwise to its flow,
and set athwart, the way we strive to go.

* Originally titled "Columbus Goes West". See Textual Sources.

WATER-LILY

When the red water-lily was touched
By the flank of my woman,
What spirit-child then took delight
In the youth of her body and leapt?

My woman among all the women . . .
While digging for lily-roots
Deep in the mud with her fingers
Was struck by a stone in the belly

And suddenly called out shrilly,
Called as the child
Kicked, and she wearily
Pushed back the hair from her eyes

And waded out and was sick.

IMMARNA

Myself with an empty tin,
The lid bent back to make a handle,
Sit with Birrahlee. The ants
Are busy at an old bone. Very sad
Is the sound of the wind that comes
To wash itself in the leaves of the tree,
Cool itself in the thin shadow. We sit and wait,
Myself and Birrahlee,
Sit on our heels and wait.

And sometime during the afternoon, a cloud,
A small black cloud on the far horizon . . .

I weep, Birrahlee, for things you have not known:
How once I sang up such a cloud for rain.
Now set your face, Birrahlee, for the train.

CANDLE ON A STUMP

On a stump a bit of candle, wax
dribbles and sets in fantastic icicles.
Between gusts, up like a flower grows the flame,
symmetrical, with specific zones of colour,
a black tongue of wick at the centre.

A caterpillar nibbles at the leaf
with the yellow of sere at the heart,
fastens a thread of gossamer and hangs
idly oscillating at the end. Huge jaws
come out of the floating sea, the bed of the sun.

Misalliance. A noble takes a serf to wife
and kicks her from his bed. His will
he improves with deep thumbs. Surely
his eyes are the eyes of a madman, one
with the serious pressure of an old skull wound?

The widows have put on white clay,
yet, with the vow of silence still upon them,
have burst their bonds of mourning.
But gestures are not enough, lips are distorted
and limbs in rigid anguish twisted.

I hear a song as from a distance,
and one saying to another Let me
finger the cloth of your garments. Surely
your eyes are the eyes of one very sick,
with the weight of an ancient sorrow in your heart?

I hear a song of broken twigs and brittle leaves,
scattered with sweet white scales of manna;
and in the murmur and confusion of voices
a tearing down and a building up;
and sun and moon are stepfather and stepmother.

Grey sheep nibble among the stones:
not the reed flute, not the broken white columns,
not the legendary heroes, not the familiar names,
but a black stockman with a chew of straw,
his warm lips pursed into silence.

Grey ships bunt at the wharves:
now we shall cover the heads of the women with skins.
A ritual dance is done by butterflies
over the needlebush in the twilight
then drift in a cloud of petals to the sea.

Whirlwind that walks on the plains,
pours like a trunk of red smoke out of the forest,
what do you bear this time, the breath
of a man child or a woman child?
Grey sheep nibble among the stones.

Things fall into the candle, shrivel their wings,
patter against my cheeks, against
my shielding hand interposed
between the flame and the wind. Transparent, hot,
down spurts the wax like tears.

FLAME THE CAT

Flame about its business
Licks over all morsels,
Flame the wild cat, paws
With the broad pad.

How the belly sinks down
Low upon the ground,
Along the earth, crouching,
Edging forward! the snarl, the spring!

Flame goes up trees, needle
Claws in bark. That red
And terrible cat is hunting
Along the horizon tonight.

Flame you have a sister
With a kinder tongue,
Saliva for black wounds and no
Searing smoke from her

Mouth, only sweetness, a sweet breath.
Her flame is green leaf
Very silent and cool,
A green and delicate flickering

All along black limbs, rippling
From bole to smallest twig,
And single green candles
Burning on the bare ground.

POST MORTEM

Not the spirit but the body
Flowers, breaks into glorious colour.
Deftly the edge of the knife
Begins its revealing work and the still
Wax is shaken into colour.

You who were sobbing last night
In the corner of the ward behind
The cotton screen in the corner
And heard my curses cried through many
Screens, are wax on veined white marble.

Not the spirit but the body
Flowers and your name is
Passed from mouth to mouth.
They say you received no letters;
They say you wrote to no one.

There is a measurable limit to this
Depth now that the statement is moulded
Wax with all the skeletal structure
Prominent and the flesh concave,
A depth of wax for the knife.

Quiet yellow of primroses, white
Cotton and spun linen. Not
The spirit but the flesh
Flowers amazingly. I beg
Reverence of the gloved hands.

BAIAMAI'S NEVER-FAILING STREAM

Then he made of the stars, in my mind,
pebbles and clear water running over them,
linking most strangely feelings of im-
measurable remoteness with intimacy,

So that at one and the same time I
not only saw a far white mist of stars
there, far up there, but had my fingers
dabbling among those cold stones.

BECAUSE THE CATERPILLAR

Because the beautiful caterpillar
Which accordioned itself along my desk,
Set me yelling,
Sucking my fingers and dancing . . .

Because the harmless green grasshopper
Suddenly bit like hell
And a fist of revenge
Defeated the entomologist,
And flattened the specimen . . .

How can poetry here be anything else
But prickly, highly-coloured, treacherous,
Both reverential and extremely vulgar? . . .

I hear a kitten, but it's a bird;
I see a bird, but it's a bat;
I see a bat, but it's a butterfly. Here,
Ladies and gentlemen,
Birds and frogs may sing in the self-same tree!

THE SURPLUS

Singing troubles me, the
singing of a bird.
Reason tells me that

Whether or not he takes
joy in it, all puffed up and
a tree his high dais,

Song is for mating only. She
listens, he pours it out.
Song is for mating in season.

But the surplus, the
overflow. More than is
necessary comes

From that bird, far
more than is wanted I'm
positive, positive!

EAGLEHAWK

Eaglehawk is like a leaf in the air
All day long going round and round in circles,
Sometimes dark against the sky
And sometimes with his great wings tipped with light
As the sunset edges the clouds . . .
Only when night comes and the fire-beetle stars
Twinkle overhead,
Is the sky empty of Eaglehawk.

Eaglehawk sees all the world stretched out below,
The animals scurrying across the plain
Among the tufts of prickly porcupine grass,
Valleys to the east and plains to the west,
And river-courses scribbled across the desert
Like insect tracks in sand; and mountains
Where the world sweeps up to meet him and falls away.

The animals live in the dust,
But Eaglehawk lives in the air.
He laughs to see them.
And when the pans dry up and the rivers shrink,
He laughs still more, and laughing
Sweeps half across the world to drop and drink.

OPEN AIR PICTURES

Strange, when all the night watches us
Looking at a square of light, trees
Peering over each other's shoulders,

Poor drab moths and insignificant
Flies should dance overhead and be
Lifted up, borne like sparks in a

Beam of smoke, a tunnel of rays,
Borrowing therefrom a radiance,
A transient beauty. Maybe our hearts

Are likewise lifted up to become
Fireflies, to become
Like stars for a little while.

MARY

The bishop came, the bishop
Made a most uncomfortable journey
On foot, deplorably thirsty; also
By camel and by lugger

To visit his black
Congregation, all turned out in full
Muster because of a promise of
Tucker a'plenty . . .

Seven hundred and twenty
Miles of withering, blistering
Heat, on foot, by camel,
And by lugger:

"Mary," he said, "do you pray to God?"
"Yes," smirked she, "Me talk-talk
Longa that cranky beggar!"

NULLARBOR

Here earth and sky are reduced to an ultimate simplicity,
The earth to a completely flat circle,
An ocean-circle of red soil with flecks of white limestone,
Patches of dead brown grass and stiff dead bushes
And tuft-like clumps and knots of dwarf bushes
That look dead,
But really grip their lives tightly away from the sun,
Grip hold of their lives with little hard fists.
The leaves
Are leathery tongues with a small spittle of salt in them.
And the sky is a pure thing,
A flawless cover of glass,
An inverted glass cover upon a table.

When the train stopped I swung my legs over the side,
Jumped down from the roped truck and sat on the dry hot
    boards of the flat-top,
My feet dangling over, idly swinging, my hands behind me,
The palms taking a print from the rough wood
And the cinders and grit,
Making up my mind to take the next jump, the leap to the
    track,
And curiously examining a reluctance to do so . . .
Sleepers, a slope of cinders and metal, then
The desert, the miraculous, empty, utterly pure desert,
The clean desert and the clean bright wind,
The rim out there
Not abruptly ending, but broken,
An undercutting and a flowing into,
The sky running into the earth and the earth running into the
    sky,
Long liquid lines of sky, opaque, making inroads into the rim,
The edge of the world,
And long low islands floating . . .
Mirage.
It is the hot air rising,
The air becoming hot and beginning to tremble and throb and
    dance,
Destroys the abruptness, the clean cut-off.

And then you appeared. There you were, suddenly there in
    the desert
Beyond the train, beyond the line of waiting trucks,

William Hart-Smith

As if you had suddenly appeared out of nothing,
With your black body, your brush of sun-bleached hair
And the stick stuck in your belt
Behind you, sticking out like a tail.
You were not looking at us. You were walking away from us
  when you appeared,
Walking away in a queer loping fashion
Going off at an angle with your back to us.
My legs stopped swinging and I stared at you, fascinated,
Looked into your back and wondered what it was you were
  after,
You, boy . . .
I saw you were a boy.
You stopped then, turned back and ran a little distance,
Then turned again and walked straight towards me,
Closer and closer, till I could see into your eyes,
Closer, without stopping; then you swung yourself up onto the
  flat-top beside me
And sat there looking out over the desert.

How long did we sit there? How long was it we sat there saying
  nothing?
Perhaps an eternity. Sat there saying nothing.
I could hear your breathing. Your body had a familiar strong
  smell,
An earth smell, a special earth smell;
And I thought of the leaves with the taste of brine in them,
The spicy tang of them, the gnarled old bushes,
Life bunched up in their fists.

I changed. Slowly I changed. I became a grotesque thing.
I became white-skinned, a human being with a white skin . . .
Grotesque!
A thin being with a sharp nose and a strong reek,
Huddled into myself, covered up, cowering away from life,
A distorted thing with my senses only half awake,
My eyes only half opened, my nostrils clogged with a numbing
  deadness,
My ears with a pressure on the drums,
Only partly sensitive.

It was an eternity. I know it was.

Did you break it because of me? Did you speak at last because
  you knew what was happening to me?
Did you do it to save me?

You moved,
You pointed upward with your finger at a bird, a solitary great
    bird with white wings tipped with brown,
Spiralling, making circles, great wide circles and spirals with
    motionless huge wings
High over our heads . . .
"Eaglehawk," you said. "Eaglehawk."

It's funny, but you accepted me then. We used the code of
    stranger approaching stranger.
You came and sat down beyond the limits of my camp,
The camp of my personality and the small fire of my heart,
Waiting with your back to it before my thoughts sent out their
    women
With food and drink, went out and brought you in. We talked.
You asked for a cigarette. I gave you one and lit it for you.
I can see my white hands cupped against the brown skin of
    your face,
The deep ridge of brows as you bent over my hands and sucked
    in the flame; the tuft of beard on your chin.
A boy.
I remarked to myself on the rich body quality of your voice
And unconsciously deepened the tones of my own.
You talked as you smoked, the cigarette looking silly and
    pathetic in your fingers,
Held between ball of thumb and forefinger.

Then my own world broke in. It came
Out of the future, out of the future from a terrible distance,
Roared down on me and shrieked, and pounded fists on my
    heart.
The clash of jerked couplings shattered something in my head.
You jumped down. I heard above the noise the soft crunch
    of your feet as they hit the ground
And you looked at me over your shoulder, then turned away,
Turned your back on me and walked away
With that queer loose-swinging lope of yours,
That straight-backed, loose-limbed walk full from the hips.
You walked away and never looked back.

I sat there as the train moved
And the ground began to slide sideways under my feet,
Sideways under my boots,
Until the blur made me giddy and sick.
And when I looked up you had gone.
I looked back, but you had gone.

The desert was flowing away to the left
Bringing the clean wind strong on the right side of my head;
And the stones and low bushes were flowing away, faster and
     faster,
Faster. Only the desert remained itself, remained unchanged,
Flowing away from itself,
Yet continually renewing itself from right to left, faster, faster,
And the wind a gale,

And under me a grind and clatter of wheels.

PICTURE IN BRIGHT COLOURS

Stripped to the waist, he makes the middle-distance,
And being brown and heavily limbed, his skin shining with
     sweat,
Commands attention and holds it.

Behind him are trees, paper-crisp in hot, dry air,
Yellow-green, burning, not moving a leaf, shadows
Mauve, or amethyst, trunks and limbs charcoal on chrome.

An arch of branches frames the man: a fig
With shining leaves, and clusters of hard fruit
Like marbles in yellow wood; and a kapok tree
With bright red flowers and no leaves at all.

Now he tears a scrap of blue from the blue
Sky and dabs, dabs his forehead.

WILLIE WAGTAIL

Then Willie Wagtail hopped along the branch
Closer and closer as if to speak,
So close I could see the whiskers bristling
At the root of his beak,
And the black beads that are his perky eyes.

"Dee Ree Ree," I said, "I've heard tales about you,
That you're the bird of indecision,
And that you're a tittle-tattle!"

Then up in the air he hopped
And turned a somersault
Making a quick rittle-rattle
With his bill, as if to say:
"You attract the most succulent flies!"

"Listen!" I said. "Why do you always
Swing your tail this way and that way
Every time you settle!"

"Just to remind you, my friend,
Just to remind you
And keep you on your mettle!"

THE LIFE OF ROCKS

Taking a piece of quartz, napping it
And having it shatter
Into white, sharp flakes, if you find
A cavity inside with crystals
All in a cluster,
Like teeth, like sharks' teeth, mind
You do not forget that rock lives.

Walking at the base of a hill, round
The gibber stones and pebbles
That skirt the central mound,
Mind you trouble
To remember that rubble
Is rock in the making.

And if you should see that a people's
Heart is breaking
Into pebbles of innumerable small griefs,
Mind you remember
That rock is in the making.

DEATH OF AN ANT

Supposing the ant knew it was doomed,
of no account from the moment in the cloud
the peak was reached and the descent began,
a blurr of protest spun about a soft
body falling in a slant across
the green mounds of the rounded
trees, drawn inevitably down by earth itself
to itself. Suppose it knew.

Flying ant on the grass with a stiff
skirt of wings it treads on, an awkward
train it cannot discard. It came
down from the clouds in a slant because it failed,
was one of too many. Clouds
above the cubed buildings of the city
are banked up in a wave of yellow hair, yellow
light that descends
even to illuminate strangely an ant's
yellow body, soft maggot body with wings.

So far, having fallen among blades, struggling,
at times tipping over sideways, wings all spread-eagled,
folding them again with care,
so far has achieved
one ambition, mounts the tip
of a leaf
of grass a little sharper than the rest.

LEGEND

Because it was the last and lightest,
the spirit of water went furthest after the Sun,
smoked invisibly upwards
with all its vaporous hands imploring
the light of all living creatures to return.

But She, with her orders from above,
continued on her journey upward, through
to the place ordained for her, while piteously
the water, trying to follow, softly fell
exhausted back to the waiting earth as dew.

SPARROWS

Tell me, how do sparrows recognize
one another in a crowd?
How do they know their friends
when they have the whole world
to fly about in?

I saw two sparrows mating in a gutter
and all the time both sought invisible crumbs
as if only crumbs matter,
and the rest
inconsequential fluttering, only a small
brown fraction of the darker-speckled male
toward her with interest.

And then she flew away and was lost
among the trees.
And trees are so large;
and sparrows are so small.

SMOKE ON THE PLAINS

I can follow with my eyes a scarf of haze
fifteen miles back into the hills
from the plains, where someone started a blaze
this morning of broom and gorse.

Tonight it twinkles like a window
winking back the setting sun.
It seems an old legend recurs
continually in the soul

and here is yet another variation.
And so I feel I want to go and take
a hand in what they make.

IN SYDNEY

Mr Marsden is off again to New Zealand,
to the island home of these impassive chiefs
who regard us, be it known, as critically
as we regard them. Cunning natives,

who for some dark reasons of their own
lead the sincere Mr Marsden to believe
it's Christ they've come to seek, not muskets.
Yet it is true enough they conceive

genuine affection for him. He treats them
with deference, respects their dignity,
that grave imperious dignity conceals
so much of evil and mendacity.

And he sees nothing whatever amiss,
he is blind in Christ, in faith, and zeal
to convert them, having planted in their bosoms
motives and sentiment unreal,

and noblest inspiration. But he is proud
and fearless, single of purpose, self-doubt small.
Each likes the other, man to man,
muskets and souls withal.

NUMBER

What is there to set against Number
but the number One?

What is there to set against the number
of mankind, sandgrain, sperm?

Number overwhelms me,
my mind goes numb

considering Number.
When the stars were countable,

when they hung low
as if let down on strings

I could reach and touch them
and set them ringing,

start the whole chandelier
of the night sky swinging.

I was a child then.
Number was my friend.

It was only a phase—
World, world without end.

But now, now I must
acknowledge that the stars

are numbered as the dust.
Let me establish one

moon, and a singular Sun.
No, there is nothing

to set against Number
but the number One.

Roland Robinson

EDITOR'S NOTE

Roland Robinson was born in 1912 in County Clare, Ireland, and was brought to Australia (Sydney) when nine years old. He had no extensive education but has followed a wide variety of employment, beginning when a youth as a rouseabout on a station in New South Wales. He worked for a time with the Kirsova Ballet and has been a script writer and a green-keeper at a golf club. During the war he worked in the Civil Construction Corps and gained a wide experience of Northern Territory and Aboriginal life. He has written two volumes of autobiography and a number of works about Aboriginal mythology.

Among his books are: verse , *Beyond the Grass Tree Spears* 1944, *Language of the Sand* 1949, *Tumult of the Swans* 1953, *Deep Well* 1962, *Grendel* 1967, *Altjeringa* 1970, *Selected Poems* 1971; prose, *Legend and Dreaming* 1952, *The Feathered Serpent* 1956, *Black-feller, White-feller* (short stories) 1958, *The Man Who Sold His Dreaming* 1965, *Aboriginal Myths and Legends* 1966; autobiography *The Drift of Things* 1973, *The Shift of Sands* 1976.

THE CREEK

When other creeks are dry and filled with leaves,
This one still springs from back of Maynard's place,
Where the dead gums stand that the bushfire killed
When it roared through there and left the old farm
Nothing but ashes and scattered iron. This creek
Runs over sandstone shelves and dwells in pools
Hidden by scrub and tangled vines, and has always
Given me billy-fulls of clear cold water, dipped
Where the boronia hangs its showers of bells
Above it, or at their time the saplings stand
Against the light with young leaves in pale fire,
Or the waratah burns in these green depths of bush.

I MADE MY VERSES

I made my verses of places where I made my fires;
of the dark trees standing against the blue-green night
with the first stars coming; of the bare plains where a bird
broke into running song, and of the wind-cold scrub
where the bent trees sing to themselves, and of the night
dark about me, the fire dying out, and the ashes left.

AND THE BLACKS ARE GONE

But this sea will not die, this sea that brims
beyond the grass tree spears and the low close scrub,
or lies at evening limitless after rain,
or breaks in curving lines to the long golden beach
that the blacks called Gera before the white man came.
And the blacks are gone, and I frighten the crimson-wing
and the wallaby in gullies where the rock-pools lie
fringed by acacias and stunted gums. And I come
out on to open ridges flowering before this sea.
And the blacks are gone, and we are not more than they,
to-night as I make my camp by the rain-stilled sea.

FLOWERING TEA-TREE

I could not sleep, but listened to the sea
sending its thunder, endless, out of the night:
the rollers curling over and crashing down,
and the white water breaking out of the darkness.
Quietly, in its visitation to the room,
a gust of wind came laden with the scent,
the drugging scent of the white flowering tea-tree,
flowering alone, out on the distant hillside,
sending its native fragrance out of the night.

THE INVOCATION

Last night I spoke to you from where I lay
under a banksia-tree at the top of the gully.
Come, I said, out of the distances of cliffs
in the mists of after sunset, out of the gully
filled with the light of the soaring insects, come
out of the saplings standing against the sea,
against the mountains of clouds, come from the south
with cold first breath; and then above the sea
appeared the evening star, pale golden, swimming
with its smaller companion into the trailing rain.
Come, I said, and you stirred the trees and wreathed
the smoke of my fire and came in the night with rain.

COMING WITH DARKNESS

And, looking up, white flowers were outspread
into the darkness all about my tent;
making a pure religion in that place,
a prayer that came unbidden except by Spring
and rain that left the sandy ridges cool.
So that I lay with all the width of land,
in pause and flow of gullies, slopes and hills,
open to the stars and the faint cold dew,
at one with the night and the flowers and the stars.

CLIMBING THE GULLY

I rest with my hand on the cool bark of a gum,
and look down through the rocks and tangle of boughs
to the white anger of the sea spending itself
at the hot golden sands. And in the gully where saplings
stand in auras of burning leaves, a whip-bird
draws out his call that ends in a liquid lash.
I smell many scents and memories that are scents:
the honey smell of the gum-blossom, the yellow broom,
and native jasmine, and the hot earth with rain in it,
and shed bark and dry curled leaves and last year's bushfire.

COMMUNION

Listening, I lie and hear the rain come on,
steadily falling through the dark and cold:
it seemed far in a forest I had gone,
I made no sound upon the deep leaf-mould.
All round that forest rose sheer mountain walls,
day long I'd walked to reach that camping place,
hearing the sound of streams and waterfalls;
I stopped with the last sunlight on my face.
I stood and listened in that forest deep,
hearing the rain, the drip drip of the trees;
from this dark room communion now I keep:
there are no comrades as such thoughts as these.

MORNING

Morning so beautiful that the breathing trees
had spread their boughs against the moving sea
in adoration. And in sparkling grass
and leaves of light I woke after the rain
that comes by night drenching the earth and leaves.
And, lying there, I heard the constant surge
marbling the waters round the broken cliffs;
spreading its lawn of foam before the sands:
the timeless surge that washes round the world,
older than life and death and the giant wars.

DEPARTURE

Beautiful even as Death this rain on the sea,
and the long thrust of land with its jagged pines,
the hush of the valley beyond and the night-purple mountain.
And the rain has gone. But large and shining drops
cling to the branches. Beautiful my leave-taking:
the bar of silver water, the dark thrust of land,
and the dusk of the valley hushed and vast as death.

CALL ON THE SEA TO BE STILL

Call on the sea to be still this night of the moon,
the sea in its molten brimming beyond the scrub,
this night when the ridges are dim and the gullies lie
silent and dark to the scattered stars; or call
on the swans going past between sunset and darkness,
making me wonder whose was the cry that seemed
lost in the gully, as call on this my unrest,
on this my unrest at one with the sea, with the swans
passing in querulous cries against the stars.

THE DROVERS

Over the plains of the whitening grass
And the stunted mulga the drovers pass,
And through the dust on either side
Of the herd the native stockmen ride.

And day after day lays bare the same
Endless plains as the way they came,
And ever the cloven ranges lie
At the end of the land and the opal sky.

With creak of pack and saddle leather,
And chink of chain and bit together,
With moan of the herd, with hobble and bell
They come to the tanks at the tea-tree well.

And through corroding blood-red hills,
By sanded rivers the Gulf-rain fills,
Far where the morning-star has shone,
And paled above, their tracks are gone.

BLACK COCKATOOS

Rise then, you screaming flight of black cockatoos,
and spread your red barred tail-feathers out and scream
over the spears of the reeds and the purple lilies,
over the red rock walls of this sun-gashed gorge,
and gather in broken and screaming flight and turn
heading far up this jade-green river's reaches.
So shall I find me harsh and blendless words
of barbarous beauty enough to sing this land.

WOULD I MIGHT FIND MY COUNTRY

Would I might find my country as the blacks
come in and lean their spears up in the scrub,
and crouch and light their flickering fires, and spread
their mission blankets on the ground beneath
the dark acacia and bauhinia trees.
Would I might find my people as the blacks
sit with their lubras, children and tired dogs,
their dilly-bags and bundles of belongings
tied up in strips of some old coloured dress,
and pass the long straight smoking-pipe around
and talk in quiet calling voices while
the blood-deep crimson flower of sunset burns
in smouldering ash and fume behind the trees,
behind the thin grassed ridges of their land
that is their home wherever they may camp.

DEEP WELL

I am at Deep Well where the spirit-trees
writhe in cool white limbs and budgerigar-
green hair along the watercourse carved out
in deep red earth, a red dry course that goes
past the deep well, past the ruined stone
homestead where the wandering blacks make camp
(their campfire burning like a star at rest
among dark ruins of the fallen stone)
to find the spinifex and ochre-red
sandhills of a land inhabited by those
tall dark tribesmen with long hair, and voices
thin and far and, deepening, like a sea.
I am at Deep Well where the fettlers' car
travels towards the cool blue rising wave,
that is the Ooraminna Range, and starts
those pure birds screaming from the scrub to swerve,
reveal their pristine blush in wings and breasts,
to scatter, settle and flower the desert oak.
Here I have chosen to be a fettler, work
to lay the red-gum sleepers, line and spike
the rails with adze and hammer, shovel and bar,
to straighten up and find my mates, myself
lost in the spinifex flowing down in waves
to meet the shadow-sharpened range, and know
myself grown lean and hard again with toil.
Here, in the valley camp where hills increase
in dark blue depths, the desert hakea stands
holding the restless finches and a single star.

CASUARINA

The last, the long haired casuarina
stands upon the hillside where,
against the turquoise night of those first
yellow stars, she shakes her hair.

She shakes her hair out in her singing
of cliffs and caves and waterfalls,
and tribes who left the lichened sandstone
carved in gods and animals.

This is her country; honeyeaters
cry out its aboriginal name
where on her ridges still the spear-tall
lilies burn in flame and flame.

I listen, and our legend says not
more than this dark singing tree,
although her golden flowering lover
lies slain beside the winter sea.

I HAD NO HUMAN SPEECH

I had no human speech. I heard
the quail-thrush cry out of the stones
and cry again its crystal word
out of the mountains' crumbling bones.

I had no human word, beyond
all words I knew the rush of ash-
grey wings that gloomed, with one respond,
storm-grey, to swerve with crimson flash.

The speech that silence shapes but keeps:
a ruin and the writhe of thin
ghost-gums against their rain-blue deeps
of night and ranges I drank in.

I lived where mountains moved and stood
round me; I saw their natures change,
deepen and fire from mood to mood,
and found the kingfisher-blue range,

and found, where huge dark heliotrope
shadows pied a range's power,
mauve-purple at the foothills' slope,
the parakelia, the desert flower.

Yet, human, with unresting thought
tormented turned away from these
presences, from converse sought
with deserts, flowers, stones and trees.

ROCK-LILY

The rock-lily's pale spray,
like sunlight, halts my way
up through the unpierced hush
of birdless blue-grey bush.
The rocks crouch on their knees
in earth, torsos of trees
and limb-boughs lead up where
the cliff-face scales the air.
Out from you, rock, my friend,
I lean and, reaching, bend
the scentless pale spray back
to me and see the black
spots in each orchid flower.
O, my love, what power
keeps you curled and bound?
Tormented, the earth's round
begins again. What rock
holds you where you lock
yourself from me? Alone
this spray breaks from the stone.

EMU

Cock-bird, solitary emu pacing
out of the gidgee's zigzag
line that traces the dry silted
watercourse to stone-knife jag
of ranges, here I recognize
you: your lust in me compels
this my exile, you ascetic
drinker at the secret wells.

THE DESERT

THE BLANKET

I found that blanket branded "Alice Springs",
and made my bed with it in stones and sand
where like a lyre the casuarina sings
across a region like a shrivelled hand.

And I, too, lost it in some place, for then
possessions wearied me, and it seemed best
to travel light and clean as other men
who tramped towards a campfire in the west;

who came and made their fires beside those scant
waterholes where thin acacias dream
and painted finches drink, or the hesitant
red-gold-ringleted lorikeets swoop and scream.

THE BROLGAS

Because I came at dawn and stood
outside those ruins on the plain
where, spilt among the stones like blood,
the desert-pea spread out its stain,

and saw, out of the pale dark sky
where solitary stars were dying,
those five oncoming brolgas fly
with "*quoak*" and "*quoak-quoak*" of their crying,

to pass, with outstretched necks and fringed
beating wings above my head,
towards the fire of day that tinged
eroded ranges parrot-red,

I stood immortal there. I burned
in ageless youth and, from its mood,
renounced the world again, and spurned
all but that fierce proud solitude.

THE DANCERS

I reached that waterhole, its mud designed
by tracks of egret, finch and jabiroo,
while in the coming night the moon declined:
a feather floating from a cockatoo.

Ten paces more and there, in painted mime,
against the mountain like a stone-axe dropped,
the spirit-trees stood stricken from the time
the song-sticks, song-man and the drone-pipe stopped.

Some thrust their arms and hands out in the air,
and some were struck, contorted, on their knees;
and deep and still the leaves like unbound hair
lay over limbs and torsos of those trees.

Over their limbs their night-still tresses slept;
faint in the stars a wandering night-bird creaked.
Then, as towards their company I stepped,
the whole misshapen tribe awoke and shrieked.

And, beating from their limbs and leaves, white birds
like spirits in a terror of strange birth
streamed out with harsh and inarticulate words
above the mountains, trees and plains of earth.

THE PAEAN

Daylight, and the desert stars
blaze in fires blue and cold.
East, the bounding line of earth
quickens, runs with livid gold.

Dark the circling regions lie:
ache of gibber-plain, the yawn
of barren, ravined ranges, while
the bore-head smokes into the dawn.

From the hollowed purple plain,
clamour wakens shrill and loud.
In their thousands rise the birds
streaming in a far dark cloud.

On the burning east that host
soars, then bursts in shrill, prolonged
crescendo; there, the molten gold
with the showering birds is thronged.

Circling, all the screaming cloud
planes to earth, its paean done,
as the desert's raw bare wound
stares into the rising sun.

THE RABBIT

In lignum, near the low hills' gap,
the carrion crows are ringed around
the rabbit held there in the trap,
its body flattened to the ground.

Disturbed, each evil creature keeps
watch on me. Towards the plain,
ghoul-voiced, they rise. The rabbit leaps
screaming on its jangling chain.

I take the rabbit's legs and stand
on the trap, release those fangs.
Hand's hatchet-blow and, from my hand,
heavy, limp, the rabbit hangs.

I walk on through sparse silver grass
waved by the desert's scented breath
in flowing beauty: waves that pass
through me of terror, life and death.

THE WANDERER

Travelling again, his swag
tossed in the rack above his head,
he thought about his mates: "You'll find
gibbers and bloody sand," they'd said.

He watched the desert wheeling round.
A symbol of his mind's despair,
alone out on the plain a yellow
whirlwind writhed through trembling air.

He closed his eyes against the scene.
Then, jolted, jerked awake again—
red sandridges beneath a merciless
sky shut in the halted train.

And there, unloading sleepers, men,
the fettl s, with gaunt faces, spoiled
by lusts, by exile, trod the desert
parakelia as they toiled.

His mental hell looked out upon
this other hell at last made known.
He wiped his sweating face and in each
ravaged face he found his own.

Ahead, the locomotive's scream
called on its freight of heavy cars.
The train ran on, beneath a turquoise
night, the galaxies of stars.

When daylight, delicate, parrot-breasted,
dissolved the stars, the moon's white rind,
scenting the wind, he knew that heaven
or hell were regions of the mind.

THE IBIS

Look! And the ibis, like a drifting smoke,
hung in the sky. And there the wind, that was
their purpose, swirled, distended them, and broke
their drift above the seas of red-brown grass,

the ribbed backbones of ranges, gleaming chains
of lilied billabongs fringed with reeds and trees
and, serpentine, through swamps and plains,
the rivers flowing to their different seas.

Drifting, in skeins and skeins, the ibis passed
far down the opal sky, where still I traced
their legend's poetry, until at last
from that oblivion it was quite effaced.

FOR REX INGAMELLS*

Sword-grass, sword-sharp to the grasp,
stunted banksia and tea-tree
hold those sandridges that clasp
the hard bright jewel of the sea.

* Rex Ingamells was killed in a car accident, December 1955.

Camped there, we heard the ageless hoarse
ocean down the long sand-bars,
and cries of swans that held their course
across the galaxies of stars.

I thought of you, there, Rex, my friend.
I shall not grasp again your hands,
nor see your face. World without end,
the ocean thundered down the sands.

THRUSH

Ah thrush, limpid thrush, O like lightning under
the mountain-piled white clouds, the caverns of the thunder,
O call, call, in cold cadenzas call the rush,
the hush of rain. O drench, quench the summer bush:
the thronging fires of red and yellow Christmas-bells,
the sapling flames, each heat-hushed gum that shells
its sun-burned bark. O let the creek speak from soak
to soak; let the frogs croak, in chorus croak.
Ah thrush, limpid thrush, ah let the rain be spent
night-long on the leaves, the mould, my stretched-tight tent.

PASSAGE OF THE SWANS

How could I sleep? The moon rose at its full,
broadening the night. Through mauve-grey gum
and gum I heard, in distant swell and lull,
thunder and crash of ocean never dumb.
I lay and waited for the light, to hear
the first birds, wakening in the silent bush
and, rising through their chorus, loud and clear,
on and on, the day's harmonious-thrush.

Too late, too long I slept. It was a wind,
a rush of wings, a storm of blendless cries
that brought me, stumbling, in the daylight-thinned
darkness, to stand there, in a dazed surmise.
Far down the dawn those trumpet-throated ones
called, and I knew them . . . the swans, the swans.

SUNDOWNER

Old sundowner, in shake-down overcoat,
under the store veranda staring
out at the rain. His pug-faced dog
shivers beside his battered suitcase.
—Who's the old man? I ask in the store.
—Camps on the river, been routed out
by the rain.
    I drive off through the rain.
—Is it pity? It's ourselves we pity,
ourselves we recognize and renounce.
I go back, make some remark on the rain,
pass him a hand-out.—Thanks, son.—

It's Langland lances me, though, as I leave:
Christ pursuing us in a poor man's apparel.—

THE PIONEERS

Camped above the Fitzroy River Crossing,
under white-limbed river gums. Gathering
firewood this evening, I'm walking over
graves and headstones in the dust and grass.
A red, protruding boulder is inscribed,
"James Lennon. Prospector. Died 14–9–08."
I stand with the firewood under my arm,
and a voice speaks to me out of the dust.
"It was a wild country when I came here.
I searched for gold. The Aborigines were wild.
They circled my camp, dragging their spears,
gripped between their toes, through the grass.
A black woman was my mate. She eased
my terrors and loneliness. You, who see
the sun and stars, the river and white-limbed
trees, who hear the screaming cockatoos,
you ponder on this grave, and that grave.
You search for poetry. Some search for wealth,
love, or fame, leave children, books or poems,
that they may live on in the living. It's all
meaningless. You, who stand beside my grave,

listening to the whispered speech of the dead,
your words may be remembered, or forgotten.
You'll not know, nor care, as I do not care
nor remember if I found gold, or love, or fame."
It's a name, cut into a sandstone boulder,
above the Fitzroy River Crossing. My fire's
leaping up and flowing on the wind.
Summoned from the darkness, muscle-rippling
torsos fling their forked-lightning limbs
against the stars. Turn in. Lie down.
Those other sleepers will not trouble you.
Those pioneers are sleeping in the mother-
earth. Her blanket covers them from the cold
stars, merciless suns of the days and years.

ONE EYED NALUL SPEAKS

Listen, Balanda, because you come here,
bring cattle, build up stockyard, homestead,
this is not your country. Every waterhole,
plain, river, rock, billabong is our dreaming,
belong to my people right back to Dreamtime.

THE CHILD WHO HAD NO FATHER

(Related by Fred Biggs)

Before the white man came here
with his sheep,
the plains were covered with
all kinds of flowers.

Two sisters would go walking
at evening through
the flowers, looking for any
food they could find.

And when those sisters walked
among the flowers,
there were no mai, no men,
in all the world.

One evening as one sister
walked along,
she saw one flower, and stooped,
and broke it off.

Inside, the flower looked like
a baby's face.
She got two bits of bark
and put the flower,

between them, underneath
a log. She thought
no more about it, and walked
on through the flowers.

Next evening this sister came
again. "Oh, more
and more this flower has
a baby's face."

She took some possum fur,
and wrapped it
round the flower, and laid it
beneath the log.

Next evening when this sister
came to find
the flower, she found a baby
sleeping there.

She found her breasts had milk.
And every evening,
she went out through the flowers
and fed the child.

Her sister saw her sister's
breasts had formed.
"Oh, you must have a baby."
"Yes." "Oh, where?"

"Out there among the flowers."
The sisters went
and found the child and brought it
to their cave.

That child became a wise
and clever man.
And, afterwards, he went up
into the sky.

And always, when I hear the
white men preaching,
this story comes into
my mind. That child,

he was like Jesus, he came
into the world
without a father. He was
formed from a flower.

That woman touched that flower.
If she had not
plucked that flower, this could
not have happened.

JARRANGULLI

(Related by Percy Mumbulla)

Hear that tree-lizard singin' out,
Jarrangulli.
He's singin' out for rain.
He's in a hole up in that tree.
He wants the rain to fill that hole right up
an' cover him with rain.
That water will last him till
the drought comes on again.

It's comin' dry when he sings out,
Jarrangulli.
Soon as ever he sings out,
Jarrangulli,
he's sure to bring the rain.

That feller, he's the real rain-lizard.
He's just the same as them black cockatoos,
they're the fellers for the rain.

He's deadly poison. He's
Jarrangulli.
He'll bite you sure enough.
You climb that tree an' put your hand
over that hole, he'll bite you sure enough.
He's black an' painted with white stripes.
Jarrangulli.
He's singin' out for rain.

MAPOORAM

(Related by Fred Biggs)

Go out and camp somewhere. You're lying down.
A wind comes, and you hear this "Mapooram".
"What's that?" you say. Why, that's a Mapooram.
You go and find that tree rubbing itself.
It makes all sorts of noises in the wind.
It might be like a sheep, or like a cat,
or like a baby crying, or someone calling,
a sort of whistling-calling when the wind
comes and swings and rubs two boughs like that.

A Wirreengun, a clever-feller, sings
that tree. He hums a song, a Mapooram:
A song to bring things out, or close things up,
a song to bring a girl, a woman from that tree.
She's got long hair, it falls right down her back.
He's got her for himself. He'll keep her now.

One evening it was sort of rainy-dark.
They built a mia-mia, stripping bark.
You've been out in the bush sometime and seen
them old dry pines with loose bark coming off.
You get a lot of bark from them dry pines,
before they rot and go too far, you know.
That woman from the tree, she pulled that bark.
It tore off, up and up the tree. It pulled
her up into the tree, up, up into the sky.

Well, she was gone. That was the end of it.
No more that Wirreengun could call her back.

Mapooram. Mapooram. "What's that?" you say.
Why, that's two tree boughs rubbing in the wind.

CAPTAIN COOK

(Related by Percy Mumbulla)

Tungeei, that was her native name.
She was a terrible tall woman
who lived at Ulladulla.
She had six husbands,
an' buried the lot.

She was over a hundred, easy,
when she died.
She was tellin' my father,
they were sittin' on the point
that was all wild scrub.

The big ship came and anchored
out at Snapper Island.
He put down a boat
an' rowed up the river
into Bateman's Bay.

He landed on the shore of the river,
the other side from where the
church is now.
When he landed he gave the Kurris clothes,
an' those big sea-biscuits.
Terrible hard biscuits they was.

KIMBERLEY DROVERS

I am drained out. All day I have driven
through a barbaric country of burning colour.
Fire-red mountains, fissured and caverned,
lilac-hazed ranges, red-purple ravines,
have reared round, receded, and reappeared
all day through my vision. This is the region
of the baobab trees, of monstrous, obese
baobabs squatting in chaos of sun-fired,
sun-blackened boulders in the ranges' ravines.

I set down my swag. Against the sunset
amber-red dust is rising. I rest
camped close to drovers settling their cattle
down for the night. Out of the haze comes
the muted, mingled moan of the mob.
I hear from behind me the sharp "Crack-crack"
of the stockwhips. Stockmen are driving
their horses, donkeys, and mules with hobbles
and jangling horse-bells back from the bore.

It is after sunset. A star burns above
the bushfire haze of bellowing beasts.
Whistles, shouts of stockmen, unseen,
ring out as they ride the restless mob.
My campfire blazes in the baobabs.
A mopoke calls from the stars. Crickets sing.
Clear on the night, an Aboriginal stockman
ceaselessly sings as he rides round the mob
his savage songs. And I cannot sleep.

PART 2

The Jindyworobak Anthologies 1938–1953

Editor's Note

The Jindyworobak *Anthologies* began in 1938 and continued until 1953. All were under the general editorship of Rex Ingamells, who personally edited the first three annual issues and that of 1947. Other editors were: 1942, Victor Kennedy; 1943, Flexmore Hudson; 1944, W. Hart-Smith; 1945, Gina Ballantyne; 1946, Ian Mudie; 1948, Roland Robinson; 1949, R.G. Howarth; 1950, Nancy Cato; 1951, Gloria Rawlinson and W. Hart-Smith; 1952, Arthur Murphy; 1953, Colin Thiele. Ingamells had two principles of selection, which the other editors respected. Poetry that he thought good in its own right merited inclusion; but he always hoped for good Jindyworobak poetry.

It is necessary to enter a warning that inclusion in the *Anthologies* does not commit any individual contributor to a wholehearted espousal of every item in the Jindyworobak programme. I think it is fair to assume that every piece that was submitted was motivated, at the time, by a genuine sympathy, but it may at times have been no more than a desire to contribute to the progress of a movement which the poets thought generally well of, and hoped would in due course come to a clearer definition of its function than appeared, so far, to have emerged. It was the weakness of the editorial situation that too rigid an insistence on the Jindyworobak philosophy might have checked the flow of contributions; Ingamells's two principles were really a dilemma. Between "good poetry" and "good Jindyworobak poetry" even some of the main original Jindyworobaks were in a disequilibrium; they at times denied the affiliation while they continued to support the cause. Little wonder, then, if certain others, especially those who have since achieved distinguished independent reputations, were nervous of being classified with them. They had contributed helpfully and with genuine sincerity, but they did not regard themselves as active members of the Jindyworobak movement. Judith

Wright, among others, wished this to be clearly understood when giving permission for work to appear in this anthology.

Several such contributors do appear in this section, however, and it may be reasonable to suggest why. The section is a broad survey of the *Anthologies* as a whole. The five Jindyworobak principals are excluded because they are separately represented; but the rest is meant to give a broad impression of the movement, for which the *Anthologies* provided a focal centre. Names of poets like James McAuley, Douglas Stewart, David Campbell and Judith Wright appear, but it should be remembered that these writers are represented, not necessarily by their best and most mature writings, but simply by a few such pieces of theirs as happened to get printed. They all had something to offer freely at the time; they gave what they thought suitable, and their pieces fit into a general context to which, if they contribute highlights, they do not in effect give a main determination. The Jindyworobak line is still the dominant one and on the whole it survives; the broad effects are stronger than the particular instances.

I have included a number of poets of more enthusiasm than talent, because they were earnest Jindyworobaks; and I have excluded a few who were better poets, mainly because I found it difficult to think that, in their cases, there was any Jindyworobak affinity in them strong enough to justify inclusion. Shaw Neilson appears once but he could hardly be claimed as a Jindyworobak even of remote sympathy. A.D. Hope also contributed. I could see very little in the verses of R.G. Howarth to make even a temporary Jindyworobak of him, though he was obviously a sympathizer as he edited one of the *Anthologies* and worked hard in various ways to promote the movement; I have represented him once. At least his inclusion shows how widely the editorial interest ranged. But if the *Anthologies* demonstrate anything clearly, they show that it is not the impact of individual authors, but of the whole movement, which counts.

1938

WOLFE FAIRBRIDGE

THE BANKSIA

The spear blades of the Xamias are erect
And menacing, slanting from the direct
Drive of the wind where it rubs the dried skull
Of the hill; and below that single gull
Harries the ridges of the approaching sea.
This banksia, all knots and tangles, is less tree
Than the crushed roots of an upturned thornbush—
Disorganized and bare; its straggling brush
Of leaves seems a poor instrument to achieve
That growth of wood. Does it too wish to leave
The place where fortune dropped a seed? unwind
Its fingers from the soil, and further back find
Space between the giant strides of the jarrah;
And under those august eyes, a stranger
Be, waiting—waiting for a voice before
The window, and the knock upon the door.

PAUL L. GRANO

OUT SAMFORD WAY

Tall trees and hills, and winding roads;
Odd fields of varied shape
Whose fences meet in casual corner crowds;

Unwilling mountains, nursing farms upon their steep-hung
                                            breasts;
Whip cracks, and barking dogs,
And cows herding to the milking sheds;
Broad paddocks pimpled with gray-grassy dung;
Smoke, and the flames of burning stumps;
Brown streaks on hillsides where the last fires swept;
Fowls, and the rich ammoniated air of poultry farms;
A store where villagers debate the news
And scandalize their friends, and talk of cow;
Where daily papers jostle with the pills
And lipsticks nestle next to swinging bars;
A pub as secret looking as a bank . . .
All these, and more, I found out Samford way.
But, brooding over all, on every side
The bush, dark-sweeping to the sky,
Hemming and hating the work of Samford men.

VICTOR KENNEDY

QUEER LITTLE ALMOND EYES

Queer little deep brown almond eyes
Turned to me now with grave surprise.

What are the secrets tarrying there
Baffling the world's inquiring stare?
What is the wisdom so intense
Masked as a great grave innocence?
Born of the rich romantic East
Mysteries flash as fires released.

Reach me the depth that herein lies,
Queer little deep brown almond eyes.

GEOFFREY READING

SILAS

It seems unfair to call Silas a coward
Just because Silas turned away.
Is there one soul who would not choose
To die on a fairer day?
And at sight of hangman and hempen cord
Shudder and turn away?

Silas burnt a swagman's candle
Under a mulga sky,
And kept his house below blue-gums
When the wind spears whistled by;
But a man cannot live on blue-gum leaves,
A man cannot live on sky.

The Lord forgot that Silas needed
Each day daily bread.
And now at the end of a hempen cord
Silas is swinging dead.
For Silas slew a man whom God
Had given two men's bread.

Starving Silas slew a rich man!
Silas had to pay!
We made him dance a jig-time with
The floor two feet away.
We slew the slayer and I wonder
Who now has a debt to pay!

IAN TILBROOK

GUMS

Aboriginal . . .
grey-grown and old . . . so old beside the river reaches;
aged and bent like a white-haired black
whose hunting days are at an end.

Boughs . . .
thick and thin twisting, spreading
like wrinkles across a gin's emaciated brow;
knotted dead ends ready to drop
and flame at a nomad's fire.

Leaves . . .
spear-points drooping to earth
with sun-sharp edges;
wind-travailed through ages, they have known
the wurly and the fire, the naked men
writhing contortions round flares writhing smoke—
corroborees . . . disrupted forms of freedom they enjoyed
tottering to decay like totem gods . . .
Years have untribed them
as age unlimbs the fire-charred native tree.

RUSSEL WARD

THE KANGAROO

The great red kangaroos bounce in the air
resiliently across the tablelands;
now one stops short, swings on his bole and stands
bolt upright, head back, haughtily astare;
like some proud Argentine who does not care
to be thought curious, but still demands
to know who dares to trespass on his lands;
yet some deep instinct warns him to beware.
We are the callous banditti who trade
upon this old lord's foolish uprightness:
with ill-bred haste a gun is cocked and laid;
I hear the bullet thud into his breast;
I see him clutch his wound, the red blood rise;
we run. He stares at me with great, brown eyes.

BRIAN ELLIOTT

BLACKBOY

Out of the legended
limitless past
dimly remembering
dangers and fears
sparse-rooted he grips
with desperate dignity
fast to the soil
where scornful men glance.

Only he thinks
one thought in the sun:
grimly to gather
the tribe that is gone.

With a charred anger
and smouldering cheer
the thin spear he poises
in threat to the foe:

yearning by day's end
to slay the intruder
Time moving subtly
by silent decay.

1939

WOLFE FAIRBRIDGE

WRITTEN AFTER FLYING PERTH–ADELAIDE

Stand on the land's edge here. Let the dulled mind
Drift above the sea's shadows with their ripple
In impatient movement.
Hang in the wind's eye; the air dried and refined
Gives to the brain an infra-red moment.

North and Southward the vertical ribbon
Of cliffs borders this world abrupt;
A bare block of earth's crust;
A bass-relief of land; stone
Sand, ore in the sea's trust.

History and use have made no softening yet.
This is what the sun and rain have left for you;
Geologic ages
Evolving stoney waste
Under the unmentioned, oppressive blue.

Shut those deserts out! Sever the nerve! Close
The perceiving eye or stifle the brain's
Interpretations. I dare
No longer see these miles of uselessness,
Reflections can alone make poor repair.

It is the bare immensity appals;
Amundsen said his huskies would not pull
Without some mark to break
The uniformity of that full
World of desert white.

Effortlessly Nature's presence
Holds the bush, where we men find ourselves
Dishonourable graves.
The sun's impartial eye, in this land sees our edifice
As scratchings in a crust of verdigris;

While the world's mind comes as from an outer star
That may have vanished centuries ago,
And little strips of sea
Fence us against the felt proximity of war
That wakes so well the wage-slave and the free.

This is a helplessness unsuited now!
The world to Pithecanthropus
Looked just as hopeless then;
And the ape-like eyes looked up beneath the brow,
And lifting his fore-paws peopled the world with men.

JOHN OPIE

TALLABILLA

Far from the tribe look-out
where your claw-arms shout
warning, you will go . . .

                Tallabilla

among the driftsands
and hill-rocks your hands
will squander life . . .   Tallabilla
the pursuing song
of age, darrenderong,
will whistle . . . from cave-holes
soon . . . one day
as the clouds pass
like barrarangs
in their grave grey clouds
in the sky

              Tallabilla
              my heart,

you will die.

P. PFEIFFER

AT THE WINDOW

The last dismantled star flung into space,
In swift gradations
Night ripens into day.
Thought patterns flailed like octopus
Dichotomize.
Hen-coop cocks crow up the dawn . . .
"The guttural goose hath ushered in the day!"

1940

NANCY CATO

RIVER SCENE

Slowly rose the crane, blue crane
Long legs idly drooping
Sweep of wings, curve
Cutting the sky arclike. Again
Above the river
Green slow lethargic river
He circles once, and now
With lazy dignity
Sweeps out across the plain.

Unseen
The reed-warbler babbles in that clump of sedge
While little lizards, leaf-marked grey and brown,
Pause by a fallen log
Or slip to the water's edge.
Limp in the sun
Long-leaved, the coolibahs droop down.
Slow windmills turn
High on the yellow sandstone cliff.
White sands burn
The shrinking feet.
The river drowses, tired and still with heat.

JAMES McAULEY

ENVOI FOR A BOOK OF POEMS

There the blue-green gums have a wild precision, a strict
                                        disorder,
And the brown sheep poke at my dreams along the hillsides;
And there in the soil, in the season, in the shifting airs,
Comes the faint sterility that disheartens and derides.

Where once was a sea is now a salty sunken desert,
A futile heart within a fair periphery;
The people are hard-eyed, kindly, with nothing inside them,
The men are independent but you could not call them free.

And I am fitted to that land as the soul is to the body,
I know its contractions, waste and sprawling indolence;
They are in me and its triumphs are my own,
Hard-won in the thin and bitter years without pretence.

Beauty is order and good chance in the artesian heart
And does not wholly fail, though we impede;
Though the reluctant and uneasy land resent
The gush of waters, the lean plough, the fretful seed.

1941

C.B. CHRISTESEN

DAWN AT FLYING-FISH POINT

Full moon floods and vast Pacific tides
That bathe the tropic coast all through the night
And break with thunderous roar on coral reefs,
Transform sea-wrack with strange unearthly light;
Full moon floods that burn the mountain sides,
Awaken native age-old dark beliefs,
Cause dingo-howls to rise from timbered slopes;
And as the making tide insinuates and creeps
Past estuary and headland shoal, the unmatched
Glory slowly lightens in the east
As speeding dawn o'ertakes the landward flight
Of black and silent birds. Soon the deeps
Obliterate the beach, torn and scratched
By gull and crab that revelled in the feast
Of pungent weed. And so the morning light
Revealed what moon had silvered secretly—
Crab's claw and trochus-shell, tar-stained ropes,
An ocean-tarnished hull, a chest of tea,
Salt-sodden fruit, a shell-encrusted spar
With copper legend green: *Calcutta Star*.

MAX HARRIS

HARRIS THE HOBO

each pang bites grooves into the plasm of being,
the fool has not yet unlearned to feel;
what the tear requires, the mind releases
is not yet born into the strength of steel

I can still be humble, imploring
now the ivory handtouch, because pain
shapes patterns across the visual plains
of love, whose sun still sends no bills.

each pang calcifies the fibre, the human will
to live love with the rebel's poker-face
before the fall of each day's cards, and still
accept defeat with the poet's grace

I am no lover's attorney; have wept
the midnight cold, into a dreary myth,
the core of history's countenance, have kept
it secret in the grooves of the understood

tonight I have been a lover, your lover,
revealed the weakness of the tear spent,
and known the poet's welcome, the placid hobo
turned away with dogs and Christian sentiment.

PAUL L. GRANO

PRIME MINISTER TO GO HOME

(News Heading)

"I'm going home" said the Minister.
"He's going home" cheeped the Sparrow,
"Home" squeaked the Starling,
"Home" cracked the Gorse,

"Home" blinked the Capeweed,
"Home" said the Prickly Pear,
"Home" barked the Fox.
"How nice" said they all,
"Let's go with him."

THE AUSTRAL–ANGLO

Not Murray water nor the Darling runs in their veins
But by some treasoned alchemy
The Gulf Stream courses in them
And its fogs glow golden in their eyes;
And on their tongues no honest Austral drawl
But a tonsillar attempt to dag their vowels.

JAMES DEVANEY

BAMBA

A! Where this night fares Bamba, Bamba the boy-hearted?
A woi! that the dead cannot be tracked to the strange country
Where wanders the ghost of Bamba, the sky country of stars—
The scattered camp-fires of the vanished tribes.
Sleeping, he sways in the swaying branches, and below him
Squats the starved dingo with noise pointed, howling,
There in the big timber by the Lake of Shags.
Hu! but the wind is bitter by the shore of the Lake of Shags,
Sharp the wind as the tooth of the fierce yoornara;
Sad is the night-wind there, like a child crying,
Where Bamba the boy-hearted is lost to us for ever.
The warm days will return, filling our swamps with wild fowl,
Boondoon the kingfisher will come again to us out of the north
  land,
The little tribes of the flowers return, but never Bamba!
The wagtail, deereeree, will sing his song and will not cease,
The little kangaroo out of the pouch lean over
To crop the tall green grasses come again;
The quandong month will come again, but never Bamba!

A woi! the butterfly that loves the sun will come,
Sweet as a wandering thought of him who is lost to us—
Bamba, lost to us now by the Long Brown Water.
Happy and free the quips of the young men and maidens
By the wandering camp-fires of the Karamarras;
Happy and free now the loud talk and the laughter,
But Bamba the boy-hearted is gone from us for ever!
Many a long day from the dew-fall to the laughing-star
We flung our lines and nets in the Long Brown Water;
Many a long hunt we had in the days past over,
But Bamba the boy-hearted is lost to us for ever!
We will hear at night the far cry of the wild swans passing
over,
We will go out again with spears to the hunt at daybreak;
The alowan and the kanowar we will snare on the river,
But Bamba is far from us this night in the big timber,
In the big timber by the Lake of the Shags.

"RICKETY KATE"

WARATAH

How many dawns and sunsets came
Across the valley of the years
Before your heart of sculptured flame
Blazed through its galaxy of spears?
Green spears that lift with one desire
To shield your heart of chiselled fire!

GARRY LYLE

RAINMAKER'S STONE

O oodoolay
bring us our desire,
bring men rain.
Long have we awaited
the little cloud, the evening euloowirree
in vain,
          Come rain,
          Come soon,
come in the night
fall
steadily down heavily down, fall
soaking all,
refresh and cleanse.
Men's minds are more
than desert-arid, lacking
even the strange burnt desert beauty,
their false thoughts
are ugly, mulga-statured.
Let truth have rain, oodoolay
ere she dies
lost within the wilderness
of lies.
Blows the north wind,
the shrivelling wind,
and still no little cloud, no eulowirree.
Before the dark
give answer oodoolay,
eehu
come.

1942

"E"

RETURN

The ruthless Bush is grown along the track,
The rude and ruthless Bush—
So that I come again at last,
Through winding weed and willow push.

How busy has the pungent dog-weed been,
The purple peppermint!
The upstart ferns on loamy floor
Show many a spoor and padded print.

F.T. MACARTNEY

DIDJERIDOO

Didjeridoo—didjeridoo!
A blackfellow blows through a length of bamboo
To the regular beat of an ironwood stick,
Click-click, click-click-click;
And the throb of his breath is the ghost of a drum
With a madness of apathy muffling its thrum.

The sun, a red gasp, sank down in its throes,
And the night waits for wind as a coward for blows;
And all that the world ever wanted or knew
Is dark while you hark to the didjeridoo.

Didjeridoo—didjeridoo!
A nursery rhyme and a history too.
Black faces lean over a flickering fire;
A nasal chant rises, drops low, rises higher,
Then wearily fades to an echo of wind
Over withering grasses that footsteps have thinned
Through nomadic ages, space without scope,
Unscarred by regret and unharassed by hope;
For primitive ages are distanced into
A groan to the bone by the didjeridoo.

Didjeridoo—didjeridoo!
Even the pastorals, lyric with dew,
Piped in Arcadian meadows, so green
And so golden and glad and so mythically clean,
Are not so remote as this shudder of sound,
Which broods like a beast nuzzling close to the ground
For the track of its mate or an answering wail.
This piper sits playing and knows all things fail.
The days are so many, the years are so few,
Says the thud, as of mud, in the didjeridoo.

LEONARD MANN

TO YOUNG SOLDIERS

Young soldiers who go out to die in battle,
The boisterous and tinted winds of Spring
Have woven wisps of cloud for garlanding
Of Donna Buang above the Yarra Valley.

The hill's fat cheek beneath a fringe of bush
Is mantled with an apple orchard's blush
Where bees contend to rape each virgin blossom.

Green now are the fenced paddocks that will mellow
To summer's stubble and the brittle yellow
Of grasses dried beneath a sky of glass.

And soon will show in autumn's elegy
Summer's dun death, winter's austerity,
Echo of spring, the last and that to come.

Young soldiers who go out to die in battle,
Children of yours though not by you begotten
Will live on here and this your native land
Will be yours yet though you be all forgotten.

BRIAN VREPONT

THE FISHERS

Two men stood thigh deep in the sea,
Their bodies braced against the pounding surf,
    Hauling a net of fishes;
Heel-deep in shifting sand, inch by inch the fishers neared the
                              shore,
For heavy was the brown net with sea and fishes,
    And the pushing of a great sea-wind against them,
But already gleamed the silver sequins of creatures of the sea,
Their round eyes goggling, and mouths agape for breath.

The two men leant against the wall of wind,
    Calm in the sureness of their plunder,
And one, the taller by a head, cried: "John,
    The net is heavy with big fishes,"
And laughed and hummed a chantey.

But the man John did not hear, for the wind had him,
Whispering the lisp of his dead love of the spring,
The wind whipped him, but the fires of his heart were
                                drowned,
And the fisher John fished not for fishes,
Nor braced his thighs against the piling sea,
But loosed his tug and let the net go slack,
And the other cried: "John, the net is loose,"
And urged him stiffen 'gainst the fish escape.

The man John heard the voice as one hears shells
    Murmuring of things long gone—
Irredeemable springs, and love's laughter dead,

And John the fisher let his net-hold go,
And a great surf took his feet, and tangled them,
Wrapping him to his thighs in twisted flax,
    And drew him down,
    And sucked him to the deeps.

The net unbent its brown salt length,
And heavy of its trove of man and fishes,
Came shorewards inch by inch to ankle shallows.

While John the fisher lay so still upon the sands,
The fishes quivered, then blindly stared;
So stared the man John—at some far nothingness,
Where the fishes' breath slept, and his one Spring song.

JOHN INGAMELLS

PROTEST

The rose must wither, and sighing we must go,
we who are young, whose youth grows old
weighed down with emptiness and the dreams we know
come but go with the night once grown so cold.

If war once fills the emptiness with terror
or fancy fills the timid soul with hell
must Memory sleep to wake in nights of horror
tossing restless words they cannot spell?

My love, you must not see me with these angry eyes
persistent with an agony of dread
of each dull answer to my unwept cries
and veiled in memory of my vacant years.

Your red mouth burning bravely dries such tears
and briefly for a spell now no silence mars
together we are awhile no more alone as when we read
stark poems of consolation in the stars.

DOROTHY HEWETT

FLAME WOMAN

Woman full of flame trees
Why do you pick on me
To throw your negro passion?

Why do you stand at the edge of the street,
Staining with thick green-blood eyes,
    And brown temples
    The square.
    Whimpering skirts
    In a tugged wind,
    Like a man's hand.
    Your bare legs
    Dark trunks
    By a moving mass of cars.

O woman full of flame trees
Why do you rise up
To embrace me with
Your scarlet horror of death,
And your blood heavy imagination?
Flung heavy, top heavy, dead at my feet
The red braceleted slave girl—flame tree.

JOHN SHAW NEILSON

THE SUNDOWNER

I know not when this tiresome man
With his shrewd, sable billy-can
    And his unwashed democracy
His boomed-up pilgrimage began.

Sometimes he wandered far outback
On a precarious tucker track;
    Sometimes he lacked necessities
No gentleman would like to lack.

Tall was the grass, I understand,
When the old Squatter ruled the land.
  Why were the conquerers kind to him?
Ah, the wax matches in his hand!

Where bullockies with oaths intense
Made of the dragged-up trees a fence,
  Gambling with scorpions he rolled
His swag, conspicuous, immense.

In the full spendour of his power
Rarely he touched one mile an hour,
  Dawdling at sundown, history says,
For the pint pannikin of flour.

Seldom he worked; he was, I fear,
Unreasonably slow and dear;
  Little he earned, and that he spent
Deliberately drinking beer.

Cheerful, sorefooted child of chance
Swiftly we knew him at a glance;
  Boastful and self-compassionate,
Australia's intestate romance.

Shall he not live in robust rhyme,
Soliloquies and odes sublime?
  Strictly between ourselves, he was
A rare old humbug all the time.

In many a book of bushland dim
Mopokes shall give him greeting grim;
  The old swans pottering in the reeds
Shall pass the time of day to him.

On many a page our friend shall take
Small sticks his evening fire to make;
  Shedding his waistcoat, he shall mix
On its smooth back his Johnny cake.

Mid the dry leaves and silvery bark
Often at nightfall will he park
  Close to a homeless creek, and hear
The bunyip paddling in the dark.

1943

KENNETH H. GIFFORD

GALAH SONG

Bird-song at evening of the shrill galah,
Fraught with the night-tinge of the waking star,
Echoes in dune and on the russet sand,
Tapping the life-blood of the dreaming land.

Echoes re-echo as the sunset dies,
Shattering the wavelets in the western skies,
Probing dim caverns of the Nullarbor,
Tracing their night-ways to the deep sea floor:

Charged with the sound of billabongs at night,
Tuned to the sun-filled rocks in rugged light,
Borne through earth's night-walks to the waking morn,
Breath of Alchera to a dream-flecked dawn.

JAMES McAULEY

TERRA AUSTRALIS

Voyage within you, on the fabled ocean,
And you will find that Southern Continent,
De Quiros' vision—his hidalgo heart
And mythical Australia, where reside
All things in their imagined counterpart.

It is your land of similes; the wattle
Scatters its pollen on the doubting heart;
The flowers are wide-awake; the air gives ease;
There you come home; the magpies call you Jack
And whistle like larrikins at you from the trees.

And there, too, the angophora preaches on the hillsides
With the gestures of Moses; and the white cockatoo,
Perched on his limbs, screams with demoniac pain;
And who shall say on what errand the insolent emu
Walks between morning and night on the edge of the plain?

And northward, in valleys of the Fiery Goat
Where the sun like a centaur vertically shoots
His raging arrows with unerring aim,
Stand the ecstatic solitary pyres
Of unknown lovers, featureless with flame.

1944

GINA BALLANTYNE

NOSTALGIC

This is not a lament:
of the September sun
we take our daily superficial share
and with it the inevitable
nostalgia for suns well spent.
It is part of the good sun's heritage
that its bright spears bring
more than the momentary warmth to chilled bodies,
more than the hidden fire of latent summer:
they carry the cryptic power of all those suns,
the long sweet ancestry of seasons,
the piled-up perilous beauty of every Spring.

OLIVE PELL

REACTION

England's rural poets sing
of stately oaks and winding lanes
of buttercups and daffodils and meadows lush
of kingfishers and nightingales
and of the thrush.

But I.   I want to talk
in language brief and plain
of brown-green leaves and naked earth
and ring-barked ghosts that burn a fertile pyre
for gold wheat's birth.

Yes.   I want to talk
of loneliness and flies and dust,
and corrugated roofs that heat-waved mean
death to a diving thirsty bird, hot oppression
to a woman lean.

I want to talk
of eucalypts and stony ridges
of droughts and old gold fossickers that push
out to the great grey dusty plains
out to the bush.

F.B. O'CONNELL

RAIN AT CALOUNDRA

Rain in the ti-tree,
Wind in the gums . . .
High over Glasshouse, thunder comes.
Blue is the sand,
Yellow the clay;
The world is miserable, gloomy, grey.

Strain on the drag-ropes,
Bend your backs,
The rain will fill the new gun-tracks.
Your clothes hang heavy
With misery;
There's more rain coming across the sea.

Never a break
In sullen skies,
The raindrops seep through leaky flies.
Nothing to do
But suck your thumbs . . .
Wind in the ti-tree, rain in the gums.

R.G. HOWARTH

LOVE IS CRUEL TO THE LOVER

Love is cruel to the lover,
  To the loved it brings distress;
Spite of legend it is truly
  A fantastic happiness.

Shall we turn and try to master
  It before it masters us?
Be as neighbours, comrades, only,
  And conclude our loving, thus?

No! we'd curse the care of friendship,
  And this truth of nature prove:
Much the worst of tyrants is the
  Obligation not to love.

BRIAN ELLIOTT

THE GOLDEN EAGLE

Sick bird aspire: the sun's bright rings
by cold faint tangents touch your wings.

Moult no more O dull of eye
O but embrace felicity.

Leafless tree and droughty plain
vitiate the numbing pain.

Take flight: arise. The sacred fire
beckons in the broad empyre.

Above these wasted ways repair
through light-saturated air

past the desert's shallow fountains
past the amber tops of mountains

and earth's circles of despair.

Be adamant. Within the light
dissolve amazing mortal sight

and at the bright periphery
slough unvalued entity.

In the coronal of death
immolate exhausted breath,

let eternity consume
joyless beak and claw and plume.

Resolution fortified
shall a miracle betide:

for in the naked focal point
of creation all conjoint

ashes shall enclose some part
of the imperishable heart,

speck of spirit, pure gold
no other crucible may hold—

element, hypostasis,
predestined metamorphosis.

So rise up and re-emerge
purified in fire's purge

reforged, annealed; changed yet the same
and bearing banners of the flame.

Rejuvenation thus begun
descend again and leave the sun.

From the conflagration scatter
feathers of the fire matter

falling like a fiery snow
to fecundate what lies below:

rendering the fallows red
and enkindling us the dead.

Forests of forgotten trees
standing grim and dry shall seize

budding branches, sap shall run
substantiated in the sun:

so from our saddened roots shall spring
transcendental quickening.

1945

PETER MIDDLETON

CANE SAGA

Cane, in green lakes,
shimmers in the sun,
lapping the dark hills silently,
islanded with homesteads,
fringed with trees.

Flows from these green waters the sweet sap
that children love
and men grow strong upon,
through the long channels
of mill, machine and trade
to fill the swelling breast to the clutching babe,
lend subtle aid to lovers,
ease children's pain,
closing its secret circle in man's blood,
telling once more the sweet and ancient story
of how, like the trees,
man's roots still suck the earth
for sustenance.

Now, as the curtain of the season rises,
the green lakes burgeon like the tides of spring,
breezes whisper through the rustling cane-stems
words of doom to the expectant sap;

and in the sunrise of a golden morning
above the waters, questing eyes behold
the pearl plumed spears unsheathed
and massed in silence
in last defiant gesture and salute.

Now will the rites begin.
The sun-browned priests
cast their torches on the green-gold shores,
and soon the ranks of spears
are ringed with fire.

Night looks benignantly
upon the rosy clouds
that billow from the sacrificial field.
And morning brings the reapers;
the rock is struck,
the honey-golden sap begins to flow.

1946

KEN BARRATT

BURKE AND WILLS

1

So all men come at last to their Explorer's Tree,
whereon they carve their valediction to the world.
Whether as they, we explore a continent, or are content
to explore ourselves, we find that mysterious centre,
that vast and utter loneliness, which is the heart of being;
we hear that silence more fatal than the siren's song.

2

Silence, like sound, has its eight note scale.
There is the silence after sound.
(After the farewell speeches, the well wishings,
the cheering as they rode proudly from Melbourne Town,
the silence of the bush.)
There is the silence of sound we cannot hear.
(The black men, always lurking, always watching,
never speaking, merging in the frieze of great untidy trees.)
There is the silence amid many voices.
(Often they spoke loudly, hoping to drive their fears away,
hoping to fill the empty air with assurance,
but the silence was in them.)
There is the silence of Death, of the voice that can never be
                                      heard again.

(After Gray died, he seemed to march with them still,
the invisible companion, not answering their questions,
not questioning their answers.)
There is the silence of Desolation.
(This was no Egypt, but cresting a sand dune,
they yet might discover the stones of a city, time devoured,
or glinting in the sun, a golden helmet, become a hive
for the patient labour of the bees.)
There is the silence of Despair.
(Returning to the depot, finding it deserted,
they knew that words could buy them nothing
in this land of Nothing for Sale.)
There is the silence more ancient than man.
(Wills, the scientist, said it: *These rocks
are so old, they have forgotten the singing
and the shouting of the sea, the violence
of the earth in the making.*)
And last silence of all, completing the octave,
the silence that was before sound.
(Waiting for the end, life flowed backward to its source.
Voices, like a spring uncoiling,
receded and were superseded.
The last cry of hunger and pain
became the first cry for breath,
and now at last there was only the silence,
and they and the silence were one.)

3

Yet one man survived, one man returned
a little while to the world of men,
telling how Burke and Wills had died,
wresting the secret from a continent;
when they asked him to expound the secret,
he would speak of other things, saying rather,
"The camels gave us trouble from the beginning,"
or, *"Nardoo is no fit food for white men."*

JOHN W. EYLES

DESERT CROSSING

Twin rails, polished by pounding steel,
Stretch in the limitating distance beyond the sight
On either side; all sound is dumb
But the low soft-whispering wind in the lonely night:
Drifting sand and the wind's chill touch
Filling the dark with moment; all the light
Of the burdened day is gone with the day.

A thin vibration throbs in the desert's throat:
A low pitched humming burns within the rails,
Swelling—a glow, then a broad bright blade of light
Scatters the startled shadow; wheels
Thunder, and, nearing, clack in the vasty night
And pass with a roar of movement; steel
Grinds on steel—and fades to a whispering note
Far (like a thin elastic thread
Stretching), rises in pitch till the quiver of sound
Throbs on a single soundless key,
And the night and the wind are one with the silent sand.

GEORGE FARWELL

MALLEE SONG

Grey as famine the dust walks
stooping under its shroud of sky,
dust over the darkening mallee,
billabongs bone dry.

Yet down by the bend of the river
where great pumps are singing,
the vines grow silky-leaved,
swollen grapes clinging.

Track's dust is a loping dingo
to leap the silted fence
while sun without shadow stares
at sown wheat's impotence.

Ripen the veins of this sere flesh
pumping the river's blood,
give to these withering loins
the Murray's fecund flood.

HARLEY MATTHEWS

THE VINEYARD

When I came home from the last war
The place seemed strange—no sign of drought,
Everything green, and it full summer.
My mother closed the window to shut out
The locust just beginning. More
And more the room grew in around me.
Gone the time when a double-drummer
Could lead my mind off. Weeks before
My father, they told me, was dead.
Back now, and a new duty bound me,
All the longed-for calls found me
Unstirred. My mother moved and set
By me the wine she had decanted.
"The bottle of the Hermitage
Put down the day you left," she said.
Few the wine's years, but it had age.
It tasted cool, gentle, and yet
It carried strength, like grown-up men
Moulded by stern events. Outside
The grape-vines that my father planted
In a flush growth of weeds stood dead.
I knew the boy in me had died,
That I had matured like the wine,
When I came home from the war then.

And when I go home from this one?
A vineyard in the years between
I planted, vine and vine and vine.
The way it tilted towards the sun,
And the bush came and sheltered it
Did gladden every vigneron.
It was pleasure to prune or plough
Up its rows, grey with winter, green
In the heat; a comfort to savour
An old wine when the lamp was lit
At evening; peace to wonder how
The sun of future years would flavour
The juice just rising in the buds
Of some vines newly grafted. Roughened
With work these hands. It only toughened
The mind to take the fires and floods,
Spring frosts that blasted every shoot,
And hail that stripped us bare of fruit.
But, sleep-freed from its grief, awoke
The soil, and stirring, yielded all—
Its love, itself—up at our call.

People, the world over, said meantime,
That peace could be perpetual;
The nations need no more dispute
With armies, once they made a crime
Of war. So it was signed with stroke
Of pen and pen. And most believed
The old stern ways were done; no more
Would men fight, all would be secure,
And those flush, pleasant days endure.

But harshly they were undeceived:
For all those beliefs there came this war.
Over this planet it has shed
Its dooms and terrors; to this land,
Hardly prepared for fire or drought,
Has brought new forms of death; here bred
Mad hates which make men prisoner
Now.

The soil's love, my love are wasted.
It lies unploughed, the vine-rows stand
Unpruned; and vintages that were
To grow will never now be tasted.
And this? This had to come about:
Soldier or prisoner he must be
Whose pay is not in currency.
Although the vines are dying out,
The wine is turned to vinegar,
My land sleeps, sleeps, dreams, waiting for
Her own to come home from this war.

Anzac Internment Camp, N.S.W.,
1 August 1942.

1947

EDNA TREDINNICK

ARUNTA

Slim boy, scraping war paint,
Listening to the wise men,
Listening to tales of terrible encounter,
Told in the only tongue.

Slim boy, following hands,
Shaping again adventures
In the uncertain light.
Slim boy, wanting years,
Tree-climber,
Dog-lover,
Youngest of the tribe.

North, to the land of yellow men,
They said, and more.

Slim boy in a salt wind,
Gazing beyond the decks;
Slim boy,
Listening.

LLEWELLYN RHYS

AROULTJA

Gone forever is Aroultja from her side,
Gone seeking euro by a new dawn's rhythm.
Out where the totem wears many strange masks
And warriors dance in the fire's flood-tide
In the hunting grounds of no return.

As reeds on a clayflat Aroultja's spears
Dried and withered are, nor tribal strife brings
Coal-kiss of flame to love-denied flinthead,
Chilled by cold airs, and still colder tears
From the hunting grounds of no return.

High among treetops his bones rap soft message,
Thrummelling paper-bark. Taking her dilly-bag,
She gathers memories far from the water's edge,
Sucks of their juices while yearning fleet passage
To the hunting grounds of no return.

E. M. ENGLAND

CORROBOREE FOR A DEAD WARRIOR

From long ago, in the mists of the dark man's dreamtime
The corroboree of the dancing brolga comes,
Soft at first, to the beat of half-heard drums.

On, on, they beat till their rhythm shakes the shadows
Where the wind strums out a theme as on taut wires,
And ruby light plays upward from the fires.

The words drop smooth as honey, wild and sweet.
All meaning's lost, but the burthen lives, as though
Brolgas pace here as they did long ago.

(Long, long ago in the mists of the dark man's dreamtime
When men were giants on uncharted shores
With isles like stepping-stones to Eastern doors.)

It's like wild music that one hears in storms
When spirit-voices pipe long-drawn and shrill
Over the tumult that sweeps sky and hill.

Dance, brolgas. Fling wide your wings and make
Obeisance to the dazzling western skies
Shatter the sunset with your sad sad cries.

Mourn for young Kwalin where so low he lies.

JOHN T. KIRTLEY

WRITTEN FOR IAN MUDIE DURING MY SOJOURN IN POLITICAL CONCENTRATION CAMP NUMBER 14D, AT LIEBESTAG,* SOUTH AUSTRALIA

The willy-willy curls, the dust assembles
upon the ground sun-warmed to vapour heat.
I see the Spirit of the Land—it trembles
before it spins away beneath my feet.
What agony of pride this flight discloses
I sense myself with ever-mounting pain,
knowing a Land, unloved, sometimes deposes
its men, when all their natural virtues wane.
Only the race persists which is heroic
as Time has shown us with its pulsing tides;
for soil is greater than its flesh the stoic
by instinct knows, and in his faith abides.
All native vision has a narrow arc,
parochial, shrewd, observant, earthy, stark.

---

* i.e. Loveday. A facetious allusion to the war-time alteration of a number of place names, originally German, in South Australia.

1948

COLIN THIELE

SWAGMAN DAY

Day, gone, lights his camp-fire in the west—
an hour smouldering—
flame walking over the water,
licking the crests of the hills.

Day, gone, pays for his stay in gold—
each nightfall a hoard flung to half the earth
we take as ours, yet issue no receipts—
we, the world's dull tills.

Day, our guest departing, has short shrift—
bundled out unceremoniously in towns
with factory hoots and whistles—
spurned to make room for Night . . .

Yet here that gay old swagman rests awhile,
loiters about a valley, stoops to infuse
the blush on the face of the sea, and eases his swag—
his great burden of light—

on a mellowing hill-top . . . And pauses there too,
fumbling in gully-niches and the pockets
of old cloud-tatters for the sum
of his world rental owed,

And, finding it, pours in a breathless glow
his gold on the floor of the sky . . .
turns graciously, closing the door behind,
and takes once more the road.

ARTHUR MURPHY

SWAGMEN

With heads bent against the sun
They stride along,
Blackened billies swinging in gnarled hands—
Their throats alert with song.

Their loves are unchanging stars,
Green sweep of water and tree,
Strange red drive of roads
Towards night's illimitable sea.

Their dawn is a wild duck crying,
A swan in flight
For the blood of a billabong,
Away from the nausea of night.

1949

MARY GILMORE

THE WORD

In the Beginning Was the Word

I am the maker,
I made man,
Who, in the ooze,
His life began.

On me, as stair,
Upward he climbed,
Word after word
Meted and primed—
Uttered by man,
By reason heard,
I, the beginning,
I am the Word.

Earth, air and sky,
Deep of the sea,
The might of man
Lives but by me.

Take from the world
Its robe of words,
Man lives again
With beasts and birds.

LILITH NORMAN

THE COLOUR OF SORROW

A Lament for the Aborigines

I am the dark one, I am the unknown,
Born long ago in Yamminga, the Dreamtime,
These are my people, these I created,
Am one with their longings, and struggles and fears.

Out of the wild quarrelling of the wind,
That they might be venturesome and brave,
I created them.
From the far stars I drew forth wonder,
Melted in the misty green of the distance,
And from the savageness of the dingo,
I created them.
Black as the black satin of the night,
Upright as the lance of the red gum,
And from the laughter of the kookaburras,
I created them.
I drew strength and cunning from the gnarled crocodile,
Keen sight from Neeyangarra the eagle,
And awe was in them.
For their mystical souls I created the dew-laced morning,
The soft warm corroboree clay,
The sparkle of the waters of life,
The cicada-throb of twilight,
And in their sleep I unfolded these mysteries.
I showed them the sweet land of Jimbin,
Under the earth and the water it lies,
Where all is the dim white light of love,
And each unborn baby, Ngargululla,
Laughs with its comrades
Laughs until, summoned by the dream of its father,
It slips into the warm velvet of its mother's womb;
All this I showed to my people, and then rejoiced.

Then, one night,
Fearing lest they grow too proud,
I plucked the timbre of the mopoke's sob,
And as a curse, planted in the heart of my people . . .

A great loneliness.
Since the wild rock that is their land
First rose from the sea,
My people have gone searching down the years.
Their footprints mark the great eastern valleys,
Where, in the frosty hoar of early morn
The long silver fingers of the gums
Tickle the chuckling breeze;
There where the delicate-spiked bottle-brush,
And the flamboyant waratah,
Quiver with the day's awakening yawn,
Have my people passed silently by,
And all the land bears the imprint of their passing.

ALEXANDER CRAIG

ELEGY

Above the clouds that mask the air
No sun so much as tints their screen.
The troubled people everywhere,

Who gaze upon a bare, cold scene,
Are turned to stone. Now they have scope
Only to roll like rocks between

The ridges of time's downward slope.
And human nature grants to these
Its futile paradox—the hope

Of what they dare not hope. One sees
Them pattering from caves, to be
Soon lost on lonely promontories

Of unacknowledged grief. The sea
Roars in their ears like history.

GEOFFREY DUTTON

WOOL-SHED DANCE

The dust shaken and stamped from their feet
Is red as autumn in the rain-soft south
Where leaves by boot and hoof are mashed
And mingled in the grass, and vine-roots
Slip as surely into the dark earth
As an arm into a sleeve. A trace of it clings
Still in the cracks of their bouncing boots
As the saltbush and myall to their crumbled ground.
The air, heavy with the smell of wool,
Leans to a lamp by an empty bench
From the wool-bales of watchers, the non-dancers,
As the floor slopes down to the open
Double doors where the lamp makes yellow
The posted night. The jigging shadows
Ripple on the corrugated wall with the dancers,
Heel and toe in a clacking polka.
And a sturt pea on a faded dress
Burns like the black heart of autumn.
The accordion squeezes a new tune
And peg-leg waltzes with a ten-months baby,
Beer to ballast his wooden knee,
And the mother is proud that it does not cry.
A bottle rings on the earth like a stone
And the cook finds a tortuous path
To bed, like a myall root through rocks
Winding heavy and dark as iron.
Past midnight in the brightest moonlight
The lamps will glow black and go out,
Till sober and drunks go home,
And each year the seasons, like the accordion,
Squeezed in the cracked hands of the earth,
Play the same tune over and over again
To grey saltbush on the red land,
While in the south the rainwet trees
Strip boughs as bare as roots for winter.

1950

JUDITH WRIGHT

WONGA VINE

Look down: be still.
The sunburst day's on fire,
O twilight bell,
flower of the wonga vine.

I gather you
out of his withering light.
Sleep there, red;
sleep there, yellow and white.

Move as the creek
moves to its hidden pool.
The sun has eyes of fire;
be my white waterfall.

Lie on my eyes like hands,
let no sun shine—
O twilight bell,
flower of the wonga vine.

ERNEST G. MOLL

FARM DAY

The magpie's meditation is
Mother of morning melodies;
The kookaburra's laugh at night
Remembers some obscene delight;
And I between the two have done
A good day's work beneath the sun,
Just pausing by the stable fence
To applaud the magpie's eloquence,
And at the other's merry din
To smile at a remembered sin.

K.E. MURRAY

From NULLARBOR

I threw the spear and the leaping one, the kangaroo,
Died at the height of his leap, and the wallaby and wombat.
I threw the boomerang, it came to my hand
As a bird returning to its nest.
The emu ran before us; spear in hand
The fleet one was beside him
I brought him down with the spear.

Great heat came and the river dried to a trickle
Over the stones. We marched at night,
Yetarli gave light, Mirrabooka guided us!
We drove the women, the timid ones, and the man-children
That live in the women's camp, not having come to manhood.
These do not know the white courage of warriors,
They have to be driven.

We knew thirst in the great heat, and hunger.
Our tongues swollen and black filled our mouths,
Our bellies sank against the backbone,
Our navels were only pits.

Fire was master!
Fire ran among the hills and leapt higher than the kangaroo,
The leaping one.
Fire leapt to the tops of the gum trees.
We spent days in the river bed
Where the water trickled over the stones.
The women cried, it is the way of the timid.

We cried for rain as we cry for rain in the corroboree
In the time of the half-moon.
Um-gum-bk-ula sent us the rain bird, Pil-pilpa, who cries
Kurreke-ta-ta!
As she flies under the storm-clouds.

There is a sound of rain in our ears
The smell in our noses,
Coming from the place of the setting sun, so we cry
Kurreke-ta-ta!

In the rain dance where we make corroboree
In the time of the half moon.
Pil-pilpa brought rain;
Grass grew, the nardoo, and munyeera;
The kangaroo, the wallaby, and the wombat
Came again to the great plain.

RAY MATHEW

WHOSE COUNTRY?

How long have the cockatoos beaten, white blossoms,
Among the green leaves; the galahs grey and the parrots
Flitting like flame among the darker green?
How long have the sheep nibbled at the green shade,
The man waited, his arms gleaming sweat,
With his big-breathing horse beneath him and shade pressing
                      down?

How long?
Now the real master has taken his own,
Driven the green and wandering tribes away;
Left only wind-wood black essentials, bearing
Red leaves like tiny spears of fire and saying
This is his country: Fire walked here.

KEVIN E. COLLOPY

CHILDREN OF THE DESERT

Here in the desert, in the silent places;
In burning sand; on ridges of red stone;
Here in the stillness, their little days alone,
Their chatter and their black, forgotten faces
Stand in the way of death; though over all
The spirit of this dying land remains.
When each day ends, then lightly on the breast
Of that old lubra whom they call the Night,
The hunters sleep with day's red spears laid by.
These are the kindly hours, when worst or best
Seem more like God; when hatreds seek respite
And children all, we sleep and do not die.

NANCY CATO

MALLEE FARMER

You planted wheat but you reaped white gibbers
You ran some sheep but the crows were robbers
Of eyes and entrails and even the wool,
Plucked from the carcase before it was cool.

You cleared the mallee and the sand blew over
Fence and road to the slow green river,
You prayed for rain but the sky breathed dust
Of long-dead farmers and the soil's red rust.

You ploughed up the paddocks with a stump-jump plough,
But the gates were open and the drought walked through.
Now the old house crumbles and bares its bones
And the land is left to the crows and the stones.

ROSEMARY DOBSON

CHILD WITH A COCKATOO

*Portrait of Anne, daughter of the fifth Duke of Bedford,
by S. Verelst.*

"Paid by my lord, one portrait. Lady Anne,
Full length with bird and landscape, twenty pounds
And framed withal. I say received. Verelst."

So signed the painter, bowed and took his leave.
My lady Anne smiled in the gallery
A small, grave child, dark-eyed, half-turned to show
Her five bare toes beneath the garment's hem,
In stormy landscape with a swirl of drapes.
And, who knows why, perhaps my lady wept
To stand so long and watch the painter's brush
Flicker between the palette and the cloth
While from the sun-drenched orchard all the day
She heard her sisters calling each to each.
And someone gave, to drive the tears away
That sulphur-crested bird with great white wings,
The wise, harsh bird—as old and wise as Time
Whose well-dark eyes the wonder kept and closed.
So many years to come and still, he knew
Brooded that great, dark island continent
Terra Australis.
                To those fabled shores
Not William Dampier, pirating for gold
Nor Captain Cook his western course had set
Jumped from the longboat, waded through the surf,
And clapt his flag ashore at Botany Bay.

Terra Australis, unimagined land—
Only that sulphur-crested bird could tell
Of dark men, moving silently through trees.
Of stones and silent dawns, of blackened earth
And the long golden blaze of afternoon.
That vagrant which an ear-ringed sailor caught
(Dropped from the sky, near dead, far out at sea)
And caged and kept, till, landing at the docks,
Walked whistling up the Strand and sold it them,
The curious bird, its cynic eyes half-closed,
To the Duke's servant, drunken at an inn.

And he lived on, the old adventurer,
And kept his council, was a sign unread,
A disregarded prologue to an age.
So one might find a meteor from the sun
Or sound one trumpet ere the play's begun.

R.A. SWAN

EPITAPH TO THE VANISHED TRIBES

This, the land of the ancient folk,
The empty plains;
A few thin bones in the sand-dunes,
The silent rains.

DAVID ROWBOTHAM

ROOFS

Beetle-backs at a standstill under rain,
   Streaky red, sea-weed green, dun-grey,
Hunched together, similar, dissimilar,
   Streaming with the weather fogging the bay.

Uncouth tops of crowds with sunken legs
   And heads withdrawn beneath their angled shards,
Urbanized on a great sea coast, like a local
   Thought of love cramped blindly near the words

To give it transmutation into action:
   Dead roofs carpented on living flesh,
On loving, hating hearts, iron covers for golden
   Dreams undiscovered by circumstance or wish:

Corrugated simplicity, something that grew
   From galvanized endeavour, then stood still
In utter, dull content beside the sea
   That challenged, and the unattained hill.

IRENE GOUGH

NARRINYERRI*

When the last hot blow is beaten on the brass bowl of the
                                                                     sky,
And day is lying blood-stained on the reach,
The Narrinyerri children, once the warriors of their tribe,
Come from the wading trees and climb the beach.

Let theirs be children's joy at close of day,
The joy those warriors never could forget;
But when my time is come at last to go
Beyond the swan's road and the swallow's way,

Let me come back to earth only when the grey dawn's breaking
                                                                     cold,
And all the River lies in mist asleep,
To stand sharp-poised a moment as a white crane watching
                                                                  where
Spiralis and the water-lily creep.

---

* The Narrinyerri, a tribe on the lower Murray, had the belief that warriors returned after death, and, as young boys, lived in the trees along the river.

1951

DOUGLAS STEWART

THE ABORIGINAL AXE

Hyacinth orchid, butcher bird,
Rain on a sharp black stone:
What years like smoke and years like mist
While the butcher-bird sang in the banksia tree
And, lovely and leprous, flushed and spotted,
The hyacinth orchid bloomed and rotted,
That wet black stone has known
Since first in the scrub where the butcher-birds call
And the orchid stands up glowing and tall
Those coppery fingers let it fall
And down the track by the stony tree
The shade slipped by like a ghost.
Shaped with such care to fit the hand,
Polished and washed by the crystal shower
From stain of clay and smother of sand,
Now it lies in my own,
Warm to hold as the butcher-bird,
Cold as the rotting flower.

DAVID CAMPBELL

THE WATERHOLE

What my ma calls dirt is a turkey-egg spot,
But I hide my boots in the vacant lot
And drop my h's for a lighter load,
And we stalk like cripples down the blue stone road.

There's an old dope living in a field of fowls
We shout "Good mornin'" when he turns and scowls
With a face that's wattled like a bleeding nose,
For he's got his suspicions where the poultry goes.

It's noon till six at the waterhole
Where the yabbies are coloured like a cloudy pearl,
And we boil them gold in a rusty tin,
Screwing up our eyes as we drop them in.

Then the cock cries warning, the world is still,
And the day dies burning in the crayfish pool;
But we'll stone our terrors on the old street sign—
There'll be men in the world when we're fifteen.

FRANCIS WEBB

HENRY LAWSON

Death had you: quiet, shrill, it was all the same.
But for others a Sunday came
With its leisurely blue and white,
Twelve-footers rakish in a freshening wind,
An old man's moody pipefuls, and a boy's mind.

An old man's moody pipefuls—give us a light—
Grey ash and dust to fight
The shepherded, breathless red;
Random jowl of a smoke-puff—this life, did you ask,
Or was a burned-out lantern driven to frisk

By a tactless hand at the tent-flap? Back from the dead
For sodden conjecture spread
Over black fences: the ear
Might spare you something of this, but never the eyes
Could miss sour vapour on shambling footpaths and bays;

Dawn's broom in the gutter: like a label the sneer
With every doled-out beer
And landlord's mercy; the alloy
Rusting each sense when from a ferry's box
Of roped-in glitter swam night, and those faces empty and
 lax.

But chance rites of sunshine, an old man's pipefuls, a boy:
Had these no wings for you, joy
To push at the creaking gate
Of water and words? No, the caged shag could not pass
To his rightful distance and silver and singleness.

Back to the grave with this, then—but remember, wait:
The pub's fool, Macquarie's Mate,
Can hear them mocking his buried thought and stress,
Rises, becomes his dead friend—having nothing more—
And will fight to a standstill. Someone watches at the door.

1952

PETER HOPEGOOD

SONS OF THE SURREAL REFABRICATE THE DRAGON

Salute, jongleur of fireflies,
many lands you liberate with lutes,
radium is a captive rotting all dungeons,
whose surcease in lead is assured yet afar!
Salute, riding a hedgehog
to the assault of an anthill,
this juggler swallows swords
to belch hokkus of fire,
only thus, empirically, may it be affirmed
that the surreal is the true dragon.

1953

MARGARET IRVIN

PADDY MELON COUNTRY

The paddy melons lie among
the springing wheat like yellow balls
the sun has bounced. O green and gold
the rind around my winter world,
where leaves of pine and kurrajong—
whose seed was blown from colder hills—
litter the south with secrets brought
from time beyond the cattle-bells;
and slope to slope the land is linked
in anapests that measure, prove
the beat of my astonished thought—
the singing stress of love.

PART 3

Jindyworobak Prose

Fiction

James Devaney

TWO EXTRACTS FROM "SANCTUARY", *THE VANISHED TRIBES*

MOORA-WATHI-MEERING

"Old wrinkled Mum-garry-wee squatted on the ridge and looked intently across the country outspread below her.

"What is it you see, old mother?"

"I see the lonely camps of the lost ones, the hunted wait-jurks, away off there in the Moora-wathi-meering country. E! the heart inside me jumps up when I look over that mournful country of the hunted ones."

"E! that is the desolate place yonder, the Silent Country, the sacred sanctuary of the tribes," said Windara in a whisper.

Some of the women joined them, and all gazed out in silence across the solemn-folded bush to where the great region known to the tribesmen as Moora-wathi-meering lay dark and level in the distance. It was the ancient sanctuary of the surrounding tribes, a long, narrow tract which even Kewora the runner in a whole day could not hope to travel round, and which if a wanted man once reached he was sacred from all enemies. All knew its exact boundaries and none would dream of setting foot across the border of that solemn place, or of harming a refugee there; and even game that reached the stunted boxwoods at the edge of Moora-wathi-meering was pursued no further. It was a place always avoided, the land of banished men.

"Jalan is in that place; I saw big hairy Jalan the gin-killer chased into that place," said one woman. "He killed a Marakaraka gin for her fat one time with a strangling-cord, and the men tracked him and chased and chased, but that fellow Jalan ran over the boundary just before them. E! then he sat down, panting, and all the men stood only a spear's length away, yelling out at him and shaking their spears, but that fellow was safe in sanctuary and so the men could not throw a spear or harm him then. That is what I saw."

"My old man Dundur says there is plenty game in that country," said old Mum-garry-wee, "but there are no corroborees and almost no gins and children at all, because only the hunted wait-jurks go there."

"E! they are hunted men, and sometimes they are lonely sitting down without any gins at all, and they steal out to make raids and catch gins. Then they are speared if the men catch them; that's how Yaranga was speared at last up in the gullies after he was in that place a long time."

"Ah, they are poor lonely fellows that sit down in Moorawathi-meering," said another. "Look now, here and there you can see smokes going up over yonder in the Silent Country of the lost ones."

. . . . .

On the first evening of the Boodther gathering some of the men found old Warrhul lying on the bank of the billabong, all wet from his fishing, and groaning with great pains in the back. He knew well what it was, he told them; some one had stolen his kidney fat, some one had put strong magic upon him and taken away his kidney fat. They carried him back to his little gunyah and sang healing chants and steamed him with the steam of eucalyptus leaves, but old Warrhul had made up his mind that he had to die.

Warrhul's two sons were very angry. There was the thin and gloomy Thundung, the elder. The other was Kaat the great talker, squat and very strong, an ugly one with a great wide mouth, and a cruel beater of his gin.

"Now I am a darranderong, an avenger," he said often, "and I will find out who killed that old dead one. I can kill any Wallanbang or any Wonamara man here, I will fight anyone who is not a coward and afraid of me, like the scared reedhen that runs away."

One evening Kewora the great Wonamara was returning from the hunt at dusk. Suddenly he realized with horror that he had come right up to the grave of old Warrhul.

He was awakened at dawn by a great hubbub outside, and presently his father the old white-headed Dundur rushed into the gunyah with terrible news. Kewora's tracks had been recognized by Kaat and Thundung—he must rise and run away to the high ridges before the whole Mara-karaka camp was upon him.

"Did you steal that old fellow's fat?" asked Dundur.

"No, no, I made no magic against that one at all," said Kewora. "I followed a pademelon close up to his grave, that is how it was. Now perhaps I must go to Moora-wathi-meering, that gloomy place. I do not want to go into the terrible Silent Country!"

"E! it is a desolate place over there," agreed old Dundur.

"All the tallabillas sit down there," said Kewora.

So they sat and talked and planned, till at last old Dundur took another firestick and made his way down the slopes towards the far-off sleeping camp.

After that it was noticed that old Dundur often went away by himself into the hills. One day old Dundur came into the camp carrying a short Wonamara coffin of tea-tree bark sheets; and all guessed what it meant.

He said, "Now at last I have found my son. I do not know if the avengers have killed him or if he was lonely for his own people and died."

Old Dundur journeyed with his tribe but still often went out hunting to the ridges alone. Once he came into Windara's gunyah looking troubled and said: "Kewora is a lonely fellow now". He told her of the meeting place arranged.

Then one day the squat and strong-limbed Kaat strode into the camp and cried out: "I have seen the tracks of Kewora in this place all about!"

Then suddenly Kewora himself dashed out of the scrub in full view of all the camp. Kewora was standing with his arm round the trunk of a shapely boxwood that stood alone in the camp clearing, a minggah or spirit tree, the occasional desperate refuge of despairing men. It was a bold stroke, but for the moment he was safe. Not even Kaat would dare to launch a weapon.

"Dundur! come forward and undergo punishment!" roared Kaat. "Where is the old liar who deceived us? Let him now be speared like Wimba the scrub wallaby!"

But old Dundur was safely perched in a leafy apple-gum near the edge of the encampment.

The crowd began gradually to disperse, for the evening meal was now ready and gins at every fire were calling to their own men. None would think of setting a watch during the night; the blacks disliked the dark.

An hour later Kewora and old Dundur were sitting together over a small fire in a hollow half-way up the slopes. "It is finished now; tomorrow the horde will swarm over this place," said the old man.

"E! now it is finished," said Kewora, "but since we must go, first of all I would do a thing. We will go into the Silent Country when the moon rises, but first we will sneak up and kill those two."

There was no corroboree at all that night, but a fire showed that the Mara-karaka men were holding a Jun or conference of the fighting-men. Thundung and Kaat were there, but for half an hour the two avengers moved about in the darkness. At last Thundung came and sat on a fallen log near the edge of the cleared space and just then Kaat stood up in the midst and began to address the meeting with angry words. Kewora gave a sharp cry and the two spears left the woomeras together. Old Dundur from short range transfixed Thundung through the side; Kewora's long spear passed swift and true between several pairs of men and took the squat Kaat full in the middle of the back.

When the broad red rim of the moon first showed above the ridges, Kewora and old Dundur stood together at the edge of the tribal sanctuary.

"Plenty wallaby and wild turkey sit down yonder," said Kewora. "E! it is a good and desirable place."

"We will make our gunyah and will eat and sleep without fear," added old Dundur, "It is better than crouching out on the windy ridges, hunted always and without rest."

"Come!" whispered Kewora.

Together they crossed the boundary, and walking slowly they disappeared among the stunted boxwoods into the Silent Country of the lost.

Rex Ingamells

TWO EXTRACTS FROM *ARANDA BOY*

In spite of the serious feeling about the camp tonight Gurra decided he would follow Arriaka in the morning, if only he could wake in time.

What woke him Gurra did not know, but he was suddenly wide awake. He sat up. He soon saw that his father was not sleeping alongside him. There was no moon, and the campfire had smouldered down to glowing coals covered with grey ash; but, in the gloom under the huge ghost gums, the boy could make out the sleeping forms by his own fire and by the other fires on the creek sands. His heart thumped as he thought to himself, "Now's my chance to follow the men to the Euro Rock Pools. They can't have much of a start on me; I shall run and follow them. I shall stalk them as they stalk the kangaroos and, when I've seen them spear the euros, I shall run back before them to the camp. If I run a little wide of the creek, they will not see my tracks as they come back, and will not know I've followed them. Perhaps I shall be able to return to camp before the women are stirring. But it's a fair way to the rock pools, and I must hurry . . ."

Thinking these thoughts to himself, Gurra rose and moved carefully away from his family's fire. Even as he did so, he noticed a pale glow in the east suddenly brighten. It was the moon rising before the sun, and it would light his way before he had gone very far. Quickly now he flitted away in the direction he meant to go. As he passed the last of the fires, one of the dogs growled, and Gurra stopped, standing very still, his body pressed behind the trunk of a ghost gum. It was Brinia's fire, and Brinia called out sleepily to the dog to lie down and be quiet. In a flash, Gurra moved away; softly and swiftly, he put the camp behind him. For a time, he decided, he would follow the creek at its edge, and then, as the men did, he knew, he would leave it and cut off the wider bends; but, in doing so, he would keep off the beaten track. He settled down to a slow, steady run, weaving his way in and out of the gums at the edge of the sands. The rising of the bright Moon gave him light. Soon he saw him, large and glowing, peep and climb over a far ridge on his left hand. How smooth and misty-white in the centre of the creek, the sands shone in the light!

The boy ran steadily for a time down the creek, until the camp was well behind him and he was far past the tree where he had seen his first cicada. When he passed it, he had thought of Rira for a moment but his mind returned quickly to his new adventure. He had almost reached the point at which he would strike away from the creek across country, when there was a sudden loud burst of shouting from the trees ahead of him. Terrified, he stopped. The words were strange, and he could not understand them. He had not expected such a shock as this, or he would not have dared to leave camp. He wished now that he had not left the dying fire. A number of men or spirits—Gurra knew not which—were making a terrific noise. If they were men, surely they must be evil strangers. He could hear the noise coming from the thickness of the trees ahead of him, but he could not see any movement there. He believed in evil spirits and was afraid that he would see them rushing out to carry him away at any moment. His legs were so shaky with fear now, as he cowered back into the shade at the butt of an old ghost gum that they failed him and he sank down on to the sand.

The shouting continued, rising higher and higher, becoming a deafening din . . . but, suddenly, Gurra found a shred of comfort. One of those voices was surely Arriaka? Gurra could not understand the words, for strange words were being chanted. Yet the voice was Arriaka's, sure enough, although it was fiercer, angrier than he had ever heard Arriaka's voice in the past. This was strange, and he was still afraid. However, Arriaka was no evil spirit. As the din went on, Gurra gathered his scattered wits, calling on the strength which had deserted his legs to return. He would hurry back to the camp at once. Something had gone wrong with his little plan. Hunters would not make such a noise, he was certain, when they went after euros. Hunters worked quietly. Gurra's heart thumped heavily and fast with fear. What was going on? He knew only that something was happening which neither children nor women were supposed to know about. He must get back as quickly as possible. He stood up to run.

No sooner had he risen, however, than he threw himself down again. At that very instant, the frantic shouting ceased as suddenly as it had begun. The instant silence was as shocking as the loud sound. For a moment, he was again too afraid to move; and, before he could gather his courage, another terrifying shock was upon him. As he caught the sound of men running swiftly towards him, Gurra flattened himself again against the large gum-bole. His eyes, even as he crouched close to the ground, caught sight of something which brought back his first terror of spirits. A dozen weird figures—much weirder than any he had seen on the Corroboree-Ground at Manna Creek—were racing towards him over the moonlit sands, running like the wind; and they were covered strangely with white streaks, like bones, all along their dark bodies from head to toe. They looked fierce and horrible. Gurra closed his eyes against the sight even as he drew his head back. Eyes shut, he waited to be caught up and carried away. The sound of this rapidly moving group of awful beings was like a wind in the air; their feet scarcely touched the ground, and made a low fierce whisper as of wind on bark and leaves and sand, as of wind along the bough of a tree. Now Gurra felt all his strength go from him before these terrible evil spirits. They were already on him, he thought. Head in hand, at the tree's root, he closed his eyes tight, waiting to be seized and lost forever to the camp from which he had so foolishly stolen away; but suddenly his ears told him that the running figures were turning away from him, in single file at the other side of the tree—so close that the sand from their flying feet sprayed into his hair and upon his face. None of the runners saw him crouched there! Relieved, he opened his eyes and saw, as they ran, that the daubed face of their leader was that of Arriaka but he was still terribly frightened. He knew that he had seen something he ought not to have seen, and he connected this awful mystery in his mind with some magic to do with the death of Napanna. The sound of the feet of the rapid runners faded like a whisper into silence.

He heard voices now, and lay still while Yilta and Jira went past him and back towards the camp. They had been present at the great noise, thought Gurra, but were too old to join the swift runners. He must himself get back to camp, get back to camp! He thought he would go a roundabout way, but go quickly so that he would arrive there before Yilta and Jira, who were slow. He rose to his feet.

But Gurra was in for one more shock tonight.

"Stop, boy!"

It was the voice of Irritcha behind him; but it was not a kind voice in the night.

Gurra stopped. He was more terrified than ever. He had been caught! How he wished he had not left the friendliness of the camp-fire circle! The wind now, before the dawn, was cold, cold like his fear of what would happen because of his meddling.

Irritcha, although not nearly so old as Jira and not quite so old as Yilta, was too old to go with the Vengeance Party on its journey to overtake the Unmatjera Traders. He had arranged the magic ritual and prepared the warriors before they set out on their dread errand of revenge. The Trader, Tungulla, was blamed for the death of Napanna, and now Tungulla was being hunted. Waving his arms wildly, Irritcha had urged the men away on their mission of death, after which he had remained to remove traces of the rites, while Yilta and Jira had departed; then he had turned his own steps for the camp in time to catch sight of the boy's figure as it left the cover of the tree.

Irritcha's eyes were very angry. He came up to Gurra as quickly as his legs could carry him. His face looked hard and flinty; Gurra saw Irritcha's eyes gleaming into his from many footsteps away, and they looked cruel, like those of a hawk. When Irritcha stood before him, Gurra saw that there was no kindness left in the Medicine Man's face. His mouth was drawn so thin that no lips showed through his scrubby beard, until he opened his mouth to snap out a question.

"What did you see?"

Irritcha had to speak again before Gurra could find his tongue to answer.

"Wicked boy! You have no right to be here. Tell me at once what you have been looking at."

"I left the camp to follow the men to the Euro Rock Pools, but—but . . ."

"The Euro Rock Pools!"

Gurra went on: "I heard a great noise of shouting from over there."

He nodded his head down the creek.

"Did you go over there?"

"I stopped. I was too frightened to move at all."

Irritcha spoke again and, although he said harsh things, Gurra knew from his voice, and from the fact that the cruel light went suddenly from his eyes, that the old Medicine Man was somehow very relieved and comforted by what he had last been told.

"You disobedient and unruly dingo pup, where were you when you heard the shouting?"

"I was by this tree. I was afraid to go forward and afraid to go back. I hid here, and the swift runners did not know I was here, I was so quiet and still."

Irritcha wanted to be quite sure.

"You did not go beyond this tree tonight?"

"I have told you. I was going back to the camp after I heard the shouting, but, before I could find strength to move, the runners were coming towards me."

"Come back to the camp," commanded Irritcha.

They began to walk, and they went all the way in silence. Irritcha watched the boy creep up to his fire, where it showed the faintest trace of light in the first raying of dawn. Irritcha was glad that it had not been necessary for him to kill the boy with his hands, where he had found him on the creek. If the boy had seen the magic rites of the terrible Vengeance Party, Irritcha would have had no choice but to destroy him. It was the Law.

. . . .

As season followed season and year followed year, Gurra, tall and strong, a leader in the hunt, advanced in his knowledge of the Tribal Country as he roamed it with his Family Group, and grew in his knowledge of the sacred lore. Always his love of beauty stayed with him. Each year, he watched for the flowers of the bloodwood trees and the mulga trees. In all seasons, he looked for the flocks of white cockatoos, the scarlet and green parrots, the pink galahs, and the bright grass-green budgerigars. Passing through the high and rugged gaps in the ranges, his senses were stirred by the splendid strength of their rock sides. The yellow, red and brown, the grey and white, of rock and earth and creek-bed moved him to endless pleasure. The wisps of smoke rising from his people's cooking-fires as he approached them at the end of the day always made him warmly happy. All his natural surroundings, the lives and the ways of his people, were beautiful beyond words to Gurra, and he would often make up little songs expressing his pleasure. Gurra's songs were popular in the camp, and every now and then somebody would be heard singing one or other of them, such as—

The tall ghost gums of Lilliri Creek
stand dreamily quiet in the still noon.

Their clouds of green leaves make great shadows
on the white sands and their own white branches.

It is very pleasant to shelter from the hot sun
under the strong branches of the ghost gums.

All is still and quiet. Even the black crows
are quiet, and the heat-haze shimmers noiselessly.

All is quiet. All is quiet. Then suddenly,
as if from nowhere, comes a great clamour.

The budgerigars come, with a great clamour,
twittering and whistling along Lilliri Creek.

The budgerigars come in a green cloud,
brighter green than the green leaves of the ghost gums.

We lift up our heads to look at the twittering budgerigars,
as they sweep out of sight along Lilliri Creek.

There were other songs which Gurra had made up about the birds and animals, trees and flowers, of the bush, and about sunrise and sunset. Now people called Gurra the Song-maker. Whenever he made up a new song, there would be a new interest and excitement in the camp; and, indeed, if more than one moon went by without a fresh song from Gurra, the campfolk would begin to twit and pester him. "What is the matter with our Song-maker?" they would say, or "It's time somebody made up a song about the way the leaves talk to themselves," or "A brown hawk flew overhead just now. There should be a song about that particular brown hawk. Did you see it, Gurra?"

And sooner or later, Gurra would begin to think about this new song. Sometimes he would have one ready very quickly, but, at other times, it would take him several days to make up a song that pleased him well enough to give to the camp.

As the features of Gurra's Tribal Country and the customs of the Tribe gained special meanings through his experience of sacred ritual, his admission into the Secret Life, their beauty blossomed and enlarged in his mind and heart. The early childish delight and love he had felt, when a small boy, for familiar things never faded as he grew older; although the mysteries that had alarmed and frightened him then no longer existed as dark and fearful. They were explained to him one by one, as he grew to manhood and, once he understood them, the mysteries themselves he found beautiful.

Roland Robinson

TWO NARRATIVES FROM *ABORIGINAL MYTHS AND LEGENDS**

THE STAR-TRIBES

Look, among the boughs, those stars are all mai, men. There's Ngintu, with his dogs, he guards the skins of Everlasting Water in the sky. There's the serpent, Thurroo, he lives up there. There's Moiree mulleirn, the emu. There's Warkin, the crow, carrying Keerki, the wounded hawk-man, on his back. There's Kapeetah, the moon-man, sitting in his mia-mia.

There's Mullorkurra, that's those Seven Sisters. They're winerr, they're girls. They make the real cold frost. They're travelling across the sky. In the old times when we had the fires, when the old people were camped out, those girls would look down from the sky and see the fires. And "Mai, mai, mai", they'd sing out as they ran across the sky.

We'd say, "O that's the Mullorkurra, they're going back east". They make water, you know, when they run back. They make the real cold frost. And when you'd wake, you'd find your swag, the camp, the plains, all white with frost. Tukurr, we call it, the real cold frost.

MAPOORAM

You go out and camp somewhere. You might be lying down and a little bit of wind comes. You hear this "mapooram". "What's that?" you say. Why, that's a "mapooram". You go and find that tree rubbing itself. It calls out, "mapooram, mapooram". That's two trees rubbing together in the wind.

That tree, it makes all sorts of noises in the wind. It might be like a sheep, "maa-maa", sometimes like a baby crying,

---

* As related to Roland Robinson by Fred Biggs, Ngeamba Tribe, who, "now deceased, was one of the few de-tribalized Aborigines whose narratives were of a tribal nature". New South Wales location.

sometimes like someone calling, sometimes like a sort of whistling-calling when the wind comes and swings two boughs like that.

When this Wirreengun, the clever-feller, sings that tree, he hums this song, it's a song to bring things out, or close things up. He fetches that girl, or a woman of some sort, out of that tree. She's got long hair, right down to her back. She's a nice build, you know. He's got her for himself. He'll keep her now.

One evening, it was sort of rainy-dark. They started to build a mia-mia, stripping bark, lots of it comes off by itself. You've been out in the bush and seen that old dry pine with the bark coming off. Well, you get a good lot of bark off them old pines, before they go too far, you know.

Well, that woman from the tree, she got hold of the bark and pulled it. It tore off up and up the tree. That bark pulled her up into the tree, and up into the sky. She has gone from that Wirreengun. That was the end of it. He never seen her no more.

Well, that's all I know. It's no use me telling you a lie. That's all I heard about that from the old folks.

Origins and Theory

James Devaney

TWO EXTRACTS FROM *THE VANISHED TRIBES*

[The following extracts from the story "Broken-Face" exhibit the only occurrences in *The Vanished Tribes*, apart from the glossary, of the name Jindyworobak. The glossary lists:
Jindy-neelingo: Gaunt or thin
Jindy-worabak: To annex; to join
Note that Ingamells changed both form and spelling slightly.]

They were silent as they approached the old swimming-place of Erra-go-din, long abandoned because the terrible Wootcha lived there. Wootcha had belonged to the strong Jindy-worabaks, the enemies of the thin-legged Jindy-neelingos, a shaggy giant in the tribe, and a hated boaster and bully. None could stand against him, and he had been a tyrant and a nuisance in all the camps, doing whatever he would, until at last the whole tribe in self-protection turned against him. He was called Broken-Face because in the far days when he was still a young man he had been tracked and attacked by the men of his tribe for taking their gins, and left for dead, with his face gashed across by a heavy war boomerang; but his strength was wonderful and he had got well again.

[After Broken-Face kills Dherang.]

Then [Wawoon] got mud from the river bank and honey from her dillybag, and with these she filled his wounds.

"That fellow close up finish," said Broken-Face, speaking the Jindy-worabak words which sounded strange to her. "Lonely fellow me, nobody to make fire, nobody to sit down and catch nits out of my head."

"I am Dherang's gin, I am not your gin," cried Wawoon.

Rex Ingamells

EXTRACT FROM A LETTER TO MILES FRANKLIN, 16 MARCH 1948

"Jindy-worabak"—as the word appeared when it first hit my eye—appears in the glossary of Jim Devaney's *The Vanished Tribes*, where it is given the meaning "to annex, to join". I found it there in 1936, and have seen it dictionaried nowhere else, but Jim assured me it was a word of "a Queensland tribe".*

In adopting it for a special campaign, I reckoned it to have the following merits:

1. It is *Aboriginal* and therefore apt in denoting interest in the indigenous.
2. It is (or was) *outlandish* according to fashionable literary tastes, which deserved a shock.
3. It has an apt *symbolism* from its meaning:
    (a) denoting synthesis of our European cultural heritage with our Australian heritage. I've expressed this variously—e.g., "our English Mother tongue and our Australian Mother Land".
    (b) specifically "directing the attention of Australian writers and artists to what should be their distinctive material".

Part 3 has the real answer to what you want, so please forgive the long prologue. In the first Jindy publication *Conditional Culture* (1938) I gave 3b as the intent of the application. A few weeks later, in the first newspaper report on the Movement, "The Jindyworobaks Come Forth" (Adelaide, *The News*), I gave the reporter 3a as the intent. Both are right, obviously bound up with one another. Some people assume that "Jin-

---

* Although Ingamells says above that he "found" the word Jindyworobak in *The Vanished Tribes* in 1936, in his *Selected Poems* he dates the verse fragments "Garchooka" and "Garrakeen" 1934 and 1935. A curious observation may follow. Both these names for parrots are used by Devaney; therefore Ingamells must have *read* the book before 1936. Since his use of the word Jindyworobak corresponds with Devaney's glossary entry, but not with his use of the word in the story where it occurs, he evidently "found" it again in 1936 in the glossary and used it in the sense there defined without referring to the story.

dyworobak", meaning "to join" signified the joining of the Club; and they can have that meaning too, if they like, although it was never the basic one, and, according as the Jindyworobak publishing and ideas have advanced, the Club has fallen into the background. Instead of worrying about a host of members, we are, in the Club sense, a small group of people.

P.R. Stephensen

TWO EXTRACTS FROM *THE FOUNDATIONS OF CULTURE IN AUSTRALIA*

COLONY OR NATION

What then of culture in Australia? Here is not a mere vicinity, but a whole continent, unique in its natural features, and unique in the fact of its continental homogeneity of race and language. Australia is the only continent on the earth inhabited by one race, under one government, speaking one language. The population at present is not much greater than was that of Britain in Shakespeare's time, but by the end of the twentieth century we may expect that the population will expand to at least twenty millions, remaining of European parent-stock, but with locally-developed characteristics, and with a locally-created culture. Australia will then become indubitably recognized as a nation, and will lose all trace of colonial status.

As a colony, we exported raw material and imported manufactured goods and loans. The trade traffic was two-ways. *We imported also the imponderables, culture, by a system of one-way traffic.* As a nation we shall continue to import culture, but we shall export it also, as our contribution to world-ideas—there will then be a two-ways traffic in the imponderables.

At this present time (1935) we are no longer a colony pure and simple, nor yet are we a nation fully-fledged. We are something betwixt and between a colony and a nation, something vaguely called a "dominion", or a "commonwealth" with "dominion status". We are loosely tied to other dominions in the British Empire by law, strongly tied by sentiment and an idea of mutual protection. Inasmuch as we are politically autonomous, we have entered into virtual alliances (political, military, commercial, and sentimental) with other dominions or colonies in the Empire, including Canada, the Irish Free State, South Africa, New Zealand, Great Britain, and Jamaica. Where it will all lead to we do not know; but the virtual alliance gives us a sense of security in international affairs for the time being. The political and legal ties that bind us to the other dominions are loose enough, but the sentimental and financial tie is strong, particularly with the dominion called Great Britain. And the cultural tie is strong.

Is it sedition or blasphemy to the idea of the British Empire to suggest that each dominion in this loose alliance will tend to become autonomous politically, commercially, and *culturally*? A military alliance between the various component "nations" of the Empire may perhaps survive long after the other ties have, in fact, been weakened—though this would be contrary to the lessons of history. Such a prognostication has nothing to do with aesthetics. What matters for present purposes is that Australia has nowadays an acknowledged right to become one of the nations of the world. Australian nationalism, with or without the idea of the British Empire, has a right to exist; and there can be no nation without a national place-idea; a national culture.

HISTORY

The Aborigines, our admirable predecessors in sovereignty over the territory of Australia Felix, had their bora ceremonies, their initiation corroborees; during which the seniors took the young men away into a sacred place, knocked out with a sacred stone a tooth from each candidate for knowledge (in order to test the youths' resistance to hardship and pain), and then told them, with awe-inspiring circumstance, the holy secrets of the tribe. We white Australians should consider the advisability of doing something of the same kind.

Just as the sacred traditions and legends of an Aboriginal tribe provide that tribe with a collective soul and a continuity, *so written history and literature provide a civilized nation with a national soul and a coherence*. The recitation of national lore provides the foundation of a national survival-idea. Without this recitation of lore there can be no national centre: no nation. A nation is positively identified with its lore, which is actively handed down from generation to generation. This is the true meaning of culture in any place—preservation of tribal or national experience in a memorable form; in holy scriptures, in churinga, in *literature*; because of the coherence-value, the discipline-value, the survival-value of that experience and lore.

Those who say that Australia "has no history" are merely talking utter, arrogant, academic nonsense.

Our history and pedigree prior to the nineteenth century is the whole history of England, or of Britain; a history which belongs to us as much as it does to any modern inhabitant of Bournemouth, Leeds, Glasgow, Cork, Llanelly, Tolpuddle, Margate, or Stow-in-the-Wold. We inherit, and are proud of inheriting, British history, legend, and lore—*up to a certain point in British history*: after that point we begin to diverge, we begin to have our own history.

We have a right to our own Australian nineteenth and twentieth centuries—our first and second centuries ... In particular, the seven decades from 1850 to 1920 are the foundation decades of the Australian nation; and, as such, are of indelible interest to us.

Only an academic mugwump, blinded by the formalities of learning, could contend that nothing much of importance, *to Australians*, occurred in Australia between 1850 and 1920.

During those seven decades the merino sheep was bred, in Australia, from a mixed and dubious European ancestry, to the magnificent beast for his purpose that he is today—modesty prevents an analogy from being drawn too strongly: it is enough to say that seven decades of sheep experience was enough to produce a new kind of remarkable sheep in Australia, and that possibly something of the same kind has happened to the humans here during the same period of time.

In the matter of pedigrees, as any sheep-breeder knows, *recent history is always of more importance than remote ancestry.*

A nation can change its entire calibre, outlook, characteristics, and quality in 150 years. The French nation, for example, since the date of James Cook's "discovery" of our Australia, has experienced the enormous events of the French revolution, the Napoleonic wars, the Franco-Prussian war, and the "Great" war; has become industrialized, and has acquired a colonial empire. These comparatively recent events are of more profound significance to Frenchmen of today than the whole of previous French history from Charlemagne to Louis XV.

In the same way, the industrialization and imperial expansion of Britain, during the reigns of Queen Victoria, Edward VII and of George V, have had a *profounder mental effect* upon the inhabitants of England, Ireland, Scotland and Wales than all the events of previous British history from Alfred the Great to George the Fourth.

Recent events, very recent events, in Russia, Germany, and Italy, are certainly more significant to Russians, Germans, and Italians of today respectively than all their previous histories of a thousand years.

It is a nice point to decide at what period in retrospect history ceases to be a vital study, and becomes a mere academic exercise. It seems doubtful whether anything which occurred more than 150 years ago is of anything but academic interest for Australians of today, *or for the people of any other nation of today*. History took such a new and extraordinary trend everywhere throughout the world during the nineteenth century, with the coming of the machine epoch, changing all human categories and values so profoundly, that the relative importance of everything which happened before that nineteenth century has dwindled.

National lore, in Australia particularly, but also in every other country on the globe, should be concerned with the recitation and digestion and *vital study* of what has happened during the nineteenth and early twentieth centuries. The place for all history earlier than that is in dustbins—and universities.

Rex Ingamells

THREE EXTRACTS FROM *CONDITIONAL CULTURE*

GUM TREES IN ITALY

Norman Douglas, who has spent most of a long life in clarifying for mankind a standard of values derived from the Mediterranean, and who has never been to Australia, has written about gum trees from a rigidly circumscribed Old World point of view.

> You walk to this building along an avenue of eucalypti planted some forty years ago. Detesting as I do the whole tribe of gum trees, I never lose an opportunity of saying exactly what I think about this particularly odious representative of the brood, this eyesore, this grey-haired scarecrow, this reptile of a growth with which a pack of misguided enthusiasts has disfigured the whole Mediterranean basin. They have now realized that it is useless as a protection against malaria. Soon enough they will learn that, instead of preventing the disease, it actually fosters it, by harbouring clouds of mosquitoes in its scraggy so-called foliage. These abominations may look better on their native heath; I sincerely hope they do. Judging by *The Dead Heart of Australia*—a book which gave me a nightmare from which I shall never recover— I should say that a varnished hop-pole would be a god-send out there. But from here the intruder should be expelled without mercy. No plant on earth rustles in such a horribly metallic fashion when the wind blows through the everlasting withered branches; the noise chills one to the marrow; it is like the sibilant chatterings of ghosts. Its oil is called "medicinal" only because it happens to smell rather nasty; it is worthless as timber, objectionable in form and hue—objectionable above all things in its perverse, anti-human habits. What other tree would have the effrontery to turn the sharp edges of its leaves—as if these were not narrow enough already —towards the sun, so as to be sure of giving at all hours of the day the minimum of shade to mankind?
>
> But I confess that this avenue of Policoro almost reconciled me to the existence of the anaemic Antipodeans. Almost; since for some reason or other (perhaps on account of the insufferably foul nature of the soil) their foliage is here thickly tufted, it glows like burnished gold in the sunshine, like enamelled scales of green and gold. These eucalypti are unique in Italy. Gazing upon them my heart softened, and I almost forgave them their manifold iniquities,

their diabolical thirst, their demoralizing aspect, precocious senility and vice, their peeling bark suggestive of unmentionable skin diseases, and that system of radication which is nothing but a scandal on this side of the globe.

This piece of natural description is very stimulating. While there are certain misstatements due to ignorance, there is sincerity in the whole: it is the outcry of a civilized European who feels his sense of values to be outraged. Mr Douglas would be outraged at the thought of himself taking an attitude of orthodox respectability; yet he does so here: There is, indeed, truth in the passage, but not—as Mr Douglas has said in parallel circumstances—the whole truth. It would be as easy to caricature an oak and a weeping willow as loathsome examples of senility and obeseness: it is a matter of point of view. Mr Douglas's caricature is, indeed, so excellent that one recognizes the gum and could recognize no other tree in it. I am a devout reader of his prolific writings, have enjoyed *South Wind, Siren Land, Old Calabria* (whence this quotation comes), *Along, Looking Back*, and several other of his books; and cannot gainsay the author's fundamental sanity and genius, yet there is one thing I know well which Mr Douglas does not. I mean the gum tree in its infinite variety of species and individuality. I have yet to witness a single withered, fire-scarred, flood-marked example which does not look beautiful drenched in sun-glamour at the end of day or sparkling with dew in the early morning. And there are massive and magnificent trees which look beautiful at any time of the day or night. Mr Douglas has not seen any, as I have done, grotesque and ugly, ghastly in glare and mirage, insanely clutching and huddling under the stars, and horribly tortured under the glimmer of a red moon; yet I am not alone in seeing a stark and vivid beauty about them even then.

In spite of sternness, Mr Douglas does relent for an instant, and catches a fleeting glimpse of beauty in the gum trees: " . . . their foliage is here thickly tufted, it glows like burnished gold in the sunshine, like enamelled scales of green and gold". Thank you, Mr Douglas, for the mite! It symbolizes a first step. Before long, the strange, unorthodox beauty of the Australian gum tree, and many other manifestations of beauty peculiar to this country, will find a sure place in the standards of general culture, which will be one stage nearer universality and so much the richer.

ENVIRONMENTAL VALUES

The natural distinctiveness of the Australian continent from other lands of the world is too fundamental to vanish in the period of human history. The massive gum trees along the banks of the Murray, the gums and the mallee and the tea-tree that straggle about this vast continent; the empty spaces of our deserts; and the atonal music of the magpie and the good-natured mockery of the kookaburra—these are things that must remain. They belong to the indestructible spirit of the place about which D.H. Lawrence has written in a superb piece of natural description at the beginning of *Kangaroo*. But D.H. Lawrence realized that spirit, however intensely, only in a small part: he did not feel at home in the bush, although its power gripped him. There are thousands of Australians today who, if they have not found eloquent tongue, feel, nevertheless, with childlike devotion, the familiar beauty and utter loveliness of the outback environment in many of its moods.

Our pioneers, or the majority of them, were Englishmen who brought to this country the English manners and customs of the moment of their migration. As long as they lived they were strangers in a strange land. Many of them may have become more or less used to their new environment, but they never could become one with it. The background of their minds was made up of other associations. Yet they were isolated from the current movements of fashion and culture in the old country: in this sense they slipped behind the times. The English manners and customs which they inculcated into their children were bound to be considerably out of date by the time those children reached maturity. Thus the word "colonial" was justified, in so far as it signified rawness and lack of sophistication.

Although fresh influences were continually coming in, these were neither sufficient nor strong enough to compete with the isolation and environmental resistance, and could work only superficially. Hence any genuine culture that might develop in Australia, however it might be refreshed and inspired by English influences, would have to represent the birth of a new soul. A fundamental break, that is, with the spirit of English culture, is the prerequisite for the development of an Australian culture. Without the fact of ultimate individuality, separate identity, any general sense of culture in any country must be misty and anaemic. However strong and innumerable, however desirable and inevitable, however traditional our cultural ties with Europe may be, it is not in these ties that we must as a people seek our individuality. Its quintessence must lie in the realization of whatever things are distinctive in our environment and their sublimation in art and idea, in culture.

Australian culture is at present in a nebulous stage, because our writers have not come clearly to any such realization. I do not wish to be misunderstood. Some of the greatest Australian literature yet to be may have no local colour at all. Its settings may be in China or Mars. Our best poetry must deal with universal themes; and whether or not the Australian environment forms a background is a matter for individual poets. But all this does not affect the essence of my argument. The real test of a people's culture is the way in which they can express themselves in relation to their environment, and the loftiness and universality of their artistic conceptions raised on that basis. When, for example, someone begins a novel and sets the scene in Australia, he cannot hope to produce great art unless he has a true conception of environmental values. When our writers understand these, they will look at most of what they have written to date and say, "That is the way not to write about Australia".

The biggest curse and handicap upon our literature is the incongruous use of metaphors, similes, and adjectives. It is usual to find Australian writers describing the bush with much the same terminology as English writers apply to a countryside of oaks and elms and yews and weeping willows, and of skylarks, cuckoos, and nightingales. We find that dewdrops are spoken of as jewels sparkling on the foliage of gum trees. Jewels? Not amid the stark, contorted, shaggy informality of the Australian bushland. Nothing could be more incongruous. Jewels? I see the pageantry of the Old World, and of the march of history from the time when the Norman ladies came to England to the present day, when glittering cosmopolitan crowds mingle in the casinos of Monte Carlo and the ornate ballrooms of Venice; I see the royal courts of England, and those of France and Spain now forgotten; and I see, if you like, a vice-regal gathering or a theatrical party in Adelaide—but I do not, cannot, see jewels metaphored off on gum trees, which are so far removed from all the things with which jewels are traditionally associated. I cannot deplore too vehemently the dangerous habit of using figures of speech with regard to essentially Australian things which call up such a flood of Old World associations as to gloze over all distinctiveness. It has been a piteous custom to write of Australian things with the English idiom, an idiom which can achieve exactness in England but not here.

THE WORD "JINDYWOROBAK"

"Jindyworobak" is an Aboriginal word meaning "to annex, to join", and I propose to coin it for a particular use. The Jindyworobaks, I say, are those individuals who are endeavouring to free Australian art from whatever alien influences trammel it, that is, to bring it into proper contact with its material. They are the few who seriously realize that an Australian culture depends on the fulfilment and sublimation of certain definite conditions, namely:
1. A clear recognition of environmental values.
2. The debunking of much nonsense.
3. An understanding of Australia's history and traditions, primaeval, colonial, and modern.

The most important of these is the first. Pseudo-Europeanism clogs the minds of most Australians, preventing a free appreciation of nature. Their speech and thought idioms are European; they have little direct thought-contact with nature. Although emotionally and spiritually they should be, and, I believe, are more attuned to the distinctive bush, hill and coastal places they visit than to the European parks and gardens around the cities, their thought-idiom belongs to the latter not the former. Give them a suitable thought-idiom for the former and they will be grateful. Their more important emotional and spiritual potentialities will be given the conditions for growth. The inhibited individuality of the race will be released. Australian culture will exist.

Victor Kennedy

EXTRACT FROM *FLAUNTED BANNERS*

The word Jindyworobak is an Aboriginal word meaning to join or link up. Broadly speaking it is used by the Club in the sense of joining or linking up Australian white culture with its own environment.

Mr Ingamells defines it this way:

> "Jindyworobak" is an Aboriginal word meaning "to annex, to join", and I propose to coin it for a particular use. The Jindyworobaks are those individuals who are endeavouring to free Australian art from whatever alien influences trammel it, that is to bring it into proper contact with its material.

An essential part of its environment—its material—is the tradition of the land. This naturally involves an appreciation of Aboriginal tribal history and culture, not for its own isolated sake but for its direct bearing upon our own culture, or the bearing it should have.

Actually the only true and sincere Australian culture is that of the Aboriginal race because it has sprung direct from its own pre-existing conditions. The folk lore of the Aborigines for instance was not something imposed upon an environment; it was the natural consequence of that environment. The sunsets that blazed upon the stark forbidding hills, and shot long shadows deep into the heart of the mysterious bush did not remain forboding and gloomy and menacing when interpreted by the unspoilt children of the land itself. They were part of it all and though it had its supernatural terrors for them (as external nature still has with more of us than admit it frankly) they did not escape from it into a land of make-believe and simpering abstractions. They were swept along in it; were flesh and bone of it; were created and re-created in it. Their dream-life, more sincere than our own simulated spiritualities, was all concerned with the *alcheringas* of their own traditions peopled with the images—the good and the bad, the mean and aspiring—of their own race life. We who came later and occupied their country, the country that still reared its hills and its bush in the presence of its flaming suns, ignored all this tradition. Our first concern was to rob and butcher the first race and as they had no written language their culture

—a very high artistic accomplishment—died with them. That is to a great extent. A few painstaking investigators are rescuing some of it, a poor remnant but sufficient for appraisal. With eyes and minds set upon the origins of our own immediate forebears we have endeavoured to graft a culture born of other environments upon a new and very different country. We have not yet learned that man cannot live anywhere without adapting himself to the country and its climate and absorbing its atmosphere. The country will not adapt itself to him. In Australia the bush remains; what are called "the wide open spaces" remain; so do all the conditions that called forth the particular culture of the Aborigines. There is no question of becoming Aboriginal, or eating goannas or living a primitive existence in a gunyah. The question that does stare us in the face is that we have to let the sunlight of this land into our souls. We have to see those blazing colours that Rex Ingamells sees so vividly because he has shed from his mind the fog refractions of an alien sun:

> Garrakeen, the parakeet, is slim and swift.
> Like a spear of green and red he flashes through
> The cumbered branches of the river-bank . . .

The observation is correct in the first place but the significance lies in the simile of the second line which is derived not from the decayed romanticism of a familiar literature but from the very world around. The verse has fixed the sense of swift movement and vivid colour inherent in the subject. A feeling of the capabilities of this landscape persists, the keener because the picture is not photographic. Detail is less important than the successful expression of a character.

A smiliar effect is achieved by the same writer when he seeks to evoke a double realization of sound and vision:

> Scarlet-and-green
> sky-streaking parrot-fires, with parrot-shrieks
> Echo-shattering the shoulders of the hills . . .

I am not inviting discussion just now upon the actual technique—the compounds or hyphenates for instance—although not a little of the success of the verse is due to method. The direct approach, the elimination of all non-essential wordage, the emergence of something like a new and appropriate idiom, and the limitless conception of the third line interact to produce a definite challenge to accepted habits of observation. The one thing these lines do not lack is authentic atmosphere. Apply them to an English countryside and they become not only meaningless but crude. Apply any applicable line from Shelley to the Australian bush and it will become not crude but wretched. Yet this is just what has been going on for a century in Australia, except of course for a handful of "cranks" who constitutionally could not see inland river mists in terms of soupy Channel fogs.

Rex Ingamells

EXTRACT FROM A LETTER TO W.F. HUDSON, 27 JUNE 1941

... How does *At a Boundary* strike you? Can you stomach the political implications of "Gangrened People" for example, or do you feel the whole pome to be maudlin? When I mentioned my "sterility" to you, I would perhaps have conveyed my meaning better if I'd said "maudlinism", meaning my sterility of anything worthwhile. I wrote the "G.P." in a fever of feeling and conviction, but having finished it, instead of feeling elated and sure of myself, I'm dogged with doubts. I've preserved my faith in its ideas but have I made 'em poetry? In other words am I still a poet or am I becoming more and more of a twirp? ...

This war business. I've not a speck of imperial patriotism, but my Australianism is strong enough to get me into the air force if the Japs make a move south ...

Rex Ingamells

A STATEMENT IN *JINDYWOROBAK ANTHOLOGY 1945*

1. The essay *On Environmental Values*, upon which Jindyworobak was founded, took its rise from criticism of my early verse by Professor L.F. Giblin, Edward Garnett and John Masefield, all of whom stressed the importance of *accuracy* in natural description. Their relevant correspondence falls within the period from late 1933 to 1935. Professor Giblin's foreword to my first book, *Gumtops* (April 1935), is, so far as print is concerned, the starting-point of Jindyworobak "theory". I do not mean that Thomas McCombie, A.G. Stephens and others never existed, but that I was not aware of them.

2. In late 1935, I read the first part of P.R. Stephensen's *The Foundations of Culture in Australia* in the first and only issue of *The Australian Mercury*. I found this stimulating and provocative in the writing of *On Environmental Values*— stimulating because it treated Australian poetry seriously, and provided my first lesson on the beginnings, provocative because I considered it critically inadequate.

3. Either late in 1935 or early in 1936, I read *The Vanished Tribes* by James Devaney and decided on the word "Jindyworobak", adapted from the glossary, as the symbolic word for which I was looking.

4. It was in *Chapbook, An Australian Magazine*, edited by Alan Francis and Rex Wood, Second Number, 1936, that the word "Jindyworobak" was first used to symbolize distinctive Australian quality in literature.

5. *On Environmental Values* was delivered as an address to the English Association, Adelaide, early in 1937. Professor J.I.M. Stewart was chairman. The opinions expressed by speakers in the audience were, for the most part, vigorously dissentient. The essay was then published in *Venture, 1937*.

6. In 1937 and 1938, Ian Tilbrook, Flexmore Hudson and Max Harris were first victims to my insistence that there must be a Jindyworobak Club. F.H. did not like "Jindyworobak" as a name at all—but his help, in spite of this, was considerable and, in the circumstances, especially appreciated. The first

Jindyworobak publication was *Conditional Culture* (1938). I sent circulars to all Australian universities, asking English professors to make it known that verse was desired for the first Anthology. Silence came from N.S.W. and Queensland. Flexmore Hudson, knowing my predicament, got busy and sent me advice that there was one, Paul L. Grano, in Brisbane to whom I should airmail; and this resulted in a much stronger front for *Jindyworobak Anthology, 1938*. The association of P.L.G., Victor Kennedy and some other Queenslanders with the *Anthology* dates from the first issue. I did not know that James Devaney lived in Q., or he would not have escaped.

7. In 1939, Messrs E.B. Wichert and C. Jutsum established a branch of the Jindyworobak Club at Broken Hill, and a lively branch it was until the war cut it off.

8. In July 1940, although he had contributed when asked to the second *Anthology*, I met Ian Mudie for the first time. Aboriginal life and legend were, from the outset, fundamental to the Jindyworobak outlook, but it was I.M. who awakened me to the significance of the Alcheringa as being a symbol, and not only a subject, within Australian literature. In this year there would have been no *Anthology* had not John Ingamells attended to most of the circularizing and correspondence. In the next year that service was performed by Ian Mudie.

9. From the start, naturally, there had been much adverse criticism of the new movement, but, beginning in March 1941, a line of criticism was adopted in *The Bulletin*, the circumstances of which I investigated in *Jindyworobak Anthology, 1941*. The only Jindyworobak publication since noticed in *The Bulletin*, so far as I am aware, is *Poets at War*, which we published in conjunction with Georgian House. As the Red Page told its readers, and as acknowledgments showed, *The Bulletin* contribution to this book was important. *The Bulletin*, however, had refused Jindyworobak the addresses of its soldier poets, so that permissions were got through other channels and, in accordance with a policy which must be harder to sustain each year, *The Bulletin* did not acknowledge Jindyworobak's part in the publishing.

10. My association with P.R. Stephensen and Australia First began in July 1941. This association induced R.G. Howarth to suggest that Jindyworobak stood for "Australia Only". This he did in the editorial of *Southerly* for November that year. Breaking a seven months' silence in his correspondence to me, four months later, R.G.H., however, declared: "I was rather horrified, as a matter of fact, that Christesen took the editorial

as part of an attack on you. Nothing was further from my intention". And, subsequently, following a two-way renewal of correspondence, the matter was aired—*Southerly* fashion, as I could not see my way clear to send in an article when invited. R.G.H. has always been ready to assist Jindyworobak when appealed to.

11. P.R. Stephensen's fine book, *The Foundations of Culture in Australia*, which I read through for the first time in 1941, has had a definite effect in educating Jindyworobak. Other Australia First people have helped Jindyworobak—and helped other well-known literary institutions in Australia—with financial backing for publications. So far as Jindyworobak is concerned, no conditions were ever attached to such help. It was freely and generously given in the cause of Australian literature.

12. William Hart-Smith's association with Jindyworobak, destined to be a major formative influence, began in 1940, and 1941 marked the advent of Gina Ballantyne, as sound a warrior as any we have. Jindyworobak has rested on many shoulders besides mine, and the state editors, W.H.S., Victor Kennedy and Ian Tilbrook, besides others as well known, have shaped its character. The policy of varying editorship of the *Anthology* has increased the value of the movement. While specialization in Australian themes is our choice, truth and its expression in literature must be our justification.

Criticism

JINDYWOROBAK AND *THE BULLETIN*

REVIVAL IN POETRY?*

Recalling the astonishing renaissance of poetry during the emotional turmoil of the last war, the Red Page has several times discussed the possibility of a revival in Australian literature to correspond with the invigorating of the nation in the present crisis. It is beginning to look as if something of the sort is happening. [. . . . . .] As many as four anthologies are likely to appear in 1941.

Immediately the Red Page made its recent suggestion that there should be annual anthologies of Australian poetry and short stories as a sort of summing up of the year's effort and a spur to the next year's, Angus and Robertson got in touch with *The Bulletin*, and it is now likely that both anthologies will make their first appearance this year. Preparation of the volume of verse is already under way.

The other anthologies likely to appear are Dr George Mackaness's selections from Australian poetry from its beginnings to the present day (a collection previously mentioned on this page); the customary *Jindyworobak Anthology*, where the young writers have their fling; and a collection of contemporary writings which the Red Page understands is being prepared by a well-known critic for the Limited Editions Society. [. . . . . .]

* *Bulletin* Red Page article, 19 March 1941

All of this activity indicates at least a desire to sum up, to collate and evaluate the work of the past. This is a stage from which a new departure is possible.

Though nothing of importance has as yet been achieved, there are two indications that something is stirring, that vital writing is likely to emerge before very long. One is that, all the way from Adelaide to Brisbane, poets and would-be poets are showing an intense interest in modern experimental verse and in the possibility of evolving a distinctively Australian version of the modern movements. The Jindyworobak productions, published in Adelaide but accepting contributions from all over the commonwealth, have let loose some extraordinarily bad verse. But that doesn't say that the movement is without significance. It is proof of a desperate desire to write poetry—and to write a valuable kind of poetry, based in a pantheistic interpretation of the Australian landscape—and it is more likely than not that some genuine poet, in whom the group's feelings coalesce, will emerge.

A somewhat similar group, though wider in range, not so dominated by a single idea as the Jindyworobakians, is gathered round Brian Vrepont in Queensland, and has just issued the second of its *Meanjin Papers*, consisting of "modernist" verse, with an introduction by James Picot discussing contemporary giants and the importance of the long poem. Here, too, desire seems to outrun performance: but it is worth noting that the desire exists, and the effort towards important poetry is being made.

According to a note the Red Page has received from Queenslander Victor Kennedy, the Jindyworobak Club is preparing a critical study of the state and prospects of Australian poetry. Leading poets and critics are to be invited to answer the question "What do you think of the new verse?" and the resultant essays will be published in book form. Something valuable, it's certain, will come out of this widespread awakening of interest in what one must (vaguely and inaccurately) call the "modern" movement.

The second pointer to a genuine poetic revival is something which could safely have been prophesied, but which will come as news to most people outside newspaper offices: that is, that an increasing stream of verse is beginning to flow back to Australia from men abroad with the A.I.F. It's coming, obviously, from men who have never written poetry before [. . . . . .] So far, most of the verse that has come to *The Bulletin* has been pretty bad. But it's certain that someone will emerge to express what so many men are feeling.

NOTES ON A BANNER BEARER*

Bearing a banner with a strange device—"Jindyworobak"—Queenslander Victor Kennedy in *Flaunted Banners* (Jindyworobak Club, Adelaide) buffets his way through snowstorms of "obtuseness of thought", climbs manfully over imaginary crags of "antagonism" and "actual resentment" and, alone upon the mountain top, waves his challenge at the sky.

In reality it is only at the heavens that he can rage; for, far from attacking or ignoring the Jindyworobak movement in Australian poetry, *The Bulletin* and such other journals as pay any attention to verse, because the movement is Australian and because its writers are trying hard to do something, have given it far more serious attention than the quality of the poems in its anthologies to date have [*sic*] warranted.

Movements in poetry are judged not by their theories, but by their fruits: Milton makes good poetry out of a sonorous Latinity, so that the "grand manner" is a good theory; Wordsworth makes good poetry out of the everyday speech of the people, so that the humble manner is a good theory; Tennyson believed in a marble smoothness, Browning in a bouncing roughness; the Georgians wrote some lovely lyrics, Spender and MacNeice, who repudiate the Georgians, also write good poetry. Any theory of poetry is good so long as it works; that is, if it produces good poetry.

It's a good sign of life and vigour in Australian poetry that a new theory is being evolved, that the Jindyworobaks, in their belligerent Australianism and in their technical experiments, want to produce a kind of art that is, say, the direct opposite of Hugh McCrae's. But that theory, as far as the anthologies have indicated, has yet to *work*. It is not Mr Kennedy's pamphlet that will be the vindication of the Jindyworobak theory, but one good poem written by a Jindyworobak: one poem as good in its own way as a McCrae poem is in its own way: one poem that in its own way enriches the Australian tradition as much as "The Man from Snowy River" enriched the tradition in Paterson's way.

Mr Kennedy knows this and more or less says so. But no "movement" can have any publicity or any fun unless it has enemies, so Mr Kennedy elects the Red Page as the Jindyworobak Public Enemy No. 1. The point on which he finds the Red Page hostile or "obtuse" or "destroying for destruction's sake" is this Page's query in a review some time

---

* *Bulletin* Red Page article, 3 September 1941

ago as to whether when he said that the Abos. "despite all flesh were my people" a Jindyworobak bard meant what he said. Mr Kennedy believes that the poet meant something else. The point is of no importance whatsoever, for the cold critical truth is that this particular poem, though a pleasant enough piece of verse and though mentioned here for the sake of giving the encouragement of publicity to the Jindyworobak movement, is simply not worth discussing, on its quality as poetry, as an enrichment of the literature of Australia.

That this last point is the only one that matters Mr Kennedy knows very well. Here is his summing up on the movement:

> The main point is that they are all going somewhere and in the development of their new forms, so long as they, too, are not mere external imitativeness of similar overseas movements, they are both refreshing and significant. Out of it all I predict that this movement will produce at least one good, sound, national poet for Australia.

And here is what the Red Page also said in a summing up of that movement:

> The Jindyworobak productions have let loose some extraordinarily bad verse. But that doesn't say that the movement is without significance. It is a proof of a desperate desire to write poetry—and to write a valuable kind of poetry, based in a pantheistic interpretation of the Australian landscape—and it is more likely than not that some genuine poet, in whom the group's feelings coalesce, will emerge.

Mr Kennedy must have his fun: and to have the fun of regarding the Red Page as his enemy-in-chief he has conveniently ignored the fact, obvious from these two summings-up, that he and this Page are in entire agreement on the one great essential—that while the movement's fireworks are a healthy sign of life, it is works of art that will finally vindicate it.

REX INGAMELLS

SOMETHING MORE THAN AN EDITOR'S NOTE*

The Bulletin
Bulletin Buildings,
252 George Street, Sydney.
August 6 [1941]

Dear Mr Ingamells,

I think it would be best if I didn't contribute to this year's Jindyworobak: but thanks all the same for the invitation. If the anthology's still the organ of a "movement", then I'm off its beat, and it's off mine; if its scope is broadened, it becomes a competitor with the anthology I've done for A & R. While I, personally, would be glad to see it expanded, and wish it all success, I think that it would hardly be fair to A & R for me to come in. Not that I imagine that it matters very much which anthology my verses happen to be in; but I'm considering it from A & R's point of view.

Yours sincerely,

(sgd.) DOUGLAS STEWART

The Jindyworobak Club
3 Harcourt Road,
Rugby,
South Australia.
November 26 [1941]

Dear Mr Stewart,

I wish neither to take lightly Australia's most famous critical page, on which you are a critic, nor to affront the dignity of Australia's most famous publishers, for whom you are an editor. Could you not have prevented the first from side-slipping in a way for which it must be held responsible? Have you not inaccurately represented the attitude of the second in a matter in which you must be held responsible?

The Red Page of March 19 noticeably allied its name with that of Angus & Robertson in an article which was noticeably ungracious to Jindyworobak. Your letter of August 6, written

* Statement in *Jindyworobak Anthology*, 1941

on *Bulletin* office-paper, insults Jindyworobak, apparently in the interests of Angus & Robertson. Red Page articles are seldom signed, but your letter is: and the whole concatenation of circumstances, from Jindyworobak's point of view, is such that for me to refrain from publicizing your letter in the course of combating them would be to render protest superficial.

Do the Red Page and your letter reveal a collusion, in antipathy to Jindyworobak, of *The Bulletin* and Angus & Robertson? I am going to answer this question, and ask others which it will be for you to answer.

When, in February, the manager of Angus & Robertson advised me that his firm was to begin publication this year of an annual anthology of Australian poetry, and invited me to contribute some of my work, it did not occur to me that, as proprietor of *Jindyworobak Publications*, I ought, in any circumstances, to consider A & R's projected anthology "a competitor" to my established three-year-old. Said Mr Cousins:

> The venture is not intended as a commercial enterprise, but as an effort to foster Australian literature.

I applauded the assurance and accepted the invitation; nor did subsequent thought convince me that I should be justified in slighting A & R by withdrawing my acceptance.

In May you wrote, as editor of A & R's anthology, to ask that you might use a poem I had sent to *The Bulletin* in preference to those I had sent to A & R. Your request was friendly, the more so perhaps because, as I now realize, the poems I had sent in were inferior, though you gave no hint that such was your opinion. I acceded to your request. In spite of my personal gratitude, however, your subsequent attempt, on August 6, to distinguish between a non-competing and a competing *Jindyworobak Anthology* is something you cannot be permitted to get away with. It was because I have great admiration for your poetry that I invited you to contribute to the anthology of which I am editor. Although I indicated to you that I was anxious to broaden Jindyworobak in the sense of bringing into its symbolic annual a number of poems, not essentially Australian, by writers not yet in its pages, I did not state that Jindyworobak would be any less Jindyworobak: for consciousness of the growth and intensification of its spirit alone could justify such broadening as I anticipated. Each past issue contains clear precedent for such expansion. This year's issue will reveal the process continuing. Jindyworobak still the organ of a movement? Of course, Mr Stewart—a growing movement. Jindyworobak is a vital and expanding force of which A & R's anthology, your anthology, cannot fail to be, to some degree, an implementation. Were you conscious that simply to say that, as a poet, you were off Jindyworobak's "beat" did not apply to you as editor of *Australian Poetry, 1941*, and could not excuse you, as poet-editor, for denying a *quid pro quo*? In spite of beats, you went to some pains to indicate that it would not matter much which anthology your verses were in, were it not for Angus & Robertson.

As Mr Cousins knew when he addressed me, Jindyworobak exists precisely "to foster Australian literature". He addressed me as editor of the *Jindyworobak Anthology*, and asked for cooperation in A & R's design. Jindyworobak, "a competitor" not to be helped by A & R's anthological editor! Am I to believe that Mr Cousins' assurance was actually on a par with sales talk? Is A & R's chief desire, after all, to cash in on the spadework done by Jindyworobak? Why did A & R wait until the demand for Australian poetry was so greatly stimulated by Jindyworobak? Does A & R ever lose sight of the main chance? Was my cooperation invited, tongue-in-the-cheek, while A & R were seeking to steal a march on Jindyworobak? These questions logically arise from your letter. But I reject them most emphatically, Mr Stewart, not from any naiveté, but because the only evidence to support them is indirect, appearing in your letter and on the Red Page; and I have very definite evidence that A & R are well disposed to Jindyworobak; that Mr Cousins' letter was *bona fide*, and that the shadow cast upon it by your letter was of an editor presuming too far with the proprietors of his publication. You knew that the Jindyworobak editor was cooperating in A & R's anthology. What right had you to assume that "A & R's point of view" would not be reciprocal? A & R have, in fact, agreed to bring out a Jindyworobak publication, soon to be on the market, which surely they would hesitate to do were they countenancing any collusion of antipathy. There is no such collusion that I can see. The notion of Jindyworobak as a possible competitor to the anthology of which you are editor must clearly be your own, Mr Stewart. Ungraciousness and insult, moreover, have assailed Jindyworobak solely from the *Bulletin* quarter.

Was the Red Page of March 19, in which the announcement of A & R's anthology was made, cautiously beginning a process of smoking Jindyworobak at the altar of something still in the blue? The best your page had to say for the *Jindyworobak Anthologies* on that date was that they have let loose "an extraordinary amount of bad verse," although they reveal "a desperate desire to write poetry", which "more than likely" some Jindyworobak will. This was cautious going; yet, in that particular article, it was extremely ungracious, especially as your Red Page took unto itself credit for suggesting (an innovation?) "that there should be annual anthologies of Australian poetry and short stories as a sort of summing-up of the year's effort and a spur to the next year's". Has not Jindyworobak alone been seeing to this for three years in poetry? Your page speaks correctly of "the customary *Jindyworobak Anthology*, where the young writers have their fling": but, far from granting that youth once more has led the way in something worthwhile, your page studiously disregards the fundamental significance Jindyworobak must have for any present speculation on a Revival of Poetry for Australia. Were there not possibly truths, without negative insinuations, which it was not intended to express concerning Jindyworobak?

Was the opening pargraph of "Notes on a Banner Bearer", on September 3, primarily a silly laugh at Mr Kennedy or a more subtle but equally silly jibe at Jindyworobak? But that is by the way. Consider this:

> *The Bulletin* and such other journals as pay any attention to verse —because the movement is Australian, and because its writers are trying hard to do something—have given it far more serious attention than the quality of the poems in its anthologies to date have warranted.

The Jindyworobak theory,

> as far as the anthologies have indicated, has yet to *work*. It is not Mr Kennedy's pamphlet that will be the vindication of the Jindyworobak theory, but one good poem written by a Jindyworobak; one poem as good in its own way as a McCrae poem is in its own way; one poem that in its own way enriches the Australian tradition as much as *The Man from Snowy River* enriched the tradition in Paterson's way.

A different Red Page, by the way, had previously given high praise to some Jindyworobak poetry. The Red Page is being renovated! Why? When and where has the Red Page been dubbed "Public Enemy, No. 1" of Jindyworobak—except in the Red Page of September 3? Mr Kennedy distinctly presented a quotation of some criticism of a Mudie poem as "a case in point" of "obtuseness in thought", which seems all the more apt because, although he gave no clue to the journal in which it appeared, your Red Page hastens to claim it as its very own! Is someone on the Red Page, Mr Stewart, conscious of a special role? Your page magisterially sweeps into the circumference of the phrase,

"SUCH OTHER JOURNALS AS PAY ANY ATTENTION TO VERSE."

Southerly, in which H.M. Green says:

> "The Jindyworobak Club of Adelaide matters more by reason of the movement it has started than by the actual verse—though a little of this is notable—that its members have turned out ...

The Age, *The Catholic Leader*, *The Brisbane Telegraph*, *The Herald*, *The Argus*, and Jindyworobak's oldest friends, *The News* and *The Mail*, and the sometimes friendly *Advertiser*, and such critics as Edgar Holt, Cecil de Boehme, Noel Goss, H. K. and the immortal James Devaney. These journals and critics, and others, have said sufficient to brand the Red Page assertion false, and its author, on the most generous interpretation, ignorant of Australian journals, and incredibly presumptuous in pretending to speak for them all.

What Mr Green says is, in effect, that Jindyworobak has produced only a little good verse, but matters.

What your page seems to have tried hard to create, since March 19, is the impression that Jindyworobak has not produced a single good poem, and does not matter so much as the Red Page has perhaps led people to believe.

In our 1941 anthology, which I intend your letter and this of mine to preface, we Jindyworobaks are, I believe, pushing on with our distinctive task, which is, while respecting all cultures, to bust the enslavement of Australian to English. There are many worthwhile things we cherish in common with England, but we are sick of English-born professors and other europocentrics blinding the imagination of the Australian people.

Expressing the sincere wishes of myself and those I represent that this letter may help to re-establish good relations between us and the Red Page, and expressing confidence that A & R's anthology will be a success.

I am,

Yours faithfully,

REX INGAMELLS*

---

* The following extract from a letter, Rex Ingamells to W. F. Hudson, 2 November 1949, points to an eventual reconciliation between Ingamells and Stewart. Stewart amiably contributed to the *Jindyworobak Anthology* in 1951 and 1952.

I met Douglas Stewart in Sydney, when I went along to see *Shipwreck*. Somebody carted me backstage (Miles Franklin), and Stewart put out his paw, saying "This silly row has gone on long enough". He was extremely decent, and I liked him very much. He's reviewing *Handbook* in *The Bulletin* soon, he says—and I fancy there'll be some policy remarks, the character of which I'll be very interested to note.

JINDYWOROBAK AND *SOUTHERLY*

A. D. HOPE

CULTURE CORROBOREE*

Cultural Cross-Section. Edited by John Ingamells. (A Jindyworobak Publication, Adelaide, 1941. 3s. 6d.) *Flaunted Banners*, by Victor Kennedy. (A Jindyworobak Publication, Adelaide, 1941.) *At a Boundary*, by John Ingamells and Rex Ingamells. (F. W. Preece Ltd., Adelaide, 1941.) *This is Australia*, by Ian Mudie. (Frank E. Cork, Adelaide, 1941. 3s. 6d.)

The Jindyworobaks might be described as the Boy Scout School of Poetry. They have the same boyish enthusiasm for playing at being primitive, they lay the same stress on the moral values of bushcraft and the open air, they promise to be pure Australian in word and thought and deed, but above all there is the common determination to do noble deeds, not to dream them all day long. *Flaunted Banners* and *Cultural Cross-Section* contain the latest explanations and defence of the Jindyworobak theories. *Flaunted Banners* by Victor Kennedy is a reasoned attempt to explain just what the movement stands for and to clear up some common mistakes about it. It does not, he points out, require us to become Aboriginal, live in a gunyah or eat goannas. It is simply "an effort to link Australian thought with its own natural background". We are asked to treat "as alien everything that owes its being directly to other cultures—English cultures, Irish cultures, German, Dutch or American", and to study and make the basis of our own traditions and vision "the only true and sincere Australian culture . . . that of the Aboriginal race". We are told we must adapt ourselves to this country since the country will not adapt itself to us.

I think this is where the Jindyworobaks make their first mistake. They still see Australia as the country untouched by the white man. They call this the real Australia and they see the Australia we have made as an artificial and fictitious thing. They do not see that a windmill, a railway train, a sheep station, a vineyard, Broken Hill and Canberra are as much part

* *Southerly* Vol. ii No.3, November 1941

of our natural background today as, to quote Rex Ingamells, "the haggard outback valleys, silent deserts and scraggly scrublands". The point of view is put in the series of emotional outbursts masquerading as an argument which appears in *Cultural Cross-Section* under the title of "Politics and Aboriginal Culture", by Ian Mudie. "We are merely aliens in our own land, and nothing else. In 153 years we have failed to become adjusted to our environment."

The answer is that wherever we have settled in those 153 years, we have adjusted the environment to ourselves just as we have adjusted ourselves to the environment. To say we have not is nonsense. We have created a new European country in Australia and we belong to the European nations even though we do not live in Europe. Mr Mudie selects what he likes in the country, calls that Australia and says we should write about it. Anything he does not like he calls alien. Mr Kennedy points out that our poets too often write as if they were still living in England and so write badly, for what they write is second-hand and imitative. But to the majority of Australians, the point of view and culture of the Aboriginal is still more alien and remote, and the poet who tries to write like a second-hand Abo. is no more likely to produce sincere work than the poet who writes like a second-hand Englishman. In fact, the result of attempting to write like an Aboriginal is shown in one of the examples Mr Kennedy selects to praise:

> Garrakeen, the parakeet, is slim and swift.
> Like a spear of green and red he flashes through
> The cumbered branches of the river bank.

Of this Mr Kennedy writes: "The observation is correct in the first place but the significance lies in the simile of the second line which is derived not from the decayed romanticism of a familiar literature but from the very world around".

This illustrates the kind of delusion of the Jindyworobak mind which sees the corroboree as a literary rite. Mr Kennedy and the poet he quotes, Mr Rex Ingamells, may, for all I know, write with their spears and throwing sticks beside them, but I should like to know for how many other Australians a spear is a natural simile for a parakeet, or taken from "the very world around".

Cultural Cross-Section, as its name suggests, appears to mark stage two in the Jindyworobak cultural revolution. From a mystical nationalism in poetry it has gone on to Jindyworobak economics and a social theory which quotes Kipling, the great Boy Scout, as its text:

> Nations have passed away and left no traces,
>   And History gives the naked cause of it
> One single simple reason in all cases:
>   They fell because their people were not fit.

There are critical and historical articles by John Ingamells on the general state of literary culture in Australia, by Rex Ingamells on National Unity, in which the Jindyworobak political creed begins to take shape. There is a survey of poetry by Nettie Palmer. There is the incoherent article on Politics and Aboriginal Culture already mentioned and articles on Painting, Sculpture and Music. In spite of some fine theosophical nonsense by A. N. Ingamells, it appears that the Jindyworobaks have not yet been able to nationalize music. It does appear, however, that the Jindyworobak composer is going to get there in the end by the simple process of dieting:

> The greatest artists of the future must shun all excesses in food, drink and living that would impair their healthy receptivity. Man must vibrate to the inspirational forces emanating from the peaks of consciousness. Thus he will be able to sense, select and combine sounds, colours, forms and movements in a far finer way than any purely technical and intellectual knowledge, however great, would enable him to do.

This article represents perhaps the main fault of Jindyworobak prose and Jindyworobak argument. Most of these articles achieve the rich incoherence of the type of mind that thinks almost entirely in abstract nouns. This is a pity because there is a core of sound common sense in the Jindyworobak case.

However, the proof of the pudding is in the eating, and besides reprints of articles by J. K. Ewers, James Devaney and others, there are a number of new poems scattered through the book. The best of them, "In the Workshop" by Leonard Mann, has already appeared in *Poems from the Mask*. Flexmore Hudson's "Wanderlust" is immediately convincing and satisfying and "Address to Life" is nearly as good. The sonnet form may have something to do with the fact that there is none of the loose thin quality of much of his previously published verse.

I like too Gina Ballantyne's "Phantom: Song of the Lost Tribes", and "Nightfall: Sydney Harbour" is an adequate new expression of a rather worn-out subject. Sheila Sibley's "Song for a Man" is a silly poem, but we have all, I suppose, written this sort of thing at the humourless age when one can't hear the words for the feelings.

As a cross-section of Australian Culture the book is unconvincing and confused. As a cross-section of the Jindyworobak mind it is well worth intelligent and critical study—especially by Jindyworobaks.

At a Boundary by John and Rex Ingamells does not explain its name, but has in it several poems that I like, especially the psychological delicacy of "Written on Leave" by John Ingamells.

The chief poem in the book is a long piece of versified journalese: "The Gangrened People" by Rex Ingamells. In this, I am afraid, indignation replaces poetry altogether. Here is a sample of flat-foot verbiage which makes one wonder whether the Jindyworobaks are really competent to speak for poetry in Australia:

> We who are called Australians have no country;
> No country holds us native heart and soul . . .
> We dwell in the limbo of a harsh deception,
> A criminal betrayal, guaranteeing
> The selfish satisfaction of the cunning
> Exploiting us for money, money, money,
> Spreading the itch to purchase every day,
> Filling our hearts with fatal loyalties
> To nations not our own, nor suited to us.

There are five whole pages of this. Believe it or not! If troopleader Rex can mistake it for poetry it is high time the Jindyworobaks deposed him and took away his bushcraft badge.

I suggest that it might be given for merit to Ian Mudie, whose new volume *This is Australia*, is not only finer and rarer work than *Corroboree to the Sun*, but is the poetry of a man in love. All the poems in this book are the same poem, they all state the Jindyworobak thesis, they are all unashamed patriotic poems and, unpromising as it sounds, they are all convincing and sincere because they are all love-poems. It is a fanatic love: the love of

> sons who shall hold
> That soil sacred, sons who shall be
> Fanatic and consecrated in their loyalty.

It has traces of the fanaticism of the Hitler Youth Movement. In fact, like most love-poetry it contains a lot of patent absurdity—and yet, because it is poetry, can give the truth of the vision and allow us to share the sincerity of the experience.

> My people have few songs to sing;
> thus should it be; a people's songs
> rise from its nationhood, and we

are not a nation, shall not be
until our land in all our thoughts
looms vast and peremptory as the sea.

expresses much the same thing as the lines by Rex Ingamells. The difference is that one uses the method of poetry, the other the rhetoric of fifth-rate journalism.

EDITORIAL*

"I'm greedily looking for *Southerly* to grow more assertive", writes Mr Rex Ingamells, in a letter from which we may pardonably quote. "I'll presume to express it as my opinion, too, that the ultimate value of *Southerly* will be (as regards Australian letters) in proportion to the impetus it affords Australianism." As is now well known, Mr Ingamells was the founder, and remains the leader, of the Jindyworobak school of poets in South Australia. Four of their latest publications are reviewed in this issue. The "Jindyworobaks", as they have come to be called, believe in "Australia First"—in fact, one might almost say, "Australia Only". But their Australia is that of the Aborigines, not that of the so-called usurpers, the white men; according to some of them—if this is not unfair—to be true Australians we must trace our culture back even to Alcheringha [*sic*], the ancient native "dreamtime" or period of primitive bliss. We must disown Europe, think and write only of our surroundings and true past.

This argument Mr Hope, in his review of the publications mentioned, has answered: whether finally is for the reader to decide. It seems hardly likely that even his reduction to absurdity will daunt the Jindyworobaks, if they are progressing in the way he suggests. Meanwhile there is the question of *Southerly*'s position as a literary magazine and its attitude to the controversy. Mr Ingamells calls for a statement of that position; in effect challenges *Southerly* to become more national in the sense in which the *Jindyworobak Anthology*, say, is national. This annual harbours no work that is alien to Australia in any way—at least such is the intention, for up to the present there seems to be no real origination of verse-forms, for example, in the collections; merely development from those already used in England and America. It may be doubted whether *Southerly* is altogether bound to accept such

* *Southerly* vol. ii, no.3, 1941

a challenge, and take a definite stand; but a few words of explanation, at least, may be given.

The title of the magazine was deliberately chosen to suggest its Australian character; and also, be it noted, chosen with some thought of its relation to England. The organ of an "Australian English Association" could not well do otherwise than attempt to maintain a relationship which, culturally, is surely all-important. If the contents of *Southerly* were to be limited to articles, poems, stories, of local interest, if no contributor to it were to be allowed to look beyond his own shores, then the peculiar status of the Australian author—which Mr *John* Ingamells seems to recognize—as surveyor of the whole world from the vantage-point of its newest part, would be lost. He would be deprived of the inestimable benefit of being able to select just what he wants from abroad and here—to interpret English writers from the Australian point of view, to bring out in his verse the contrasts of land and character, to adapt and improve technique, to set past against present, and so on. Perhaps in no other nation is the writer in so favoured a position today. If he does not avail himself of his opportunities, it is his own fault. But to circumscribe himself, to disregard *our* antipodes, go to school to the Aborigines, find his landscape at Alice Springs, would surely result in ingrowth and, finally, barrenness.

The Jindyworobaks may try it. Let them—with our blessing —go as far as they can. Already they have instituted something like a poetic renascence in South Australia, and are stimulating enthusiasm elsewhere. But *Southerly*, so long as is possible, will remain non-exclusive, liberal towards the English as well as the Australian: will welcome both corroboree chants and critical appraisements of Joyce; will play its part in maintaining the cultural good relations that have hitherto subsisted between the mother and the daughter countries; and, by this means, will help to bring knowledge of Australian literature and literary endeavour, Australian linguistic variation, to English readers and writers. Thus shall we avoid any charge of regionalism, provincialism, not to say parochialism. And, by not tying ourselves, we may hope to escape finding ourselves tethered.

EXTRACT FROM EDITORIAL*

With some surprise, we learnt that our last editorial, together with Mr Hope's review of Jindyworobak publications, had been taken as constituting an attack on Jindyworobakism, and also on its founder, Mr Rex Ingamells. In the course of correspondence with the latter we have assured him that there was no personal motive in the articles—which, in any case, were independent of each other—and have tried to convince him that no real cause of offence had been given. He further complained, however, of misrepresentation of his movement: to which a reply was given that everything in the editorial had been based on a study of Jindyworobak (not merely his own) proclamation and practice, and that if we erred it was not through dishonesty of interpretation. Unfortunately, however, we had not seen two publications of the Jindyworobaks which are not readily available, and to these Mr Ingamells has now invited our notice. Furthermore, declaring that though the movement had developed from the principles laid down in these, it had never departed from them, he marked two passages for our information. It is only fair, therefore, to cite these passages in *Southerly* [See Notes below]. We feel that no apology or retraction is necessary. We are sorry to have given annoyance or pain, but it will surely be acknowledged that the fault, if any, arose more from a necessarily incomplete study of the Jindyworobak movement than from anything like hostility towards it, and readers will now have an opportunity of judging the matter for themselves. The question is still, we think, whether or not the Jindyworobaks have gone too far in the direction of literary "autarky". That they have done so, indeed, is the view quite independently upheld by Miss Herring, as critic, in this issue, of the recent *Jindyworobak Anthology*.

In this connection, it must be reaffirmed that, subject only to the ordinary restraints, our reviewers have complete freedom of speech, and that their opinions are not necessarily those of *Southerly* or of the Australian English Association. Miss Herring and Mr Hope, for instance, speak for themselves, and we may or may not agree with them. Even an editorial must be an expression of personal opinion. But the editorials of *Southerly* may also be taken as expounding the policy of the magazine. In our present policy there is nothing hostile to

* *Southerly* vol. iii no. 1, 1942

Jindyworobakism. We reserve the right of criticism, and if the grounds of such criticism are shown to be untenable, we are prepared to withdraw it. But in this instance it seems that only the impartial reader can decide.

NOTES

Jindyworobakism.—The extracts referred to in the editorial are:

(1) "I do not wish to be misunderstood. Some of the greatest Australian literature yet to be may have no local colour at all. Its settings may be in China or Mars. Our best poetry must deal with universal themes; and whether or not the Australian environment forms a background is a matter for individual poets. But all this does not affect the essence of my argument. The real test of a people's culture is the way in which they can express themselves in relation to their environment, and the loftiness and universality of their artistic conceptions raised on that basis."—Rex Ingamells, *Conditional Culture*, 1938, page 6.

(2) "The Jindyworobaks stand for a precise cultural movement. While we realize that culture springs from varied sources, we insist that a nation's culture depends for significance on distinctive qualities, peculiar to that nation alone. It is to stress such qualities in Australia that the Jindyworobaks have sprung into being. It is ridiculous to assume—as is assumed in some quarters—that we are against the appreciation of overseas art, or that we regard the only suitable subjects for Australian art to be typically Australian subjects. It is right to assume that we want to see more writers and painters dealing with typically Australian subjects, and that we are categorical concerning art of this kind . . . Mediocre work, if it fights shy of pseudo-European humbug, we encourage; and we believe we are far-sighted in doing so."—Editorial in *Venture*, Jindyworobak Quarterly Pamphlet, No. 1, April, 1939.

R. H. MORRISON

THE VERSE ANTHOLOGIES: FOR AND AGAINST*

Jindyworobak Anthology, 1946. Editor, Ian Mudie. (Jindyworobak Publications, Melbourne, 1946.)
Australian Poetry, 1946. Selected by T. Inglis Moore. (Angus & Robertson Ltd, 1947. 6s.)

The inner dialogue has many surprises. While reading these anthologies I was struck by the petulance of Contra, the agility of Pro, and the persistence of both. They paid me no heed, and didn't mind how they disturbed me with their chatter. In the end I decided I'd let them have their say, and to pass the time I made notes of their infernal wrangling. Just then one of them was becoming a little heated.

Con: You prate about "making allowances", there's too much of that in Australia. Take this *Jindyworobak Anthology*—just listen a moment to the opening lines:

> Victory Day!
> A wet wind blows and the sky is grey,
> But you've beaten the enemy, God be praised,
> So raucous and shrill (though a trifle dazed!)
> Flutter your favours and coloured rags,
> Caper and prance on the paving-flags!
> Care and tomorrow are miles away—
> Victory Day!

Tell me, do you agree or not that the collection of such lolloping jingle into anthologies can only bring ridicule on Australian poetry as a whole, and is evidence of a deplorable lack of critical standards?

Pro: No, I don't agree. You're narrow and intolerant. The poem may not be very good, but it has the virtue of sincerity, like so many others in this volume. As for bringing ridicule on our poetic reputation, that is too slighting to our numerous capable poets, who are well able to look after themselves. And the standards you mention—aren't you a little in the clouds? Not every poem can be the masterpiece you seem to expect. Every beginner has to begin. In any case, you've referred to one poem only; there are sixty-seven in this anthology, and quite a number are better than "Victory Day". For instance, "The Reef", by Paul L. Grano, is a carefully-worded and

* *Southerly* vol. ix no. 1, 1948

sensitive lyric; the same applies to "Two Poems", by an author who tantalizingly hides behind the mysterious initials "R.G.H.". "Vespers at Campbelltown", by Harley Matthews, presses home effectively and with restraint a little facet of the horror of life in a great metropolis. I could go on like this with other poems in the same varied collection, but I don't think you're even listening.

Con: Yes, I'm listening to your drivel—and marvelling that an apparently sensible being like you could be a party to the present general degradation of values. The more there are like you in our literary circles, the longer will the second-rate be so widely accepted. In our insular condition, nothing can help our literature more than the sharp knife of criticism, to cut away dead wood and leave the tree healthy.

Pro: First plant your tree.

Con: The tree's there, growing, but it needs attention. Don't pretend that a handful of what you take to be worthwhile poems can support three-score mediocre ones. Better to publish only the few, or simply admit that not enough were received to justify the anthology's publication. But don't pad; don't accept what's just "good enough", don't treat seriously the politicians, propagandists, and company-promoters of poetry; don't pretend that *vertical prose* is poetry at all; don't talk about "virtues" where the image-making fire of poetry is quite lacking; don't . . .

Pro: Hey! That'll do. My turn now: Don't be over-earnest; don't discourage anyone, in a land where the arts need every encouragement; and don't be careless with that knife, or you'll ringbark the tree. But I think you're biased, and that reference to "Jindyworobakwardness" which started this argument was really a bit feeble, wasn't it? What about changing the subject? The Old Man has got this other thing to review, this *Australian Poetry, 1946*. You may dislike a certain school, but you'll admit that this is different, a volume edited on a broad basis and representing the best of the year's output by all our poets.

Con: Don't jump to conclusions. Frankly, I think the motto of the editor of this book must have been "Beg, Borrow, Swap". Perhaps he might have done better to steal.

Pro: Your frankness seems to me a rather offensive kind of impertinence.

Con: Well, just look. Pages 47, 50, 55, 65, and 68—in this 1947 anthology there are five poems from the *Jindyworobak Anthology* of 1946. And if you study the acknowledgments in both publications, you'll see that at least one poem in Mr Inglis Moore's volume seems to appear in print for the fourth time, and others for the third time. That is surely literary inflation.

Pro: Instead of haggling like this, wouldn't it be better to sum up one's views in a brief, objective critique? I'll put mine thus: The *Jindyworobak Anthology, 1946*, presents the work of forty-two poets, and includes several successful lyrics, a number marred by technical faults or general formlessness, and a few which are apparently the first fruits of enthusiastic newcomers. The contents, though not of a very high standard, reveal a passionate absorption in the Australian scene which will no doubt lead the contributors on to more enduring work. One notes with interest that this group is planning to bring out a review of its ten years' activity, in addition to a 1947 anthology. *Australian Poetry, 1946*, the sixth volume of an annual series, contains a fine poem by Shawn O'Leary, "The Dead Soldier", with its memorable image of "the night's black swan (unfolding) slow wings". Another outstanding contribution is "Orchestra", by Eric Irvin, a poet whose work shows a sure grasp of form, unusual sense of rhythm, insight, and sensitivity. Other poems by Robert D. FitzGerald and Nan McDonald help make this collection worth while and interesting.

Con: These two anthologies contain several poems worth preserving, but the bad unfortunately outweigh the good. After all, not many good poems are written in Australia in any one year. The pity is that to compile a volume an editor will sacrifice his standards and admit work that is not even verse, let alone poetry. This in turn must lead to the production of more of this mediocre stuff by those who evidently say to themselves: "Well, it's hardly a poem, but it is much like the thing I saw in that anthology the other day, I'll send it in". By now the damage is half done; it needs only acceptance and publication to complete the delusion of the budding poet. O, editors, define your principles, enunciate your criteria, and stick to them at any cost! The results will mean more to Australian literature than all your kind-hearted encouragement.

Pro: Lord, he's started again! I'm off. Anyway, I feel it's a case of *"eppur si muove"*.

Con: He's cleared out! *Imbecile! Non si è mosso mai!!*

MAX HARRIS

DANCE LITTLE WOMBAT*

I have just read right through the file of Meanjin Papers. So much talk about Australian Kulchewer, environmental values, national beauty, and so forth, I have never read before.

True enough, this shrieking and caterwauling about a purely fictitious problem was answered from the other side of the fence by some dignified and subtle "universalists". The stream of culture will go its amiable way irrespective of the frantic efforts of these Nationalist writers to dam it up and divert its course with a rampart of theories about what artists should be doing and appreciating.

Here are some extracts from about thirty proselytizing articles:

> But as literary craftsmen our duty is plain. It is to seek out those values which we feel inherent in our country and our life. (John K. Ewers)
>
> Australia is still the Unknown Land, unknown except to a few renegades from the Gangrened clan. (Rex Ingamells)

On the other hand there has been a minority pleading for universal qualities in the poetry of to-day.

> The majority have consciously striven to be Australian or looked too much abroad. In one case they cannot see the wood for the gum trees. (A. R. Chisholm)
>
> We must learn to practice immortality. (Kate Baker)
>
> We welcome any sincere expression of an individual vision. (Clem Christesen)
>
> Our culture has concerned itself too much with petty and local envies and vanities and not enough with things of universal worth. (J. G. Holmes)

All that the critic can do is to examine the poetry that is produced according to the highest aesthetic judgment and sensitivity that he can develop within himself. But how little competent poetic analysis, discussion of rhythm, texture, poetic integrity has gone on in this country since the Jindyworobaks and others started screeching about National Resurgence and What Poetry Should Be About, and the Important National Values Poetry Should Set Up. Have they judged according to poetic standards where the best work is coming from in this

---

* Meanjin Papers, 2.2, 1943

country, how the medium is being used, the verbal success of the vision?

The sole issue of any importance so far as the literature of this country goes is the poetic quality of the poetry. I will take the poetry of Rex Ingamells as the example, simply for the reason that he is perhaps the most representative of the plague of national poets. In this series it will not be the nationalist nor the universalist that I will examine, but the poet.

Mr Ingamells's work has developed quite peculiarly along with his thought. His first book, *Gumtops*, published in 1935, contains a certain sincerity and quiet feeling that hints at poetry. At this unsophisticated stage he is most certainly undergoing sensitive feelings towards the world about him. The prevailing atmosphere is of mood and rather vague romanticism. Nostalgia does not offer a very profound poetic experience in association with certain perspectives (contrast Rainer Maria Rilke) but at times the young Ingamells gets it across through a pleasing feeling for word-texture, for hard and soft.

> I have seen a flaming peak at dawn
> Across a sea of sand. Alone it stood,
> And bare of all but colour.

But often the spasms of genuine feeling and poetry are thwarted by an uncertainty of idiom, a degeneration of the simple and genuine feeling imposed by an inability to express it. Not being at home in poetry he falls constantly into the trap of "poeticism".

> There was nought else in that vast lonely place
> To breathe of Beauty; and I gazed in awe,
> To think that even there she held her sway;
> To think that, her staunch slave, with such fierce grace
> That peak at dawn blazed centuries before,
> And so blazed now, and so should blaze for aye.

Here the verse has ceased to be the peculiar and integral vision of the poet, and is become an echo of the way Wordsworth, and possibly Keats, experienced.

As he developed Ingamells's vision became literary-political; it entered the field of attitude rather than feeling. All his later poetry has this atmosphere of attitude towards what he sees, rather than reaction to what he sees.

His technical capacity, his idiom becomes slicker, but there is a thinning out of the tension of experience underlying it. The strengthening of attitude impoverished the poetry. Being aware of this lack of poetic force behind their attitude-poetry, almost all the Jindyworobaks fell behind a developing sort of jargon. This jargon has become just as much a form of "poetic diction" as that Wordsworth and Coleridge disposed of. On sincerely studying the poetry I cannot help coming to the conclusion that it is the product of a sense of artistic deficiency.

Here are some examples:

> Spirits shall haunt this land. O we
> Shall roam a dim Alcheringa,
> Our gods shall show us mystery
> And you not know it, Waruntha.

> Far in moorawathimeering,
> Safe from wallan darenderong,
> Tallabilla waitjurk, wander
> Silently the whole day long.

The jargon consists in "Aboriginalizing" language. All Australian poets must be European to the extent of using the English language. If only for the sake of the audience and the fact that poets do feel and articulate in a language, the working off of liberal doses of foreign language should be avoided. If I were to use a Hindu or Arabic word per line I doubt very much whether I could expect it to be accepted as a serious attempt to communicate poetic experience. The subject is not the question—let it be Alcheringa if you like—but it is the inadequacy of the expression which has to involve the "exoticism" of foreign verbiage. If the subject were intensely felt it would articulate cleanly either in Aboriginal dialect or English.

Fundamentally, a serious "Jabberwocky" might be made to mean as much in poetic terms as this parochial "poetic diction".

I suppose it was inevitable that Australia should give rise to a Jindyworobak movement, and a school of young poets whose chief concern would be with what they experience rather than the way they experience. It is to be expected that such an approach would be fatal to genuine poetry, but popularly successful. The theory behind it is this. Australian poetry must not be servile imitation of European artistic forms and artistic values. If Australian writers function genuinely, they will express in their poetry the real world of their immediate experience . . . the actual material of life that will impact their consciousness. In this case poets will find, in a similar fashion to poets in other places in the world, their field of experience, and consequently of poetic expression, conditioned by the environment in which they find themselves.

This is what Mr Ingamells describes as "conditional culture". The broad striking rural environment of Australia, its peculiar archaic aspects, are the things which will play a large part in the poet's life, they are things and the mysteries of his immediate life with which his faculties would be most intimately concerned. Poetry in this country would then be expressive of its landscape, the emotional associations of its pioneering life. Mr Ingamells's own poetry for instance concerns itself with expressing two things so far—one, the disgusting and repulsive life of the city, Big Business and Small Emotions; and two, a nostalgic self-identification with the Aborigine and the spiritual values of his life (!)

Beneath the popular appeal of this unfortunately parochial theory the simple error is easily spotted. To correct the error of the Jindyworobaks may seem to indicate indulgence in stating truisms, but the simple evidence is necessary, as some critics have honoured the cause of Mr Ingamells with sophisticated repudiations which have led the issue astray.

Poetry is not concerned ultimately with visual sensation, although all poetry uses to some measure visual sensation. But poetry primarily emerges as the expression of attitude or emotion towards the facts of experience. It concerns itself with that which is peculiar and individual in the artist's vision of his surroundings. His fundamental environment is himself. The depiction of environment and landscape in poetry only exists for the purpose of the artist saying something about it. When he speaks in verbal terms he must consequently express himself in that language which is his own, that with which he thinks and that with which he articulates his feeling, and definitely not with that which will correlate most closely with the evidence of his eyes. If the poet finds that the language with which he articulates his feelings and attitudes is inadequate, then it argues either a mistaken sense of what poetry is and does, or it argues a complete poverty in artistic equipment.

I have unfortunately had to come to the conclusion that it is more the latter with Mr Ingamells and members of his school. It reveals a disintegrating instinct for poetic expression that he has come more and more to use Aboriginal dialect for its own sake in his work. It exemplifies a pitiful lack in his own make-up that he has to capture the associative values of his environment through the use of a language which is foreign to him. His capacity at this point of decline consists in conveying a sense of place, but saying nothing about it. The need for poetry at all has gone, for the emotional content of his living has ceased to be important. More generously, we may say it has been swamped.

To some readers it may seem that this analysis merely subserves a battle of school against school. I hope to offer evidence later that my aim is broader than that. This clearing up of false issues is intended as preliminary to seeing the whole contemporary landscape of poetry in this country. It is only fair that the reader should see the terms on which this survey will be conducted, the set of values which will be applied. These values will be in short a judging of our recent history in terms of poetic qualities rather than of relation to cultural theory, be it on one side of the fence or the other.

Readers who wish to see this attempt to clarify our whole perspective might refer to a long article in the March issue of the Australian Quarterly and in Angry Penguins, although the central path of the discussion will lie through Meanjin Papers.

CRITICAL EXTRACTS FROM *JINDYWOROBAK REVIEW 1938-1948*

JAMES DEVANEY (FOREWORD)

I am not a Jindyworobak, except perhaps by adoption. For one thing, this is a movement of modern young poets, and I am not young, and am accounted completely "traditional and romantic" rather than modern. But I am glad to associate myself with the Jindyworobaks because I like very much their spirit and their aims. I cannot agree with the present dead set in some quarters against the Australian theme and outlook in Australian writing, by newer critics who apparently think that a national literature need not have roots of its own.

The Jindies have set out to create something wholly Australian. They are meeting with much criticism, but I think that in the main they are right and their critics wrong. Surely any country's literature must be an expression of that country's spirit and life; a natural growth out of its own soil. These poets, who are insistent on an Australian idiom and resolved to reject anything imported, draw their very similes and so on from this country, never from the books of others in other countries. I think they go too far in their exclusions. They would not use such words as "castle", "knight", "fairy", describing the bush, because these are borrowed and do not belong here. But we can have experience of things in other ways than by seeing or possessing them. All the same what they are trying to do is wholly in the interests of Australian literature, and we should wish them well.

. . . . .

Jindyworobak "Aboriginalism" in verse seems to be a main difficulty. Anyhow it is the thing most attacked, parodied, derided. But after all, the most significant thing really indigenous to this young-old land is the Aboriginal. European writers have centuries behind them. We have not. The Jindyworobaks, native-born like the original Australians, identified like them with this land and no other, feel a far past of our own in the Alcheringa conception. They interpret it as the genius of the country. This and this only is our land, and it is older than Europe.

REX INGAMELLS (INTRODUCTION)

Mr Brian Elliott has some degree of understanding of Jindyworobak, in the initial stages of which he was distantly concerned. Much of his criticism of the movement's and my shortcomings, in his book, *Singing to the Cattle*, is moderately well-reasoned and honest. But not all is well-reasoned; not all is strictly honest. It is not suggested that Mr Elliott means to be dishonest, but his course is fixed at present in the universities, and he seems to have cast about for conclusions such as would be acceptable to entrenched die-hards, who, chagrined at the establishment of Jindyworobak, would be grateful for sops. Mr Elliott ought to have known better than to omit from his reference to facts "always present to the Jindyworobak imagination" the most essential, namely our conception of environmental values. Accoutred with this blind spot, however, he quotes, as, "making allowances", a "prime" and "octogenarian" "example of the Jindyworobak imagination", lines from J. Sheridan Moore in which the "tribe" of coral insects are "Grinding, kneading, weaving, spinning". Spinning? Mr Elliott does not, even making allowances, seem to understand. His is a refusal to see the prime point of Jindyworobak argument, which concerns the accurate use of language. He is referred to my essay *On Environmental Values*, where he will learn all over again that the kind of early bards he lists as possessing the Jindyworobak imagination possessed, if any, remarkably little of it: their vision, however sincerely held, was too much handicapped by technical flaws in expression to be reliably Australian. There is in Mr Elliott a strong disposition to pontificate.

E. MORRIS MILLER

These Jindyworobaks desire supremely that the Australian imagination shall be the fruitage of an Australian perception —the reaction to the surrounding scene as it is and not as perceived through senses bred in other climes. They have called a halt to the indiscriminate invasion of western ideas into a continent that is the first to catch the light of dawn.

. . . .

A word of caution. In an effort to build up, or recreate, a traditional element for the growth of our literature, it is not wise to brand as alien the ideas that come from Europe, including Britain. After all, English literature claimed as one of its origins the ever-pervading scriptures of the Hebrews, and its great exponents were not averse to render malleable in their own language the mythologies of Greece, Rome, and other lands. It is the human attributes in these older literatures that find favour in the mind's currency; and nothing great in man's achievement is stranger to the creative imagination. And we should remember, too, that even the Aboriginal lore, available for literary expression, has come to us through the agency of anthropologists schooled in the world's science.

MARY GILMORE

About Jindyworobak—I am, in my work, so far removed by age and custom from the young who belong to it, that I am an Alice-sit-by-the-fire in relation to it.

I see the embers of a fire gone over, and not the young wood about to be brought in.

No one, however, more endorses new and young work than I do, whether it be the result of rebellion at any age, or because of youth. Which means that I regard the Jindyworobak not only as a tree of its times, but as an essential one.

GINA BALLANTYNE

Imaginative writers are free to be either parochial or cosmopolitan in presenting any places or subjects that stir them, and some of the most enchanting literature is the outcome of writers' success in communicating their ecstasy in their own, their native lands. A great provincial literature of England has enabled many who have never seen that sceptred isle to revel in her ivied towers, her hedgerows, coppices, spinneys, wolds and woods, her brooks and rooks, cuckoos and owls, her every crocus, fritillary or daffodil. A similar desire to express an equivalent joy accumulating in this unsung continent would seem to be the non-self-seeking but sturdily self-expressing inspiration of Jindyworobak—Jindyism, as it is termed by those whom it irritates.

. . . .

A question is sometimes asked to the effect of "where is Jindyworobak going from here?" To that I would reply that a literary group or movement should not be viewed as rushing to some particular destination in the manner of a railway train: rather can it be likened to a tree, growing and increasing in strength and beauty, and in this instance sturdily rooted in its native earth. And also, like the genus eucalypt, Jindy may be expected to establish itself in other parts of the world, in the sense that it may find appreciation in the minds of overseas readers as a true representative of its own land.

IAN MUDIE

> Oh, its good to make a start, mate,
> And keep a steady pace;
> But many an honest man's lost heart
> 'Twixt here and Martin Place.

The poets found their original inspiration for the birth of a truly national poetry in the spirit-centres of the lonely and unspoiled Centre, where the land has not been completely raped, nor the Aboriginal occupiers of the land been totally degraded to the level of the whites of a spiritless and utterly mendicant character. They have now begun to move over the tracks of the explorers, which often link that Centre with the closely settled areas. But they have so far made hardly more than tentative expeditions into the settled country, nor done little more than sojourn for a few lines in the heart of the cities, have marched hardly more than a stanza or so down the centre of Martin Place.

NETTIE PALMER

Rex Ingamells, young and already a poet, became dissatisfied with his considerable tale of sonnets on conventional themes. He somehow lifted himself into the challenging air of what he called "environmental values". Arrived there, as on a roomy plateau, he pulled up several of his contemporaries after him and called the gathering Jindyworobak—a pleasanter expression than the other and serving to remind them that they were now writing and arguing in the Aborigines' country, which was partly true. But they were wrong in thinking the whole plateau had been uninhabited by poets before them.

In the life of all old countries—and ours is one of the oldest —comes a time of questioning: have we as writers a unity with the original spirit of this land, or is all our work a mere bookish echo. Poets of Peru, not content with expressing New Worldism, have tried to recover the symbols and murmurs of long-vanished Incas. So too over our bush broods a spell;

> . . . we seem to see
> Tangible presences of deathless things.

It is the intention of Jindyworobak to remind its poets of such presences, as well as assuring their fearless "direct contact with life". Their charter is good and wide.

JUDITH WRIGHT

It seems to me that the Jindy movement was essentially an effort to get the problem into perspective. I don't necessarily mean that the Jindy writers themselves have done that, but rather that in the ensuing argument the issues have found some kind of clarification: and in fact the work of the outstanding Jindy writers has to some extent already broken the problem down. To emphasize our regionalism instead of trying to ignore it, to concentrate on the background instead of trying to elude it—this has had a value in itself, and it has performed the further function of leading to a reaction against itself. That is to say, that having found out what happens when one tries to treat the problem as an end in itself, it is now possible to apply the knowledge. The regional, the national outlook *has* a value, and no doubt some writers do their best work within such a closed circuit. But there are other jobs to do; and Jindyworobak has probably contributed something towards finding the means of doing them. It may be that because of the Jindy movement, even those most fiercely opposed or most indifferent to it know themselves a little better.

MAX HARRIS

To appreciate the historical role of Jindyworobak it is necessary to go back to 1938.

In a big partitioned room, on a mezzanine floor, at the back of Cavendish Chambers, the Jindyworobak Club was founded. It was the first sign of lively literary activity in Adelaide for many years. Its moving spirit and founder was Rex Ingamells, and assisting him were myself and Ian Tilbrook. The whole atmosphere of Cavendish Chambers was one of humility and youthful idealism . . . roneoing the little magazine *Venture*, pursuing patrons, evolving the club's constitution. The excitement of publishing poetry . . . first books by myself and Ian Tilbrook appeared under the imprimatur of the club. Then the outbreak of war. As the result of a suggestion of mine a special "War Statements" issue of *Venture* was put out.

This contained statements from such notables as Norman Makin, later Minister for the Navy, but its importance lay in the fact that it was the first attempt at defining the role and function of writers in a world at war, preceding in time, so far as I know, all other discussions, such as came to be found in "Horizon", upon the artist's role in a society at war.

In our enthusiasm we set out in search of immediate and colourful experience. I remember a journey on the River Murray train, Rex woefully attempting to play "Matilda" on a mouth-organ. He was going to hike along the Renmark–Mildura stretch of the Murray. I was heading into the picking season, first the 'cots, then the sultanas at Berri and Barmera.

But these fragmentary impressions are contained within a total picture I have in my mind. To achieve intellectual stimulus it is necessary for writers to be gregarious, even if gregariousness can only be expressed in "little" magazines. The early days of Jindyworobak were to me, a process of establishing contact, contact with poetic outlooks ranging from Grano and Devaney in Brisbane to the Bread and Cheesers in Melbourne. This interchange of viewpoints, to which Ingamells's controversial theory gave rise, caused a feeling of coherence between various individuals, and a feeling that literary thought was moving ahead in an exciting way.

Poetry, expressing Jindyworobak concepts, came from everywhere, and that poetry became increasingly mature.

Some of it, to my mind, became increasingly extreme, and under the mentorship of Professor Charles Rischbieth Jury, one of the finest classical minds Australia has produced, another group was formed in Adelaide which stressed the poetic values of poetry qua poetry, and not qua environmental values.

"Angry Penguins" expressed a reaction to the ideas of Jindyworobak, perhaps extreme in the other direction . . . but such issues are not to the point in this statement, where one's concern is not the verifying of one's prejudices, but establishing the ontogenesis of our present culture.

Later, when *Meanjin Papers* came into the field, a great deal of thinking had been done about the potentials of our national culture, and people were developing their attitudes apace.

Jindyworobak, then, has an overall significance as a coordinating and liberating factor, and it has played a determining part in giving the literary whole the particular shape it has at the moment.

BRIAN ELLIOTT

I don't think any of us (I include myself at this early stage) *knew* as much about poetry as we thought we did, although Mr Ingamells had then already written some of his best verses. But we saw in the creation of an Australian myth of place and time and destiny something quite different from the vapid prettiness and the aggressive materialism of the poetry that was then dominant, and in fixing upon the Aboriginal race as a symbol of Australian nature we thought we had discovered an approach to poetry that might be intellectually and imaginatively truthful, and fruitful in sensibility. The truth was that in the poetry everybody knew there seemed to be scope for nothing but clichés; and we looked to find a poetical scheme that would give us scope for any emotional expansiveness such as was necessary if poetry were to grow to any proportions as an art in Australia. We were not very conscious of the probability that our programme itself was capable of becoming just another such cliché. But if the plan produced no other result, it did explore the possibility, in an experimental way, of developing a store of new but true emotions and associations, a reservoir of myth upon which the imagination could draw indefinitely and upon which a system might be based that would give a real and positive life to the spirit of poetry in this country.

W. FLEXMORE HUDSON

Why has the criticism of Jindyworobak been so querulous and acrimonious? I think there are at least nine reasons:

1. Most people are instantaneously suspicious of an innovator, and critics have ever been outraged when poetic techniques have changed or developed.

2. Many malicious and spiteful people resent any achievement in others, particularly one which demands the qualities they themselves usually lack—unmercenariness, unselfish patience, devotion to an ideal.

3. The term Jindyworobak offends many people's ears. I admit that I have never been able to overcome my own dislike of its cacophony. I know Mr Ingamells wanted to challenge attention and considered that a melodious word would not do this so effectively.

4. The theory is at times windy and vague—words are used in unfamiliar senses, for example "values" instead of "qualities" in "environmental values".

5. The movement has been critical of cherished notions about the British Empire, the dear "Motherland", European progress, the Banks, etc.

6. The Australian universities (perhaps with the exception of their departments of history) have, till recently, ignored our literature or treated it with contempt. Consequently, those who "did" English at the "varsity", for instance, school teachers, have seldom brought to the new poems that spirit of willing receptivity, which they bring to traditional English verse and which is absolutely necessary for the full appreciation of any work of art.

7. In a world suffering so cruelly from the effects of pigheaded national sovereignty, even a cultural nationalism is regarded with suspicion. But in the U.S.S.R. cultural nationalism is fostered and, apparently, without any catastrophic effect.

8. In their eagerness to encourage "environmental values" in poetry the Jindyworobaks have published too many poems that are slight or crude in craftmanship, even some that seem to drag in Aboriginal terms by the hair of their head.

9. A good many of us find the Alcheringa myth unpalatable and unprofitable.

R. G. HOWARTH

Rex Ingamells has advocated from the beginning what amounts to self-reliance in our writing, and if this has sometimes appeared to err into undue isolation from our Antipodes and into over-emphasis on the Aboriginal (marked by the occasional preponderance of native terms in verse), such excess may be seen to be an inevitable and perhaps only passing consequence. If Jindyworobak does no more than succeed in removing "poetic" diction for good from our verse, it will have justified its foundation.

ALEC KING

My comment, then, on the Jindyworobaks as producers of poetry, is that their "programme" billed them as spokesmen-poets, teachers and rousers of the Australian people, that it is almost impossible to write spokesman-poetry, and that the poetry they have turned out has probably been less good than it might have been, if their minds had not been directed by a programme. The gradual change in the nature of the anthologies seems to bear this out; and I feel that it has been in spite of the programme that they have produced what good poetry is to be found in the anthologies. Finally I do not for a moment doubt that the Jindyworobak movement has indirectly stimulated a kind of interest that we all want to see.

F.J. LETTERS

EXTRACT FROM *IN A SHAFT OF SUNLIGHT*, 1948

THE JINDYWOROBAK THEORY

The Jindyworobak movement has been defined as "an effort to link Australian thought with its natural background". So far we have nothing novel. The earliest Australian versifiers conscientiously attempted the same thing. But this new aim becomes clearer with the remark that "the only true and sincere Australian culture" is "that of the Aboriginal race". So speaks Mr Victor Kennedy in *Flaunted Banners*. We are told that the mentality we have brought to Australia is non-Australian, and should be abandoned for the Australian Aborigine's. English, Scottish, Irish, are equally alien cultures, and therefore cannot be really assimilated by this country.

Grave doubts may be entertained about the whole theory. It revives the extremely ticklish, never yet settled question—what does the average white Australian really think of his black compatriot? It is significant that in Adelaide, the centre of the Jindyworobak movement, Aborigines, however popular, are rare, whereas at Darwin, where they abound, they are not universal favourites. One may ask, too, why South Africa seems able to foster a distinctive poetry without professing the theory that the true and sincere South African culture is that of the Kaffir. Nor have Northern and Southern Americans found it necessary to develop their respective literatures on Mohican and Aztec lines.

I am afraid the Aborigine is not nearly so cherished, certainly not nearly so revered in Australia as Jindyworobak principles assume he is, or should be, and I understand that few Australians, whether Jindyworobak enthusiasts or not, have even taken the trouble to master the leading native dialects.

It would be no serious practical objection if the theory consisted of a grain of truth to a pound of error, provided the error were palatable to the many. On the whole, man does not like his truth absolutely pure, but prefers it with a kick, with a good heady mixture of error and folly. But the error or folly must be seductive. Now the great majority of us will not be particularly pleased to learn that the pulse of Australia is not to be found in the effete European stock forming the bulk of the population, but in the remnants of the native tribes. "Keep Australian Thought Black" is a slogan hard to reconcile with the still popular, if somewhat abashed, White Australia doctrine.

No. The Aboriginal question must be thrashed out completely before we are likely to accept or practise the Jindyworobak dialectic. Make the masses really fond of the "Abo."; that is the first step, and the hardest.

Apart from difficulties that may yet disappear at last, there is a serious initial obstacle. Our blacks may have had a wonderful culture; but it would be the only one on record that has dispensed with a written literature because apparently its genius was beyond verbal expression. Mr Ian Mudie in *This is Australia* has admitted

> My people have few songs to sing;
> Thus should it be; a people's songs
> Rise from its nationhood, and we
> Are not a nation, shall not be
> Until our land in all our thoughts
> Looms vast and peremptory as the sea.

The trouble is that though my people have few songs to sing, my Aborigines had still fewer, whence a curious dilemma. If the reason for my Aborigines' having been so unproductive is the same as my people's, namely that they were not a nation, it would seem that nationalism is not in the Aboriginal culture we are bidden absorb. On the other hand, if to the Aborigines their land in all their thoughts did loom vast and peremptory as the sea, it is reasonable to ask why on earth they had so few songs to sing? Can it possibly be that their culture, though confessedly profound, was, and remains, somewhat narrow? In that case it is unreasonable to urge that it is sufficiently broad for us to build upon, unless we admit inability to do better without it.

To apply all this more closely to the Jindyworobak theory. In the absence of Aboriginal manuscripts presumably we should saturate ourselves with the existing oral form of Aboriginal culture. But if we subtract from the native population the half-caste and Europeanized sections, the residue will be scanty and difficult of access. As things are now, we shall have to hurry to overtake the living Aboriginal tradition, since its repository is a rapidly dying race. The Jindyworobaks, one suspects, must surely have their tongues in their cheeks; otherwise how is it they never face this tragic aspect of the matter?

How do they answer the query: "What are we to do to keep

the Aboriginal culture going?" For my part, I can see only one reply. If the culture is to survive, the race that produced it must be assisted to survive at least until we in turn shall have absorbed the culture. And how are we to give this assistance? Again there can be only one answer. There must be inter-marriage of white and black Australians, since the black, left to themselves, will practically vanish in a generation or two. We must above all aim to multiply the half-castes, as these will absorb the Aboriginal culture in a way no one could suspect of pretence—through their very blood.

The difficulties the Jindyworobaks must face when driven to this conclusion will be great, but Mr Ian Mudie will no longer have any reason, if the conclusion is put into practice, to complain sadly, as he has done in his article "Politics and Aboriginal Culture": "We are merely aliens in our own land, and nothing else. In 153 years we have failed to become adjusted to our environment."*

The difficulties will be great. Two of them will probably prove too much even for Jindyworobak enthusiasm. In the first place, the reactionary White Australia doctrine, though grown rather mangy, still crouches on their path; in the second, in Australia the interests of a national literature count for little compared with the country's real or supposed political needs. Australians may say they believe of course in immigration, but that the best immigrant is the Australian. The truth is that we dislike immigrants, and most of all the Australian immigrant, and I see no reason for thinking that the half-caste baby will be any more welcome than the Aryan.

At the same time, though Jindyworobakism is riddled with so many absurdities that its advocates can be only partially sincere, it is certainly that rare thing, a genuine idea. That it is an idea based not merely on a simple error, but on a lie, does not make it nonsensical or useless. Man, as I have remarked, usually needs his truth to be mixed with illusion, if that truth is to initiate a popular movement. It is the illusion that provides the spur, and the absurd hope of bringing about a golden age may at least bring about the demolition of a good many slums. *Es irrt der Mensch, so lang er strebt.*

It is unnecessary to look for more flaws in the delightful paradox that Australia's only hope is a race of virile Euro–Australians which is unlikely ever to be born. But a final word will not be out of place. Jindyworobakism raises the possibility of a double allegiance, of two conflicting patriotisms, in a single nation. If as lovers of poetry we are to revere the

---

* *Cultural Cross-Section*, ed. J. Ingamells, Adelaide, 1941

black culture, as students of history we shall find ourselves facing a question the merely political unimportance of the Aborigine makes no easier to answer.

That question is: "How far have the blacks been ill-treated by our ancestors?" As far as I know, there is really no authoritative answer to this terrible poser ... Australian historians have exhibited first-class agility in avoiding it. But at a meeting of the Aborigines' Progressive Association a few years ago a well-known authoress, who has written much on conditions in Australia fifty years or so ago, is reported as having said that "when she was a child she had seen Aborigines massacred in hundreds. They had been lying dead around poisoned waterholes, and she had seen hunting parties gather together. Dogs had been imported from Europe because they were more savage. She had seen little children dead in the grass, and scalps of blacks paid for as if they were dingos." (*Sydney Morning Herald*, March 1938.)*

Now, if all this is true, it is extraordinary that so few of us have read anything of the kind in our historians, especially those of to-day, who are notorious enthusiasts for detailed research. In reply to the lady, indeed, a letter appeared next day in the *Herald* from a person claiming to speak as an authority. He and the lady were of about the same age, yet he had never heard of cases of ill-treatment of blacks generally, but only of isolated occasions, where the culprits were brought to justice whenever possible. His conclusion was that the massacres in hundreds, poisoned waterholes, imported dogs, etc., were "imagination run riot, and (this was bound to come) unfair to our pioneers, and also to the history of Australia". Incredible as it may seem, this was the only letter published on the subject. Verily, Australians, even those who love writing to the newspapers, are very bashful about discussing some things. It is unnecessary here to decide between the disputants. But the objector's final sentence goes to the heart of the question of our attitude to the blacks and to our pioneers. If the lady's allegations are true, the bestiality of our more recent pioneer forebears would make even a Lindsay–McCrae Centaur vomit. There may be good reasons for being proud of our original convicts, or at least for finding plenty of excuses for most of them. But we could only execrate their degenerate descendants of fifty years ago.

---

* The imaginative speaker, at a public meeting on 3 March (reported as 4 March) 1938, was Dame Mary Gilmore. The writer of the letter (5 March) was John Reidy.

If we are persuaded to do that, the Jindyworobak philosophy is likely to grow more popular. But, alas! the average Australian will probably be unwilling to spit when his Aborigine-poisoning forebears are mentioned, even though the same average Australian (I am referring to the city man) has a vague, sentimental attachment to the "Abo.". I imagine he would endeavour to avoid the dilemma this newspaper report and the correspondent's rejoinder proposed by agreeing with the lady as regards most of the facts, but by comfortably and comfortingly asserting that only an inconspicuous minority of our pioneers could have been guilty; he would not, I am afraid, be ready to exchange the culture either of Potts Point or of Woolloomooloo for that of Bulloo Downs.

JUDITH WRIGHT

EXTRACT FROM *BECAUSE I WAS INVITED*, 1975

[There was] a group which came into view in the late 1930s, the Jindyworobaks. Proclaiming the need for "environmental values", they claimed that the time lag in our adaptation to the landscape was the chief problem of Australian verse. This had some show of reason, since the kind of minor versifying that persisted in describing Australia in English terms still survived, as did the deference paid to England and all its works by Australian society at large.

One thing the movement did achieve was to make verse a subject of debate and argument. Opposition movements sprang up, and brought into the quarrel most practising poets of any stature. The Jindyworobak tenets were discussed, and their more extravagant aspects such as the recourse to "Aboriginality" was ridiculed, even in the daily newspapers (which at that time were scarcely arenas for literary debate). The fact that the movement attracted many minor and magazine versifiers, and that its chief apologists, however sincere, were not notably able theorists or practitioners, rather obscured the real basis it rested on.

Though it could never point to any major achievement in altering the literary climate, it did succeed in wiping out the last traces of the minor versifying it complained of, and the poetry of Roland Robinson and of William Hart-Smith (both, by the way, English-born) stands to testify to its real fruits in acclimatizing poetry here. It could have been—and some of its proponents insist that it was—a step towards a really indigenous poetry. But, for this to happen, Australians themselves would have had to become, and remain, indigenous; and this did not come about.

For no sooner had "Englishness" in poetry become a reproach, and the use of elves and fairies, groves and dells, instead of Aborigines and native animals, eucalypts and creeks and gullies, been finally discredited, than the second world war thrust Australia into closer contact with the Pacific and brought the real dangers (and advantages) of "outside" pouring onto her astonished shores. The Jindies had been working in a small and isolated society, trying to make it understand the value of what it had. (Even the much-scorned "Aboriginal" aspect of their credo might have made us see the values of that dispossessed culture with clearer eyes, and treat those sad remnants of it as people, not as invisible sub-humans.) Now that small society suddenly found itself part of a world on which it was dependent as never before, and by which it was imperilled as never before. The question of "environmental values" in verse seemed suddenly to lose relevance.

To a point, the argument was vindicated. The country, threatened for the first time, became for the time at least a vision of beauty and threatened security to more people than poets. There was an uprush of nostalgic feeling for its life and landscape. But increasingly, as the terrors ebbed, change and new influences came in. We were never again to be so isolated, so self-limited and self-occupied.

The Jindy movement struggled on until the early 1950s largely on the slowing momentum of that feeling for the country that war had brought with it; then it disintegrated as a movement, leaving us some poets who carried forward what was valuable in it. The inrush of new factors—prosperity, the increasing growth of the cities, the new influence of the rapidly growing universities, the decline of our once comfortable sense of security by the fact of belonging to a protective Empire —brought in new concerns and new arguments. But the movement had had its relevance to its time.

The main movement which stood in opposition to it, the Angry Penguins, had correctly assessed its weaknesses: its inherent isolationism, the fact that it depended on Australia's remaining the small non-industrial society it then was, and the over-emphasis on rescuing and translating elements of Aboriginal culture into terms of a white viewpoint which failed to understand the real basis of that culture. But the Angry Penguins had nothing to oppose to this except another, and perhaps equally questionable, kind of symbiosis with "Apocalypse" and surrealism, overseas poetic movements which were themselves even then declining.

In fact, the two movements between them illustrated the double-sided problem of writing in Australia and the imitativeness that kept us swinging uncertainly between "indigenous values" and our European origins. The crux of the problem was that both factors were needed, but that it didn't seem possible to bring them into creative reconciliation. The Jindies and the Penguins, in their extremist positions, represented the confrontation in its purest form.

. . . .

But both movements had had their value as well as their

excesses. We had realized that neither were really viable answers: we could not truly incorporate either Aranda myth and legend, or movements like surrealism, into the Anglo–Australian context. We could no longer exploit the advantages of being provincial and isolated, or bypass our provincialism by becoming parasitic on movements originating somewhere else and in a different context. The fate of both attempts, displaced by a more rational if less exciting reversion to the central tradition of English poetry, was anyway instructive. It remained to accept ourselves for what we were and work out our problems with the tools that condition offered.

PART 4

Jindyworobak Affinities

Editor's Note

Had it not been for the accident of a letter from the contemporary poet Les Murray I should have been content to rest upon my conviction that the Jindyworobak movement amounted to a "completed form" in Australian literary history. But Les Murray, if only in joke—yet half seriously—called himself "the last of the Jindyworobaks" and I felt obliged to take notice. Not until then did it occur to me to throw in the epithet "original" for the earlier practitioners and to give him the description "new". But still the question remained, what real continuity could there be? That there is one, I readily believe.

If it be true that the "original" Jindyworobak phenomenon is well and truly finished, what, one may ask, can this new phenomenon be? What was and *is* the essential Jindyworobak reality—the heart of it, the quality which, detached from all accidental circumstance, is capable of surviving into a world so much and so radically changed? I think it may be possible to attempt an answer, even if, at present, only somewhat obscurely. We have seen that several principal characteristics stand out. There is in the first place the fundamental concern with "country"—what the "original" Jindyworobaks called "environment" or sometimes "the land". In the case of the Aborigines the values were highly spiritual; the Jindyworobaks aimed at that too. Very closely associated with this territorialism was the broad European assimilation to a landscape which had in the earliest days of settlement been taken as hostile. The colonial history of Australian landscape art tells how (aesthetically) the hated became the loved. If only gropingly, the Jindyworobaks sought more than aesthetic responses: their articles of belief received stimulus from Aboriginal myth and religion, which they partially understood, and became a poetic faith that was also a philosophy. The symbolism they extracted from Aboriginal example epitomized the imaginative part of their system. It became a cliché. Yet it is not, and cannot become, a total banality. There is an energy in it which may survive in some form.

"In some form" requires emphasis; except in fairy tales it is not likely to remain the pure Alcheringa image. Les Murray at least is convinced that something can be made of it. It is for him and others who may respond to his stimulus to define the new Jindyworobak faith on the foundation of principles already laid down. That is, they must make a new harmony out of the old Jindyworobak elements of time, territory and eternity, and give it spiritual dimensions equal to the phenomena it is required to celebrate.

It now remains only to offer a few remarks about the contents of this Jindyworobak Affinities section. The fiction selections include two extracts from *Kangaroo,* showing D.H. Lawrence's sensitive reaction to the atmosphere of the Australian bush. This novel was an early source of inspiration to Rex Ingamells. Also included are extracts from Xavier Herbert's *Capricornia,* a work contemporary with Ingamells's early poetry, and his much later *Poor Fellow My Country*: the dates of the two novels (1938, 1975) virtually incapsulate the Jindyworobak movement. In the selections in verse I make no claim to comprehensive representativeness. And possibly the first poet included is not to be called a Jindyworobak on anybody's ascription, since she is Aboriginal by race and requires no further justification. That Kath Walker has an affinity with the Jindyworobaks however is clear enough, as is also the point that she captures a more recent point of view. She has clearly read the "original" Jindyworobaks and drawn encouragement from them. But the experience she writes from is real; literary in manner, but actual in substance. She can use the instrument of verse well; when she chooses to write roughly the choice is deliberate. Like Ingamells she is a "joiner" of the white and black but there is a quite different tone in her purpose. Where she is political, she is not theoretical and idealistic as the young men of the thirties were; she has something to complain of, though she manages to do so with humour and moderation. I am not aware how much she derives from Mary Gilmore; something perhaps, but the point of view is her own. Feminine indignation is something they both naturally share. She is certainly aware of much more than the injustice her people suffer, eloquent as she is about that. The exuberantly good humoured "Ballad of the Totems" makes lively fun of both the old *Bulletin* ballad style and—what Ingamells himself could scarcely have been anything but glum about—the now irrecoverable romantic mythology of the totems, the Alchera image. She is at least not labouring to preserve the unpreservable. In other poems she has less disposition to joke about the facts. "The Teachers" shows her sharply critical of the policy of racial integration. Irony, though, and not merely bitterness, is her cutting tool. I feel it is just and necessary to bring her into the picture though she is not a categorical Jindyworobak in either the old or the new sense; her value is as a touchstone of some function of poetry other than the kind they both stand for.

It was through Les Murray's allusions to him that I came to reflect on Peter Porter's Jindyworobak affinities: which I will not assert to be extensive, though interesting and pertinent in at least one poem: "On First Looking into Chapman's Hesiod". The father of the early Greek poet Hesiod had been a farmer in Asia Minor but migrated with his two sons to "new country" in Boeotia. One of the sons prospered, but Hesiod, who perhaps neglected his farm at Ascra for poetry, did not do so well, at least on the land; and the two had some disagreement. The work in Porter's mind is Hesiod's *Works and Days*, a bucolic poem which could be said to have a pioneering but not an Alcheringa-type interest. But it may be well to remember Hesiod is also credited with having written the *Theogony*, a work of mythology.

I come to Les Murray himself, and begin with a passage of prose, "The Coming Republic", which I take from *Quadrant* (October 1976, p. 37). "Waiting", he says, "for the Australian republic is like waiting for the other shoe to drop"—but I am not going to follow him into politics; and indeed his politics are mainly of the imagination. The word is also caught up in the title of a recent book, *The Vernacular Republic*, 1975. At bottom it is not so very different from what Ingamells intended: his "vernacular" has a good deal in common with the Jindyworobak "environment". "It would be altogether simple-minded", he says, "to assert that republicanism of the ordinary sort would suffice as our liberating word . . . "

> This other republic, the one we have to discern, is inherent in our vernacular tradition, which is to say in that "folk" Australia, part imaginary and part historical, which is the main matrix of any distinctiveness we possess as a nation, and which stands over against all of our establishments and colonial elites. This is the Australia of our deepest common values and identifications, the place of our quiddities and priorities and family jokes . . .

"Not", he insists,

that the vernacular republic consists merely in a tribal excitement. It is the subsoil of our common life, and to live consciously outside it or in opposition to it, without expatriating oneself, is a crippling strain . . .

Formal education and high culture in Australia, as in any other colonial country, are systems of foreign ideas imposed from above whose usual effect is to estrange people from their own culture and injure their rapport with their own people . . . *It has never been possible to get an Australian education through institutional channels.** You must either give yourself one, or be taught by your elders in a more or less informal way. This is the way all the vernacular cultures of Australia, Aboriginal, immigrant and mainstream, *are* in fact transmitted . . . the tragedy of a colonial situation in the things of the mind is that thought itself can come to seem alien and oppressive . . .

While, at its best, the main vernacular culture in Australia has always tended to revere the Aborigines, however mawkishly, as a sort of gold-standard of Australianness, a recent stream of intellectual opinion has taken them up as the *only* licensed Australians, and used the tragic facts of their cultural crisis as a weapon against, in particular, country people . . .

Dad and Dave, he suggests, have become a screen behind which we have allowed ourselves to hide our guilt at our conquest and displacement of the Aborigines. For this and similar misrepresentations he is prepared to blame "intellectuals and academics". But by contrast he has a particular admiration for certain writers who have preserved a respect for outback people: Upfield, Idriess, Durack, Xavier Herbert.

On the other hand, he concedes, "The vernacular republic is not solely rural or working class"—

Poets as diverse as C.J. Dennis, Douglas Stewart, the later Slessor, Ronald McCuaig and Bruce Dawe . . . have kept us in mind of this. In many ways the urban and middle class ramifications of the vernacular tradition are among the most interesting to trace and meditate upon, because they are subtler and less cliché. As we decolonize, we must learn to understand all the strands of our vernacular culture, as well as seeing it as a unity over against past and present streams of dependence. I have long wanted to see an anthology of Aboriginal poetry in translation, which is to say a collection of song texts of every level of solemnity translated at a proper literary standard from the original languages. There isn't as yet much decent Aboriginal poetry in English, but some of the material I have seen in translation from the Aborigines' own

---

* I italicize this observation because it is a purely Jindyworobak sentiment, and it is profoundly observed and *so very nearly* true. [Ed.]

languages is superb; the *Moon-Bone Cycle* of the Wonguri Sandfly clan of Arnhem Land, in Professor Berndt's translation, is one of the very great poems of Australia, and ought to be a part of every secondary school syllabus, as much as *Five Bells* or *The Wind At Your Door*. There is bound to be much more material of a similar standard, if we will look for it. Some is around already, in the stiff or literal sort of translation that suffices for scientific journals. A collection of translations of scrupulous scientific accuracy which still manages, often, to flower into poetry of a high order, is T.G.H. Strehlow's *Central Australian Song* [*Songs of Central Australia* 1970]; a huge and vilely expensive book, it covers only a part of the oral literature of one tribe, the Aranda. The whole extent of the literature we might retrieve must be truly stupendous.*

He is quite right to respect the translations of Strehlow and Berndt, and there are others; he is on rather rockier ground, perhaps, in recommending the texts for secondary schools unless there have been some changes since I went to one. Professor Berndt's recent publication, *Love Songs of Arnhem Land* 1976, is a major addition to the translated repertoire. It is true, love can be very frank with the swains of Arnhem Land; the *Moon-Bone* cycle is a drawing room exhibit by comparison. However Murray does not overpraise it; there is a magnificence about it, and for that matter, about Berndt's other cycles; and the praise given to Strehlow is well deserved.

Les Murray's admiration for the *Moon-Bone* can be traced in his *The Bulahdelah-Taree Holiday Song Cycle*, which clearly relates to it very closely. In fact so closely that I think it should be pointed out and readers will find a comparison both informative and enjoyable. I cannot unfortunately find space to include the whole of both poems, since both are long —deliberately, I think, Murray follows Berndt's precedent in including thirteen "songs" in his "cycle"—but the main point will be established if I reproduce something from the beginning and the end of both. Murray's poem may be read either simply as it stands, for its celebratory content, its human allusions and something very local in its mood as a document of experience in an Aboriginal-type unit of "country"; or it may be opened up to interpretation in the light of its carefully planned relationship to its Arnhem Land model. In the latter case it will be necessary, if the reader is really serious, to understand the way the Aboriginal cycles work; and that is a special study, but accessible now with the help of Strehlow, Berndt and

---

* As this book goes to press comes the distressing news of Professor T.G.H. Strehlow's sudden death. He is believed to have been working during his retirement on other translations which we must hope will some day see the light of publication. [Ed.]

others. The only warning it seems proper to throw in here, is that Aboriginal poetry is not, like ours, meant to be experienced only verbally, or as "literature", but has also complex associations with ritual, music and dancing. To read it as literature without some such awareness may be to court illusion. But that the pleasure of the poetry *is* literary in an understandable sense is evident even at a glance. Translation itself can be a source of confusion, but what comes through indicates abundantly that this kind of poetry—to which the *Moon-Bone* cycle is an illuminating introduction—is a verbal art with points of correspondence with our own experience, and capable of motivating Australian poetry in new directions. The best of Ingamells was, as I have been at pains to show, clear and bright, precise and accurate. But this poetry expands and opens out. It assumes the same landscape and environment, it postulates a similar spiritual origin or "dreamtime"; but it is also about what is now living and actual, and has a warm and social impact. It appears to facilitate new flexibilities of emotion which the original Jindyworobaks laid a foundation for, but did not themselves exploit.

The other Murray inclusions need no explanation. They are short, lyrical, and have—what is not forbidden to a Jindyworobak—wit.

The Richard Tipping piece with which the selection closes is a *bonne-bouche*; it comes unobtrusively with the coffee and cigars.

Fiction

D.H. LAWRENCE

TWO EXTRACTS FROM *KANGAROO*

In Europe, he had made up his mind that everything was done for, played out, finished, and he must go to a new country. The newest country: young Australia. Now he had tried Western Australia, and had looked at Adelaide and Melbourne. And the vast, uninhabited land frightened him. It seemed so hoary and lost, so unapproachable. The sky was pure, crystal pure and blue, of a lovely pale blue colour: the air was wonderful, new and unbreathed: and there were great distances. But the bush, the grey, charred bush. It scared him. As a poet, he felt himself entitled to all kinds of emotions and sensations which an ordinary man would have repudiated. Therefore he let himself feel all sorts of things about the bush. It was so phantom-like, so ghostly, with its tall pale trees and many dead trees, like corpses, partly charred by bush fires: and then the foliage so dark, like grey-green iron. And then it was so deathly still. Even the few birds seemed to be swamped in silence. Waiting, waiting—the bush seemed to be hoarily waiting. And he could not penetrate into its secret. He couldn't get at it. Nobody could get at it. What was it waiting for?

And then one night at the time of the full moon he walked alone into the bush. A huge electric moon, huge, and the tree-trunks like naked pale Aborigines among the dark-soaked foliage, in the moonlight. And not a sign of life—not a vestige.

Yet something. Something big and aware and hidden! He walked on, had walked a mile or so into the bush, and had just come to a clump of tall, nude, dead trees, shining almost phosphorescent with the moon, when the terror of the bush overcame him. He had looked so long at the vivid moon, without thinking. And now, there was something among the trees, and his hair began to stir with terror, on his head. There was a presence. He looked at the weird, white, dead tress, and into the hollow distances of the bush. Nothing! Nothing at all. He turned to go home. And then immediately the hair on his scalp stirred and went icy cold with terror. What of? He knew quite well it was nothing. He knew quite well. But with his spine cold like ice, and the roots of his hair seeming to freeze, he walked on home, walked firmly and without haste. For he told himself he refused to be afraid, though he admitted the icy sensation of terror. But then to experience terror is not the same thing as to admit fear into the conscious soul. Therefore he refused to be afraid.

But the horrid thing in the bush! He schemed as to what it would be. It must be the spirit of the place. Something fully evoked tonight, perhaps provoked, by that unnatural West-Australian moon. Provoked by the moon, the roused spirit of the bush. He felt it was watching, and waiting. Following with certainty, just behind his back. It might have reached a long black arm and gripped him. But no, it wanted to wait. It was not tired of watching its victim. An alien people—a victim. It was biding its time with a terrible ageless watchfulness, waiting for a far-off end, watching the myriad intruding white men.

This was how Richard Lovat Somers figured it out to himself, when he got back into safety in the scattered township in the clearing on the hill-crest, and could see far off the fume of Perth and Fremantle on the sea-shore, and the tiny sparkling of a farther-off lighthouse on an island. A marvellous night, raving with moonlight—and somebody burning off the bush in a ring of sultry red fire under the moon in the distance, a slow ring of creeping red fire, like some ring of fireflies, upon the far-off darkness of the land's body, under the white blaze of the moon above.

It is always a question whether there is any sense in taking notice of a poet's fine feelings. The poet himself has misgivings about them. Yet a man ought to feel something, at night under such a moon.

. . . . . .

He was not happy, there was no pretending he was. He

longed for Europe with hungry longing: Florence, with Giotto's pale tower: or the Pincio at Rome: or the woods in Berkshire—heavens, the English spring with primroses under the bare hazel bushes, and thatched cottages among plum blossom. He felt he would have given anything on earth to be in England. It was May—end of May—almost bluebell time, and the green leaves coming out on the hedges. Or the tall corn under the olives in Sicily. Or London Bridge, with all the traffic on the river. Or Bavaria with gentian and yellow globe flowers, and the Alps still icy. Oh God, to be in Europe, lovely, lovely Europe that he had hated so thoroughly and abused so vehemently, saying it was moribund and stale and finished. The fool was himself. He had got out of temper, and so had called Europe moribund: assuming that he himself, of course, was not moribund, but sprightly and chirpy and too vital, as the Americans would say, for Europe. Well, if a man wants to make a fool of himself, it is as well to let him.

Somers wandered disconsolate through the streets of Sydney, forced to admit that there were fine streets, like Birmingham for example; that the parks and the Botanical Gardens were handsome and well-kept; that the harbour, with all the two-decker brown ferry-boats sliding continuously from the Circular Quay, was an extraordinary place. But oh, what did he care about it all! In Martin Place he longed for Westminster, in Sussex Street he almost wept for Covent Garden and St Martin's Lane, at the Circular Quay he pined for London Bridge. It was all London without being London. Without any of the lovely old glamour that invests London. This London of the Southern hemisphere was all, as it were, made in five minutes, a substitute for the real thing. Just a substitute—as margarine is a substitute for butter. And he went home to the little bungalow bitterer than ever, pining for England.

XAVIER HERBERT

EXTRACT FROM *CAPRICORNIA*

After a moment Andy put his hand on Norman's head, and went on in the same gentle tone, "Let's consider the Old People for a jiffy, and see what's wrong with 'em. Forget the ones that live in civilization. They're starved and sickened and kicked and stupefied and generally jiggered out of all recognition. Let's consider 'em in their natural state. How do we find 'em? Big, strong, broad-browed, keen-eyed, laughing fellows. Consider their manner of livin'. Their tribes are families, in which no-one is boss, in which no-one is entitled by any sort of right to bully and grab. Then there's their laws regardin' Supply and Demand. They have a certain area stocked with game and vegetables. It's their farm. People accuse 'em of bein' too stupid to practise husbandry. Quite to the contrary. They practise it in the most amazin'ly clever fashion. They simply preserve their game and fruits and things, by drawin' on 'em carefully, and so save 'emselves the labour of havin' to till and sow and the trouble of gettin' all mixed up financially over their stock as we do. You might call that Primitive. But lookin' at it closely and comparin' it with our system of sweat and worry and sinfulness, I dunno but what it aint quite as good. The point to look at is, what are we livin' for? Is it to create intricate systems that all become obsolete after a while and have to be changed with painful reconstruction? Or just to enjoy in the simplest way possible the breath of life that's in us? What is the perfect state of society? Aint it the one in which everyone's equally happy and well fed? If it is, then Brother Binghi has it. And as to the primitive business—well, they've had the mighty good sense to limit their population to suit the natural food supply. That idea is only just occurrin' to us. It seems to me that all our intricate system of society has only been brought about by the fact that we've overstocked our paddicks with the human herd. If we'd thought of birth-control a thousand years ago, providin' we had'nt allowed a few greedy hounds to rule and rob us, today we might've been livin' as simply as the Binghis 'emselves. Do you think a Binghi livin' out in the bush in his own style would swap his lot for ours, if he knew the full strength of it?"

Old Andy looked round his audience.

He answered himself. "He'd be a blunny fool if he did," he said.

EXTRACT FROM *POOR FELLOW MY COUNTRY*

The Ring Place was anything but deserted now. At the end nearest the camp, the southern, stood a semi-circle of armed and painted men, facing northward. In that direction the scrub beyond the Ring had been cleared further, to make a passage about as long as the Ring was wide. At the end of it stood a solitary slight figure, wearing the regalia of The Snake, but accoutred with a single boomerang, one so brightly painted that it flashed like a swift bright bird in darting to meet a spear that at that moment came hurtling from one of the group still standing out in front crouched with woomera extended. The boomerang turned the spear to the right, so that if finished in the ground with haft vibrating above the scrub beyond. Two other such hafts were to be seen. Speech broke from Jeremy as a croaking: "Oh, God . . . a trial by ordeal!"

Another spearman had stepped from the semi-circle, weapon hooked in woomera, crouched. As the spear flew, a mere line of air-disturbance in its fleetness, Jeremy croaked again, "Jesus Christ!"

Up came the bright boomerang again and met the hurtling death, causing the wooden blade to split away from the haft, the latter to go spinning over the fillet-bound head that in the last rays of the Sun upon the western rampart glittered gold. The slight figure staggered slightly from the impact. The arm with the boomerang fell heavily, betraying weariness.

Here was another man out with spear and woomera. How many more before the outrage done on tradition was vindicated either with death or the magical prowess to defy it? How much longer could a scarce-bearded boy beat skill and strength and indignant purpose that themselves were in the realm of magic?

As the marksman, that tall thin Executioner, swung to give full force to right arm and to the arm's magical projection, the woomera, a yell burst from Jeremy: "Hey!"

Even the spearman looked. Jeremy started to leap down, shouting now so that the rock behind him rang his words all round, "Cut that out!"

Cut that out . . . Cut that out . . . Cut that out!

But he gasped and halted in his headlong rush to see that flicker of the air as the spear flew, and gaped as he watched the boomerang come up too late, and the slight figure stagger back impaled. The figure swayed, sagged at the knees, collapsed, while the haft of the missive of tribal justice wagged its triumph in the air.

Jeremy sprang out of immobility, turned on the group now turned from him, and got their attention again on the instant, shouting, "You bastards!" As he started leaping down again, they swung as if to meet him. He stopped again, and from using the rifle to aid his progress, threw it up to grasp in both hands, slipped the catch, and without aiming, pulled the trigger —*BANG!*

A small burst of dust from the further wall. The rocks rang all round—*Bang, Bang, Bang*! The kites whistled and flapped for height. With a single movement the arc of warriors swung towards the camp, bolted *en masse*, except for the Executioner, who was late off the mark. Again a flicker in the air. The Executioner staggered, fell to knees, with a spear-haft waving between his shoulders.

Jeremy looked to left. Risen out of the scrub was a tall skeleton figure in the insignia of The Snake, woomera still extended from the throw. He looked again to right, to see the fallen man rise and wth swaying steps vanish after his brethren. He raised the rifle and fired again at the opposite wall—*BANG*!

In a moment there were the warriors to be seen leaping up the split part of the southern wall, a couple dragging their wounded mate between them with the Pookarakka's spear still wagging like a tail behind him. Then they were gone.

Jeremy turned towards the fallen boy, started for him at a run, did not pause as he passed the Pookarakka, but glaring at him, yelled, "What's matter you no-more look-out that boy?" He burst through the scrub to the cleared space, reached Prindy to have the grey eyes so like his own fix him with the light of recognition and see a slight sweet smile move lips and release a bubble of blood. The spear had penetrated the painted breast just above the heart.

Struggling with his breathing, Jeremy stooped—only to jerk erect again with a sharp cry: "Oh!" He staggered to the right, tripped over the rifle, fell to knees. He goggled at the watching grey eyes as he swung to his left, hands groping that way, his own eyes staring astonishment. The long haft of a heavy spear protruded from his side backward, swinging out of sight as he turned, the blade buried to the hilt just above his hip. He grasped both haft and hilt. It was a shovel-spear of the modern kind, with broad blade of thinly hammered steel. He looked up to see the Pookarakka approaching, gaped at him, gasped, "What's matter you?"

How fiery the coals and harsh the cackle as the answer was given: "You been kill-him my *Mekullikulli*, Whiteman!"

The red eyes were directed at the prone figure towards which the long spidery stride was headed. With a groan Jeremy turned, to see the Pookarakka bending over his grandson, to see the grey eyes glaze, the smile obliterated by the sag of the bloody jaw. He groaned again, then suddenly drew breath and yelled, "You bastard . . . why you let that mob make boy stand-up?"

The red eyes were raised from the pale dead face, to fix the living grey. The voice was not a cackle now, but a harsh scream: "Wha's matter you come bugger-him-up bijnitch?"

Jeremy's face had turned yellowish. Sweat oozed from it. Still he clutched at the spear with both hands, but as if unaware of it now. He struggled for breath, panted, "He only young boy . . . must . . . they kill him . . ?"

The Pookarakka swung and reached for the painted boomerang, and seizing it, rose and lunged and shoved it before Jeremy's eyes, crying in the same tone, "Nobody can beat him dat *Mahraghi* . . . spone you no come bugger-him-up!" There was froth on the wide lips.

Jeremy's eyes rolled.

The voice went on: "Me been tell him you right t'ing . . . g'won you go 'way. No matter, you whiteman, you do it wrong t'ing . . . you come . . . finish *Mahraghi* . . . finish belong me *Mekullikulli*

Jeremy breathed, "Oh, Jesus Christ!"

Verse

KATH WALKER

THE TEACHERS

*For Mother who was never
taught to read or write*

Holy men, you came to preach:
"Poor black heathen, we will teach
Sense of sin and fear of hell,
Fear of God and boss as well;
We will teach you work for play,
We will teach you to obey
Laws of God and laws of Mammon . . ."
And we answered, "No more gammon,
If you have to teach the light,
Teach us first to read and write".

WE ARE GOING

For Grannie Coolwell

They came in to the little town
A semi-naked band subdued and silent,
All that remained of their tribe.
They came here to the place of their old bora ground
Where now the many white men hurry about like ants.

Notice of estate agent reads: "Rubbish May Be Tipped Here".
Now it half covers the traces of the old bora ring.
They sit and are confused, they cannot say their thoughts:
"We are as strangers here now, but the white tribe are the
                                                    strangers.
We belong here, we are of the old ways.
We are the corroboree and the bora ground,
We are the old sacred ceremonies, the laws of the elders.
We are the wonder tales of Dream Time, the tribal legends
                                                    told.
We are the past, the hunts and the laughing games, the
                                           wandering camp fires.
We are the lightning-bolt over Gaphembah Hill
Quick and terrible,
And the Thunderer after him, that loud fellow.
We are the quiet daybreak paling the dark lagoon.
We are the shadow-ghosts creeping back as the camp fires burn
                                                    low.
We are nature and the past, all the old ways
Gone now and scattered.
The scrubs are gone, the hunting and the laughter.
The eagle is gone, the emu and the kangaroo are gone from
                                                    this place.
The bora ring is gone.
The corroboree is gone.
And we are going."

THE BUNYIP

You keep quiet now, little fella,
You want big-big Bunyip get you?
You look out, no good this place.
You see that waterhole over there?
He Gooboora, Silent Pool.
Suppose-it you go close up one time
Big fella woor, he wait there,
Big fella Bunyip sit down there,
In Silent Pool many bones down there.
He come up when it is dark,
He belong the big dark, that one.
Don't go away from camp fire, you,
Better you curl up in the gunya,
Go to sleep now, little fella,

Tonight he hungry, hear him roar,
He frighten us, the terrible woor,
He the secret thing, he Fear,
He something we don't know.
Go to sleep now, little fella,
Curl up with the yella dingo.

BALLAD OF THE TOTEMS

My father was Noonuccal man and kept old tribal way,
His totem was the Carpet Snake, whom none must ever slay;
But mother was of Peewee clan, and loudly she expressed
The daring view that carpet snakes were nothing but a pest.

Now one lived right inside with us in full immunity,
For no one dared to interfere with father's stern decree:
A mighty fellow ten feet long, and as we lay in bed
We kids could watch him round a beam not far above our
    head.

Only the dog was scared of him, we'd hear its whines and
    growls,
But mother fiercely hated him because he took her fowls.
You should have heard her diatribes that flowed in angry
    torrents
With words you never see in print, except in D.H. Lawrence.

"I kill that robber," she would scream, fierce as a spotted cat;
"You see that bulge inside of him? My speckly hen make that!"
But father's loud and strict command made even mother
    quake;
I think he'd sooner kill a man than kill a carpet snake.

That reptile was a greedy-guts, and as each bulge digested
He'd come down on the hunt at night as appetite suggested.
We heard his stealthy slithering sound across the earthen floor,
While the dog gave a startled yelp and bolted out the door.

Then over in the chicken-yard hysterical fowls gave tongue,
Loud frantic squawks accompanied by the barking of the
    mung,
Until at last the racket passed, and then to solve the riddle,
Next morning he was back up there with a new bulge in his
    middle.

When father died we wailed and cried, our grief was deep and sore,
And strange to say from that sad day the snake was seen no more.
The wise old men explained to us: "It was his tribal brother,
And that is why it done a guy—but some looked hard at mother.

She seemed to have a secret smile, her eyes were smug and wary,
She looked as innocent as the cat that ate the pet canary.
We never knew, but anyhow (to end this tragic rhyme)
I think we all had snake for tea one day about that time.

From **THE WONGURI-MANDJIKAI SONG CYCLE OF THE MOON-BONE***

1

The people are making a camp of branches in that country
    at Arnhem Bay:
With the forked stick, the rail for the whole camp, the
    Mandjikai people are making it.
Branches and leaves are about the mouth of the hut: the middle
    is clear within.
They are thinking of rain, and of storing their clubs in case
    of a quarrel,
In the country of the Dugong, towards the wide clay-pans
    made by the Moonlight.
Thinking of rain, and of storing the fighting sticks.
They put up the rafters of arm-band-tree wood, put the
    branches on to the camp, at Arnhem Bay, in that place
    of the Dugong . . .
And they block up the back of the hut with branches.
Carefully place the branches, for this is the camp of the
    Morning-Pigeon man,
And of the Middle-of-the-Camp man; of the Mangrove-Fish
    man; of two other head-men,
And of the Clay-pan man; of the Baijini-Anchor man, and of
    the Arnhem Bay country man;
Of the Whale man and of another head-man; of the Arnhem
    Bay Creek man;
Of the Scales-of-the-Rock-Cod man; of the Rock Cod man, and
    of the Place-of-the-Water man.

2

They are sitting about in the camp, among the branches, along
    the back of the camp:
Sitting along in lines in the camp, there in the shade of the
    paperbark trees:
Sitting along in a line, like the new white spreading clouds:
In the shade of the paperbarks, they are sitting resting like
    clouds.
People of the clouds, living there like the mist; like the mist
    sitting resting with arms on knees,

* Translated by Ronald M. Berndt.

In here towards the shade, in this Place, in the shadow of
 paperbarks.
Sitting there in rows, those Wonguri-Mandjikai people,
 paperbarks along like a cloud.
Living on cycad-nut bread; sitting there with white-stained
 fingers,
Sitting in there resting, those people of the Sandfly clan . . .
Sitting there like mist, at that place of the Dugong . . . and
 of the Dugong's Entrails . . .
Sitting resting there in the place of the Dugong . . .
In that place of the Moonlight Clay Pans, and at the place
 of the Dugong . . .
There at that Dugong place they are sitting all along.

12

Now the New Moon is hanging, having cast away his bone:
Gradually he grows larger, taking on new bone and flesh.
Over there, far away, he has shed his bone: he shines on the
 place of the Lotus Root, and the place of the Dugong,
On the place of the Evening Star, of the Dugong's Tail, of
 the Moonlight clay pan . . .
His old bone gone, now the New Moon grows larger;
Gradually growing, his new bone growing as well.
Over there, the horns of the old receding Moon bent down,
 sank into the place of the Dugong:
His horns were pointing towards the place of the Dugong.
Now the New Moon swells to fullness, his bone grown larger.
He looks on the water, hanging above it, at the place of the
 Lotus.
There he comes into sight, hanging above the sea, growing
 larger and older . . .
There far away he has come back, hanging over the clans near
 Milingimbi . . .
Hanging there in the sky, above those clans . . .
"Now I'm becoming a big moon, slowly regaining my
 roundness . . .
In the far distance the horns of the Moon bend down, above
 Milingimbi,
Hanging a long way off, above Milingimbi Creek . . .
Slowly the Moon Bone is growing, hanging there far away.
The bone is shining, the horns of the Moon bend down.

First the sickle Moon† on the old Moon's shadow; slowly he
  grows,
And shining he hangs there at the place of the Evening Star . . .
Then far away he goes sinking down, to lose his bone in the
  sea;
Diving towards the water, he sinks down out of sight.
The old Moon dies to grow new again, to rise up out of the
  sea.

13

Up and up soars the Evening Star, hanging there in the sky.
Men watch it, at the place of the Dugong and of the Clouds,
  and of the Evening Star,
A long way off, at the place of Mist, of Lilies and of the
  Dugong.
The Lotus, the Evening Star, hangs there on its long stalk, held
  by the Spirits.
It shines on that place of the Shade, on the Dugong place,
  and on the Moonlight clay pan . . .
The Evening Star is shining, back towards Milingimbi, and over
  the Wulamba people . . .
Hanging there in the distance, towards the place of the
  Dugong,
The place of the Eggs, of the Tree-Limbs-Rubbing-Together,
  and of the Moonlight clay pan . . .
Shining on its short stalk, the Evening Star, always there at
  the clay pan, at the place of the Dugong . . .
There, far away, the long string hangs at the place of the
  Evening Star, the place of Lilies.
Away there at Milingimbi . . . at the place of the Full Moon,
Hanging above the head of that Wonguri tribesman:'
The Evening Star goes down across the camp, among the white
  gum trees . . .
Far away, in those places near Milingimbi . . .
Goes down among the Nguruwulu people, towards the camp
  and the gum trees,
At the place of the Crocodiles, and of the Evening Star, away
  towards Milingimbi . . .
The Evening Star is going down, the Lotus Flower on its stalk . . .
Going down among all those western clans . . .

---

† The phrase "sickle Moon" is perfectly intelligible in English, but at the
  same time is a vivid reminder of the unrelieved difficulty of translating
  primitive imagery and ideas into sophisticated language.

It brushes the heads of the uncircumcised people . . .
Sinking down in the sky, that Evening Star, the Lotus . . .
Shining on to the foreheads of all those headmen . . .
On to the heads of all those Sandfly people . . .
It sinks there into the place of the white gum trees, at
    Milingimbi.

LES MURRAY

From THE BULAHDELAH–TAREE HOLIDAY SONG CYCLE

1

The people are eating dinner in that country north of Legge's Lake;
behind flywire and venetians, in the dimmed cool, town people eat Lunch.
Plying knives and forks with a peek-in sound, with a tuck-in sound,
they are thinking about relatives and inventory, they are talking about customers and visitors.
In the country of memorial iron, on the creek-facing hills,
they are thinking about bean plants, and rings of tank water; of growing a pumpkin by Christmas;
rolling a cigarette, they say thoughtfully Yes, and their companion nods, considering.
Fresh sheets have been spread and tucked tight, childhood rooms have been seen to,
for this is the season when children return with their children
to the place of Bingham's Ghost, of the Old Timber Wharf, of the Big Flood That Time;
the country of the rationalized farms, of the day-and-night farms, and of the Pitt Street farms,
of the Shire Engineer and many other rumours; of the tractor crank-case furred with chaff,
the places of sitting down near ferns; the snake-fear places, the cattle-crossing-long-ago places.

6

Barbecue smoke is rising at Legge's Camp; it is steaming into the midday air,
all around the lake shore, at the Broadwater, it is going up among the paperbark trees,
a heat-shimmer of sauces, rising from tripods and flat steel, at that place of the Cone-shells,
at that place of the Seagrass, of the tiny segmented things swarming in it, and of the Pelican.

Dogs are running around disjointedly; water escapes from their
     mouths,
confused emotions from their eyes; humans snarl at them
     Gwanout! and Hereboy! not varying their tone much;
the impoverished dog people, suddenly sitting down to nuzzle
     themselves; toddlers side with them;
toddlers, running away purposefully at random, among cars,
     into big drownie-water (come back, Cheryl-Ann!)
They rise up as charioteers, leaning back on the tow-bar; all
     their attributes bulge at once:
swapping swash shoulder-wings for the white sheeted shoes that
     bear them,
they are skidding over the flat glitter, stiff with grace, for once
     not travelling to arrive.
From the high dunes over there, the rough blue distance, at
     length they come back behind the boats,
and behind the boats' noise, cartwheeling, or sitting down, into
     the lake's warm chair;
they wade ashore and eat with the families, putting off that
     uprightness, that assertion,
eating with the families who love equipment, and the freedom
     from equipment,
with the fathers who love driving, and lighting a fire between
     stones.

10

Now the ibis are flying in, hovering down on the wetlands,
on those swampy paddocks around Darawank, curving down
     in ragged dozens,
on the riverside flats along the Wang Wauk, on the
     Boolambayte pasture flats
and away towards the sea, on the sand moors, at the place
     of the Jabiru Crane.
Leaning out of their wings, they step down; they take out their
     implement at once,
out of its straw wrapping, and start work; they dab grasshopper
     and ground-cricket
with nonexistence . . . spiking the ground and puncturing it . . .
     they swallow down the outcry of a frog;
they discover titbits kept for them under cowmanure lids, small
     slow things.
Pronging the earth, they make little socket noises, their
     thoughtfulness jolting down-and-up suddenly;

there at Bunyah, along Firefly Creek, and up through
    Germany,
the ibis are all at work again, thin-necked aging men towards
    evening; they are solemnly all back,
at Minimbah, and on the Manning, in the rye-and-clover
    irrigation fields;
city storemen and accounts clerks point them out to their wives,
remembering things about themselves, and about the ibis.

12

Now the sun is an applegreen blindness through the swells,
    a white blast on the sea-face, flaking and shoaling;
now it is burning off the mist; it is emptying the density of
    trees, it is spreading upriver,
hovering above the casuarina needles, there at Old Bar and
    Manning Point;
flooding the island farms, it abolishes the milkers' munching
    breath
as they walk towards the cowyards; it stings a bucket here,
    a teatcup there.
Morning rides into the world by more and more southerly
    gates; shadows weaken their north skew
on Middle Brother, on Cape Hawke, on the dune scrub toward
    Seal Rocks;
steadily the heat is coming on, the butter-water time, the
    clothes-sticking time;
grass covers itself with straw; abandoned things are thronged
    with spirits;
everywhere wood is still with strain; birds hiding down the
    creek galleries, and in the cockspur canes;
the cicada is hanging up her sheets; she takes wing off her
    music-sheets.
Cars pass with a rational zoom, panning quickly towards
    Wingham,
through the thronged and glittering, the shale-topped ridges,
    and the cattlecamps,
towards Wingham for the cricket, the ball knocked hard in
    front of smoked-glass ranges, and for the drinking.
In the time of heat, the time of flies around the mouth, the
    time of the west verandah,
looking at that umbrage along the ranges, on the New England
    side;
clouds begin assembling vaguely, a hot soiled heaviness on the
    sky, away there towards Gloucester;

a swelling up of clouds, growing there above Mount George,
    and above Tipperary;
far away and hot with light; sometimes a storm takes root there,
    and fills the heavens rapidly;
darkening, boiling up and swaying on its stalks, pulling this
    way and that, blowing round by Krambach;
coming white on Bulby, it drenches down on the paddocks,
    and on the wire fences;
the paddocks are full of ghosts, and people in cornbag hoods
    approaching;
lights are lit in the house; the storm veers mightily on its stem,
    above the roof; the hills uphold it;
the stony hills guide its dissolution; gullies opening and
    crumbling down, wrenching tussocks and rolling them;
the storm carries a greenish-grey bag; perhaps it will find hail
    and send it down, starring cars, flattening tomatoes,
in the time of the Washaways, of the dead trunks braiding
    water, and of the Hailstone Yarns.

13

The stars of the holiday step out all over the sky.
People look up at them, out of their caravan doors and their
    campsites;
people look up from the farms, before going back; they gaze
    at their year's worth of stars.
The Cross hangs head downward, out there over Markwell;
it turns upon the Still Place, the pivot of the Seasons, with
    one shoulder rising:
"Now I'm beginning to rise, with my Pointers and my
    Load . . ."
hanging eastwards, it shines on the sawmills and the lakes, on
    the glasses of the old people.
Looking at the Cross, the galaxy is over our left shoulder, slung
    up highest in the east;
there the Dog is following the Hunter; the Dog Star pulsing
    there above Forster; it shines down on the Bikies,
and on the boat-hire sheds, there at the place of the Oyster;
    the place of the Shark's Eggs and her Hide;
the Pleiades are pinned up high on the darkness, away back
    above the Manning;
they are shining on the Two Blackbutt Trees, on the rotted
    river wharves, and on the towns;
standing there, above the water and the lucerne flats, at the
    place of the Families;

their light sprinkles down on Taree of the Lebanese shops, it
    mingles with the streetlights and their glare.
People recover the starlight, hitching north,
travelling north beyond the seasons, into that country of the
    Communes, and of the Banana:
the Flying Horse, the Rescued Girl, and the Bull, burning
    steadily above that country.
Now the New Moon is low down in the west, that remote
    direction of the Cattlemen,
and of the Saleyards, the place of steep clouds, and of the
    Rodeo;
the New Moon who has poured out her rain, the moon of the
    Planting-times.
People go outside and look at the stars, and at the melon-rind
    moon,
the Scorpion going down into the mountains, over there
    towards Waukivory, sinking into the tree-line,
in the time of the Rockmelons, and of the Holiday . . .
the Cross is rising on his elbow, above the glow of the horizon,
carrying a small star in his pocket, he reclines there brilliantly,
above the Alum Mountain, and the lakes threaded on the Myall
    River, and above the Holiday.

THE FLYING-FOX DREAMING

Now that the west
is lighting in under leaves
and Hookfoot the eagle
has gone from over the forest
there is no sound except the
tree-foxes, unwrapping from rest;

finger-winged night workers
who will soon beat up in tens
and thousands out of this daylong head-down city;
in the offing of scents above earth, they will cast for grown
and native fruit, and home in down-country for miles
on the ripe tree beacons.

Upside down all their days,
Antipodean,
night wardrobes their singleness for them. Each bat, alone,
puts off crowding and chatter, once above the perches
he becomes the unfolded, far-speeding, upward-sidestepping,
hawk-owl-outflying one.

Here, one, his fur ballast
dropped among weeds in its tightening parchment, also
disproves a bush story: they don't excrete through the mouth
to satisfy gravity. All down the valley of fig
and flying-fox men, the lights now of towns are beginning
to gleam. They will burn late. It goes on being appropriate,

even the dead one becoming a clenched oval stone
now clear of all twig-arrest, free of clambering dinners,
free at last of dawns' dazzling comedowns. Windrowing east
over the farms, adroit
at wingshrink turns
he is topping the nectar time, and the pollen harvest,
going on out continually over horizons.

THE EUCHRE GAME

So drunk he kept it at tens—and the bloody thing lost!
he bought a farm out of it. Round the battered formica
table the talk is luck more than justice, justice
being the politics of a small child's outcry.

The subtlest eyes in the Southern Hemisphere look at
the cards in front of them. *Well I'll go alone.*
Outside the window, passionfruit flowers are blooming
singly together. Many are not in the sun.

Men lose a trick, deal a fresh hand. Intelligence here
is interest and the refusal of relegation;
those who conceive it chance-fixed to their benefit also
believe in justice. Some of them are what remains of

the Revolution. *Hey, was that for us?* Footsteps
recede down the hall. One looks at the window, three smile:
Europeans! you're all suffering-snobs. Who's away?
The game's loosely sacred: luck is being worked at.

VISITING ANZAC IN THE YEAR OF METRICATION

Gelibolu, Chanakkale—
there's no place called *Gallipoli*
down there, where the summer fires strip
the hills of scrub and rosemary.

Old wire snags the steeps like thorn
and human bones come out of the clay
where squatters' and selectors' boys
and the aghas' sons and their peasant boys

met in a raked boot-scrambling roar
and the sooling prints turned black with names
when currents drifted the landing buoys
to the heights of thyme and rosemary.

Things sticking out jag at the mind,
Tooths' bottles, messtins, vertebrae
laid down in the bonzer *stoushing* days
the *spirited* and *clean-cut* days

up where the laddering trenches clung
and gravel flew in hobnailed sprays
where ripped and screaming chaps found out
that fellow humans really would,

where crimson tidemarked puttees bore
histories of crowding in the sea
below the chirrup-haunted thyme,
burst entrails, shell-brass, rosemary.

When hard-case jokes and frantic help
poured content into noble sieves
that human lives cannot keep filled
it was the day of *turning round*,

when firing, wags might turn around
and yell *How's that?* and in a push
a hundred jokers might turn round
and sprawl, and leap. Towns died of that

and the bush went underground:
the nation stalled in elegy
with a Day for massing through the streets
in pub time, wearing rosemary.

At Lone Pine and the Nek, the spinner
has scattered his cranial shilling bets
the king-and-country stones up there
mark no one's grave (Islam burns crosses)

Bowled Walers and stumped Victorians lie
in those broken hills inextricably
with their adversary, who was no less brave.
The misemployed, undone by courage

have become the Unsaluting Army
and buttoned boys, for all their trades
are country again, and that funny Missus
Porter's not yet changed poetry.

White bones, inconsolable proof
high scree, incomparable test—
on both points, class warfare has raged
but the war-pipes sail through jam-packed streets

where everyone is turning round:
old men and the ageing wear bright coins
and plain men and battlers' sons are proud
and the *flash* still trust extremity.

Our continent is uncrowded space,
a subtler thing than history.
The Day of our peace will need a native
herb that out-savours rosemary.

Down in the flatlands, coming away,
torn cotton bloomed in the few scratch fields
and conscripts on bivouac jogged by,
the Hittite face, the Turan face—

down there, in a day of rabid peace
and wartime love, one thought of how
to farm blokes, war is Sudden City.
The newchums learned the tram-routes well

but disaster is all our brotherhood,
starved height, incomparable friends,
this is the reign of the measuring god,
this is the pit of rosemary.

High, near-Port Lincoln light. Harsh places.
This is the day of Freedom, too—
like the sardine tin lid tied
to the hawk's tail, life presents new faces.

Those shelterless hardscrabble cols
where even the Heads get *knocked*, were best
assaulted in youth: we were handiest,
the climbing was overt and in vogue

and done with friends, in company.
Pioneering there, building with planks,
we showed the *battler* style to Death
amongst hoarse screams and rosemary.

LACONICS: THE FORTY ACRES

We have bought the Forty Acres,
prime brush land.

If Bunyah is a fillet
this paddock is the eye.

The creek half-moons it,
log-deep, or parting rocks.

The corn-ground by now
has had forty years' grassed spell.

Up in the swamp
are paperbarks, coin-sized frogs—

The Forty, at last,
our beautiful deep land

it was Jim's, it was Allan's,
it was Reg's it is Dad's—

Brett wanted it next
but he'd evicted Dad:

for bitter porridge
many cold returns.

That interior machinegun,
my chainsaw, drops dead timber.

Where we burn the heaps
we'll plant kikuyu grass.

Ecology? Sure.
But also husbandry.

And the orchard will go there,
and we'll re-roof the bare pole barn.

Our croft, our Downs,
our sober, shining land.

PETER PORTER

ON FIRST LOOKING INTO CHAPMAN'S HESIOD

For 5p at a village fête I bought
Old Homer-Lucan who popped Keats's eyes,
Print smaller than the Book of Common Prayer
But Swinburne at the front, whose judgment is
Always immaculate. I'll never read a tenth
Of it in what life I have left to me
But I did look at *The Georgics*, as he calls
The Works and Days, and there I saw, not quite
The view from Darien but something strange
And baulking—Australia, my own country
And its edgy managers—in the picture of
Euboeaèn husbandry, terse family feuds
And the minds of gods tangential to the earth.

Like a Taree smallholder splitting logs
And philosophizing on his dangling billies,
The poet mixes hard agrarian instances
With sour sucks to his brother. Chapman, too,
That perpetual motion poetry machine,
Grinds up the classics like bone meal from
The abattoirs. And the same blunt patriotism,
A long-winded, emphatic, kelpie yapping
About our land, our time, our fate, our strange
And singular way of moons and showers, lakes
Filling oddly—yes, Australians are Boeotians,
Hard as headlands, and, to be fair, with days
As robust as the Scythian wind on stone.

To teach your grandmother to suck eggs
Is a textbook possibility in New South Wales
Or outside Ascra. And such a genealogy too!
The Age of Iron is here, but oh the memories
Of Gold—pioneers preaching to the stringybarks,
Boring the land to death with verses and with
Mental Homes. "Care-flying ease" and "Gift-
devouring kings" become the Sonata of the Shotgun
And Europe's Entropy; for "the axle-tree, the quern,

The hard, fate-fostered man" you choose among
The hand castrator, kerosene in honey tins
And mystic cattlemen: the Land of City States
Greets Australia in a farmer's gods.

Hesiod's father, caught in a miserable village,
Not helped by magic names like Helicon,
Sailed to improve his fortunes, and so did
All our fathers—in turn, their descendants
Lacked initiative, other than the doctors' daughters
Who tripped to England. Rough-nosed Hesiod
Was sure of his property to a slip-rail—
Had there been grants, he'd have farmed all
Summer and spent winter in Corinth
At the Creative Writing Class. Chapman too
Would vie with Steiner for the Pentecostal
Silver Tongue. Some of us feel at home nowhere,
Others in one generation fuse with the land.

I salute him then, the blunt old Greek whose way
Of life was as cunning as organic. His poet
Followers still make me feel déraciné
Within myself. One day they're on the campus,
The next in wide hats at a branding or
Sheep drenching, not actually performing
But looking the part and getting instances
For odes that bruise the blood. And history,
So interior a science it almost seems
Like true religion—who would have thought
Australia was the point of all that craft
Of politics in Europe? The apogee, it seems,
Is where your audience and its aspirations are.

"The colt, and mule, and horn-retorted steer"—
A good iambic line to paraphrase.
Long storms have blanched the million bones
Of the Aegean, and as many hurricanes
Will abrade the headstones of my native land:
Sparrows acclimatize but I still seek
The permanently upright city where
Speech is nature and plants conceive in pots,
Where one escapes from what one is and who
One was, where home is just a postmark
And country wisdom clings to calendars,
The opposite of a sunburned truth-teller's
World, haunted by precepts and the Pleiades.

RICHARD TIPPING

PERSONAL OBJECT

i have become
something harder
in this land,

the hills alight
with autumn,
a strange hand

touching each
cold english tree
with alien passion,

"I have reached my prime."

Glossary

The following list, which is drawn from various sources, may be found useful. It represents Jindyworobak use but not anthropological and linguistic authority.

alchera, alcheringa: the mythical dreamtime; the eternal spirit of the dreamtime
alowan: wood duck
atninga: a group sent to carry out tribal justice; vengeance party
balanda: white man
barrarangs: ghosts
billai: crimson-wing parrot
birrahlee: small child
boolee: whirlwind
churinga, tjurunga: a small decorated object of wood or stone, highly sacred and secret, of personal significance and related to sacred traditions and dreamtime ancestry
darenderong: avenger
deereeree: willy wagtail
didgeridoo: drone pipe
douran douran: north wind
eehu: rain
Emianga: a ceremonial site (Hamilton Creek)
eulowirree: the rainbow
kanowar: (black) swan
karaman: leader
karaworo: eaglehawk
lilliri: shadow
lukara: witchetty grub
mirrabooka: the Southern Cross

moorawathimeering: the Land of the Lost, a sanctuary for outcasts
mouyi: white cockatoo
munyeera or *munyero* (Spencer and Gillen): edible seeds
nardoo: edible seeds
ngathungi: a revenge custom
oodoolay: the rainmaker's stone
pilpilpa: plover
pinnaroo: old and weak, thin
tallabilla: outlaw
tchidna: footprint
tjameta worms: edible worms
tnatanja: a ceremonial object of great potency and magic, generally in the form of a tall decorated pole
waitjurk: murderer
wallan: strong
waruntha: white man
warrumbool: the Milky Way
wilban: cave
wirreengun: magic-maker, medicine-man
wombalunga: carry
wurley: dwelling; hut or shelter of boughs
yaraan: white gum tree
yaraandoo: Southern Cross
yoorana: spotted cat
yowee: spirit of death

Textual Sources

The poems are arranged as far as possible chronologically in the order of their first appearance, whether in an issue of the *Jindyworobak Anthology* (1938–1953) or in published volumes. It has not been possible to attempt a systematic record of first appearances in newspapers and magazines but where the information was clear it has sometimes been done. Where the poets have themselves dated their work, their dating has been accepted as a rule.

PART 1   MAJOR JINDYWOROBAK POETS

REX INGAMELLS

Key		
	A + year	*Jindyworobak Anthology**
	AP' + year	*Australian Poetry* series. Angus and Robertson
	AB	*At a Boundary* Adelaide: Preece, 1941
	B	*The Bulletin*
	CH	*Chapbook*
	CQR	*Content Are the Quiet Ranges* Adelaide: Jindyworobak, 1943
	CW	*Come Walkabout* Melbourne: Jindyworobak, 1948
	FP	*Forgotten People.* Adelaide: Preece, 1936
	GSL	*The Great South Land.* Melbourne: Georgian House, 1951
	GT	*Gumtops.* Adelaide: Preece, 1935
	MH	*Memory of Hills.* Adelaide: Preece, 1940
	PQ + year	*Poetry Quarterly* (issues 1–9 undated)
	SF	*Sun-Freedom.* Adelaide: Preece, 1938

* Publishing details of the Anthologies are given in Part 2, Textual Sources.

	SP	*Selected Poems*. Melbourne: Georgian House, 1944, 1945
	T	*Torch*, Adelaide Teachers' College Magazine

1930	Luis de Torres, AP44, SP(dated 1930–1943)
1932	Boomerang, SP(dated 1932), GT
	The Afghans, SP(dated 1932), GT
1933	Forlorn Beauty, SP(dated 1933), GT
	Evening in the MacDonnells, SP(dated 1933), CH(1935), FP
	The Bullocky, SP(dated 1933), GT
1934	Excited Crows, SP(dated 1934), GT
1935	Garchooka, the Cockatoo, B(pre 1938), SP(dated 1935), A38, SF
	Garrakeen, B(pre 1938), SP(dated 1935), SF
	Rivers and Mountains SP(dated 1935), FP
	Black Children, SP(dated 1935), FP
	Long Ago, SP(dated 1935), FP
	Moorawathimeering, SP(dated 1935), CH(1936), SF
	Forgotten People, B, University of Adelaide Bundey Prize (1935), FP, SP
1936	Sun-Freedom, *The Home* (pre 1938), B(pre 1936), SF, SP
1937	Shifting Camp, SP(dated 1937), SF
	Outback, B(pre 1938), SF, SP
1938	Earth-Colours, SF, SP
	Ngathungi, SF, SP
	Boolee, SF, SP
1939	Black Mary, AB, T(pre 1941), SP
	Memory of Hills, A39, MH, PQ2(1941), A45, SP
	From a Dying People, A39, MH, SP(misdated 1940)
1940	Black Boulder, MH, SP
	Desert Dawn, MH, SP
	Dark Cry, A40, AB, SP
1941	The Swagman, AB, SP
	The Gangrened People, AB, SP
	Billai, A41, SP
	Yaraandoo, A41, SP
	Unknown Land, PQ4(1941), A43, SP
1942	Australia, A42, SP
1943	To Mirrabooka, CQR, SP
	Martin's Pub, CW, SP
	Macquarie Harbour, PQ7, SP
	Captain William Bligh, A43, SP
1944	The Tourist Dump, A44, CW
1945	Slight Autobiography, A45, CW
1951	The Great South Land, GSL
1952	The Pensioner, A52
1953	Uluru, A53

W. FLEXMORE HUDSON

Key		
	A + year	*Jindyworobak Anthology*
	AIH	*As Iron Hills*. Melbourne: Robertson and Mullens, 1944
	AP + year	*Australian Poetry* series. Angus and Robertson
	AS	*Ashes and Sparks*. Adelaide: Preece, 1937
	IV	*Indelible Voices*. Lucindale, S.A.: W.F. Hudson, 1943
	IWT	*In the Wind's Teeth*. Adelaide: Preece, 1940
	PCR	*Pools of the Cinnabar Range*. Melbourne: Robertson and Mullens, 1959
	PQ + year	*Poetry Quarterly* 1941–1947; issues 1–9 undated
	SMH	*Sydney Morning Herald*
	WFSR	*With the First Soft Rain*. Lucindale, S.A.: W.F. Hudson, 1943

1933	Song, AS(dated 1933)
1935	The Poet and the World Today, AS(dated 1935)
	Sonnet, 1935, AS
	The Farmer, AS(dated 1935), A38, AIH
1936	To a Boy on his Eleventh Birthday, AS(dated 1936)
1937	Mallee Farm at Dusk, AS, A38, AIH
	Drought, IWT(dated 1937), A40
1938	As the Fugitive Grass, IWT(dated 1938), A40
	Mallee Scene, A38, IWT, AIH
	Mallee Courage, A38, IWT
	Mail Night; Mallee Store, IWT(dated 1938), AIH
	Andrew, IWT(dated 1938), AIH
	Prayer, IWT(dated 1938)
	Song of an Australian, A38, IWT, AIH
1939	Gum Tree, A39, IWT
	To Myrle: And Then You Sang, A39, IWT, AIH
	Magpies, IWT(dated 1939), AIH
	Black Cockatoos, IWT(dated 1939)
	Sundown, IWT(dated 1939), AIH
1940	To Edgar H. Mercer, from Sonnets on the War, A40
	Galahs, IWT
	War, IWT, AIH
1941	As Seeds Through Years of Drought, A41; retitled With the First Soft Rain, WFSR
1942	Song For My Generation (Part 4 of *Indelible Voices*), A42, PQ5
1943	Indelible Voices A43, IV
1944	Hare in Summer, A44, AIH
1945	Words, AIH, A45
	Kirsova, AIH, A45, PQ11(1944), revised in PCR
1946	Giovanni Rinaldo, P.O.W., A46, AP46, PQ20(1946), PCR
1947	Nostalgia, A47, retitled Home-sick, PCR
	The Kiss, A47, PQ23/24(1947), PCR

1953	Bashō, A53 (broadcast earlier), PCR, SMH	
	Mallee in October, PCR	
	A Hymn for the Dark Age, PCR	
	Coach in Training Camp, PCR	

IAN MUDIE

Key	A + year	*Jindyworobak Anthology*
	AD	*The Australian Dream*. Adelaide: Jindyworobak, 1943, 1944
	AP + year	*Australian Poetry* Series. Angus and Robertson
	B	*The Bulletin*
	BC	*The Blue Crane*. Sydney: Angus and Robertson, 1959
	CS	*Corroboree to the Sun*. Melbourne: Hawthorn Press, 1940
	LK	*Look, the Kingfisher*. Melbourne: Hawthorn Press, 1970
	NBR	*The North-Bound Rider*. Adelaide: Rigby, 1963
	O + year	*Overland*
	P45	*Poems 1934–44*. Melbourne: Georgian House, 1945
	PQ + year	*Poetry Quarterly*. Issues 1–9 undated
	PU	*The Publicist*
	PW	*Poets at War*. Melbourne: Georgian House, 1944
	Salt + year	Army Education magazine
	SMH	*Sydney Morning Herald*
	SP	Selected Poems, 1934–74. Melbourne: Nelson, 1976
	SSU	*Their Seven Stars Unseen*. Adelaide: Jindyworobak, 1943
	TIA	*This Is Australia*. Adelaide: Cork, 1940

See also J.J. Tonkin and J. Van Wageningen, *Ian Mudie: A Bibliography*. Adelaide: Libraries Board of S.A., 1970.

1938	As Are the Gums, PU38, A39, CS, P45
	This Land, PU38, A40, CS, P45, SP
	Street Vision, PU38, CS, P45, SP
1940	Corroboree to the Sun, PU40, A40, CS, P45, SP
	Earth, PU40, A40, CS, P45
	Underground, CS, P45, SP
	Morialta Memory, CS, P45
	Galah, CS, P45
	Have Anger, CS
	Belong, CS, P45, SP

1941	This is Australia, PU41, TIA, P45
	I Would Not Go, PU41, TIA, P45
	The Young Warriors, PU41, A42, SSU, P45
1942	Glory of the Sun, A42, SSU, PW, P45
1943	If This be Treason, SSU, P45
	The Australian Dream, A43(part only), AD, P45
	New Guinea Campaign, *Salt* 43, A45, P45
1944	Unabated Spring, *Salt* 44, A44, PW, P45, SP
1952	No Phoenix Australis, A52, BC, SP
	They'll Tell You About Me, B52, BC, SP
1953	The O.T., SMH53, BC, SP
	The Wreck of the *Ethel*, Low Tide, B53, BC, SP
	One Day, Perhaps in Spring, A53, BC, SP
1954	The Blue Crane, SMH54, BC, SP
	Sitting-Room, Strzelecki Homestead, B54, AP54, BC, SP
1955	Bushfire, SMH55, BC
1957	I Wouldn't Be Lord Mayor, B57, NBR, SP
1958	In Neon Pastures, O58, NBR, SP
1959	To Me the Poem, BC, SP
	River Port, BC, SP
1963	The Crab or the Tree, NBR
1970	The Day the Rain Came, LK, SP
	Intruder, O70

WILLIAM HART-SMITH

Key	A + year	*Jindyworobak Anthology*
	AP + year	*Australian Poetry* Series. Angus and Robertson
	CC	*Christopher Columbus*. Christchurch: Caxton Press, 1948
	CGW	*Columbus Goes West*. Adelaide: Jindyworobak, 1943
	H	*Harvest*. Melbourne: Georgian House and Jindyworobak, 1945
	OL	*On the Level*. Timaru, N.Z.: Timaru Herald, 1950
	PD	*Poems of Discovery*. Sydney: Angus and Robertson, 1959
	TC	*The Talking Clothes*. Sydney: Angus and Robertson, 1966
	UG	*The Unceasing Ground*. Sydney: Angus and Robertson, 1946
	MP	*Minipoems*. Perth [1974]

1940	Avenger, A40, CGW
	La Perouse, A40, CGW
	Summer Day, A40

1941	The Fishing Lubra, A41, CGW
1942	We Are the Elders, A42, CGW
1943	April 28th, 1770, PQ8(1943), A43
	Moondeen, PQ8(1943), A43, H
	Black Cockatoos, A43
	Columbus Goes West, PQ7(1943), CGW, retitled Space, CC, PD
	Prologue (to CC), CC, PD
	The Pear-Shaped Earth, CC, PD
1944	Water-Lily, A44, UG
	Immarna, A44
	Candle on a Stump, A44, AP45, UG
	Flame the Cat, A44, AP45, UG
	Post Mortem, A44
1945	Baiamai's Never-Failing Stream, H
	Because the Caterpillar, A45
	The Surplus, A45, H, UG
	Eaglehawk, A45, UG
1946	Open Air Pictures, UG
	Mary, UG
	Nullarbor, UG
	Picture in Bright Colours, UG
	Willie Wagtail, UG
	The Life of Rocks, UG
	Death of an Ant, UG
	Legend, UG
1949	Sparrows, A49, OL
1950	Smoke on the Plains, A50, OL
	In Sydney, OL
1964	Number, AP64, TC

ROLAND ROBINSON

Key A + year	*Jindyworobak Anthology*
*ALT	*Altjeringa*. Sydney: A.H. and A.W. Reed, 1970
AP + year	*Australian Poetry* series. Angus and Robertson
BGS	*Beyond the Grass-Tree Spears*. Melbourne, Georgian House and Jindyworobak, 1944

* A number of the poems in this volume, originally given to Robinson by Aboriginal people whom he names, are reprints or revisions of prose or verse versions printed earlier (see especially the section "The Wandering Tribes" in DW).

	†DW	*Deep Well*. Sydney: Edmonds and Shaw, 1962
	G	*Grendel*. Brisbane: Jacaranda Press, 1967
	LS	*Language of the Sand*. Sydney: Lyre-Bird Writers, 1949
	SP	*Selected Poems*. Sydney: Angus and Robertson, 1971
	TS	*Tumult of the Swans*. Sydney: Lyre-Bird Writers, 1953
1944		The Creek, A44, BGS
		I Made My Verses, BGS, LS(retitled Inscription), DW, SP
		And the Blacks Are Gone, A44, BGS, LS, DW
		Flowering Tea-Tree, BGS, LS, DW
		The Invocation, BGS, LS, DW
		Coming With Darkness, BGS, LS, DW
		Climbing the Gully, BGS, LS, DW
		Communion, BGS, LS, DW
		Morning, BGS, LS, DW
		Departure, BGS, LS, DW
1945		Call On the Sea to Be Still, A45, LS, DW, SP
		The Drovers, A45, LS, DW
1947		Black Cockatoos, A47, AP47, LS, DW
1948		Would I Might Find My Country, A48, LS, DW
1949		Deep Well, A49, TS, DW, AP64
		Casuarina, LS, A50, DW
1951		I Had No Human Speech, A51, TS, DW
1952		Rock-Lily, AP51/52, TS, DW
		Emu, TS, DW
1962		The Desert (Sequence: The Blanket, The Brolgas, The Dancers, The Paean, The Rabbit, The Wanderer, The Ibis) DW
		For Rex Ingamells, DW
		Thrush, DW
		Passage of the Swans, DW
1967		Sundowner, G
		The Pioneers, G
1970		One Eyed Nalul Speaks (Nalul), ALT
		The Child Who Had No Father (Fred Biggs), ALT
		Jarrangulli (Percy Mumbulla), ALT
		Mapooram (Fred Biggs), ALT

† The volumes from BGS to DW with some continuity in ALT form a single design. LS reprints the substance of BGS and adds to it; TS is new but is absorbed with the others in DW, which is the definitive volume. In TS and subsequently sequences are named but individual poems are merely numbered. A table of titles and numbers is placed at the end of DW. In the present selections, for convenience of identification, titles are preserved although such was clearly not Robinson's final intention so far as the content of DW was concerned.

Captain Cook (Percy Mumbulla), ALT
Kimberley Drovers, ALT

PART 2   JINDYWOROBAK ANTHOLOGIES

Ingamells, Rex, ed. *Jindyworobak Anthology*, Adelaide: F.W. Preece, Ltd., 1938.

Ingamells, Rex, ed, *Jindyworobak Anthology*. Adelaide: F.W. Preece, Ltd., 1939.

Ingamells, Rex, ed. *Jindyworobak Anthology*. Adelaide: F.W. Preece, Ltd., 1940.

Ingamells, Rex, ed. *Jindyworobak Anthology*. Adelaide: F.W. Preece, Ltd., 1941

Kennedy, Victor, ed. *Jindyworobak Anthology*. Adelaide: F.W. Preece, Ltd., 1942.

Hudson, Flexmore, ed. *Jindyworobak Anthology*. Adelaide: F.W. Preece, Ltd., 1943.

Hart-Smith, W., ed. *Jindyworobak Anthology*. Melbourne: Georgian House, 1944.

Ballantyne, Gina, ed. *Jindyworobak Anthology*. Melbourne: Jindyworobak, Georgian House, 1945.

Mudie, Ian, ed. *Jindyworobak Anthology*. Melbourne: Jindyworobak Productions, Georgian House, 1946.

Ingamells, Rex, ed. *Jindyworobak Anthology*. Melbourne: Jindyworobak, 1947.

Robinson, Roland, ed. *Jindyworobak Anthology*. Melbourne: Jindyworobak, 1948.

Howarth, R.G., ed. *Jindyworobak Anthology*. Melbourne: Jindyworobak, 1949.

Cato, Nancy, ed. *Jindyworobak Anthology*. Melbourne: Jindyworobak, 1950.

Rawlinson, Gloria and Hart-Smith, W., eds. *Jindyworobak Anthology*. (Trans-Tasman Issue). Melbourne: Jindyworobak, 1951.

Murphy, Arthur, ed. *Jindyworobak Anthology*. Melbourne: Jindyworobak, 1952.

Thiele, Colin, ed. *Jindyworobak Anthology*. Melbourne. Jindyworobak Publications, Georgian House, 1953.

PART 3   JINDYWOROBAK PROSE

Devaney, James. *The Vanished Tribes*. Sydney: Cornstalk Publishing Company, 1929 (abridged), pp. 114–15, 240.

Ingamells, Rex. *Aranda Boy*. London and Melbourne, Longmans, Green and Co., 1952, pp. 58–65, 81.

———. *Conditional Culture* (with commentary by Ian Tilbrook). Adelaide: F.W. Preece, 1938. A Jindyworobak Publication.

———, ed. *Jindyworobak Review 1938-1948*. Melbourne: Jindyworobak, 1948.

———. Letter to Miles Franklin, 16 March 1948. Miles Franklin Papers, Mitchell Library, Sydney.

———. Letters to W.F. Hudson, 27 June 1941 and 2 November 1949. Hudson Papers, Menzies Library, A.N.U. Canberra.

Kennedy, Victor. *Flaunted Banners*. Adelaide: Economy Press, 1941. A Jindyworobak Publication, pp. 5-6.

Letters, F.J. *In a Shaft of Sunlight*. Sydney: Shakespeare Head Press, 1948, pp. 101-106.

Robinson, Roland. *Aboriginal Myths and Legends*. Melbourne: Sun Books, 1966.

Stephensen, P.R., *The Foundations of Culture in Australia*. First published in *The Australian Mercury* 1935; as book by W.J. Miles, Gordon, N.S.W., 1936, pp. 18-19, 98-101.

Wright, Judith, *Because I Was Invited*. Melbourne: Oxford University Press, 1975, pp. 56-58.

PART 4 JINDYWOROBAK AFFINITIES

Lawrence, D.H., *Kangaroo*. Harmondsworth: Penguin, 1923, pp. 18, 25.

Herbert, Xavier, *Capricornia*. Hawthorn: Lloyd O'Neil Pty Ltd, 1971, p. 324.

———. *Poor Fellow My Country*, Sydney: Collins, 1975, pp. 1441-43

Walker, Kath, "The Teachers", "We Are Going", "The Bunyip", "Ballad of the Totems", *My People*. Milton, Qld: Jacaranda Press, 1970.

Berndt, R.M., tr., "The Wonguri-Mandjikai Song Cycle of the Moon-Boné", *Oceania*, vol. XIX, September 1948, p. 16.

Murray, Les, "The Bulahdelah-Taree Holiday Song Cycle", *Poetry Australia* Double issue September-December 1976, nos. 60-61. "Flying-Fox Dreaming", "The Euchre Game", "Visiting Anzac in the Year of Metrication", "Laconics: The Forty Acres", *Ethnic Radio*. Sydney: Angus and Robertson, 1977.

Porter, Peter, "On First Looking into Chapman's Hesiod", *Living in a Calm Country*. London: O.U.P., 1975.

Tipping, Richard. "Personal object", *The Australian*, 19 June 1971.

Select Bibliography

All relevant Jindyworobak poetry volumes are listed under Textual Sources.

Berndt, R.M. While Ronald and Catherine Berndt have not written directly on the Jindyworobaks, their writings provide the best available introduction to Aboriginal life, culture and literature. Specially recommended: *Kunapipi*. Melbourne: Cheshire, 1951. *Djanggawul*. Melbourne: Cheshire, 1952. *Love Songs of Arnhem Land*. Melbourne: Nelson, 1976. *The World of the First Australians* (with C.H. Berndt). Sydney: Ure Smith, 1964.

Devaney, James. *The Vanished Tribes*. Sydney: Cornstalk Publishing Company, 1929.

———. *The Currency Lass*, 1927 is of lesser, but still some interest.

Elliott, Brian. "Breath of Alchera". *Singing to the Cattle*. Melbourne: Georgian House, 1947.

———. "Jindyworobaks and Aborigines". *Australian Literary Studies* vol. viii no. 1 (May 1977): 29–50.

Ewers, J.K. *Creative Writing in Australia*. Revised edition. Melbourne: Georgian House, 1956: 117–21, 142–46, 163–64.

Green, H.M. *A History of Australian Literature* vol ii. Sydney: Angus and Robertson, 1961: 983–87. A severe but discriminating assessment.

Hope, A.D. *Native Companions*. Sydney: Angus & Robertson, 1974.

Ingamells, Rex. *Conditional Culture* (with a commentary by Ian Tilbrook). Adelaide: F.W. Preece, 1938.

———, ed. *The Jindyworobak Review 1938–1948*. Melbourne: Jindyworobak, 1948.

Kennedy, Victor. *Flaunted Banners*. Adelaide: Economy Press, 1941. A Jindyworobak publication.

McAuley, James. *A Map of Australian Verse*. Melbourne: M.U.P., 1975. Contains critical allusions but no Jindyworobak selections.

McQueen, Humphrey, "Rex Ingamells and the Quest for Environmental Values". *Meanjin* vol. 37 no. 1 (1978).

Meanjin vol. 36 no. 4 (1977) is an Aboriginal Issue and contains relevant material. Particularly recommendable is the article "The Human Hair Thread" by Les Murray.

Robinson, Roland E. *The Drift of Things*. Melbourne: Macmillan, 1973.
——. *The Shift of Sands*. Melbourne: Macmillan, 1976. Both volumes are autobiographical; much Jindyworobak content. Tends to be anecdotal.
Spencer, W.B., and Gillen, F.J. *The Arunta*. London: Macmillan, 1927.
Stephensen, P.R. *The Foundations of Culture in Australia*. Gordon, N.S.W.: W.J. Miles, 1936.
Strehlow, T.G.H. *Aranda Traditions*. Melbourne: M.U.P., 1947.
——. *Songs of Central Australia*. Sydney: Angus and Robertson, 1971.
Wright, Judith. "Some Problems of Being an Australian Poet". *Because I was Invited*. Melbourne: O.U.P. 1975.